MASTERING MONEY

How To Create Your Own Financial Plan

Anne M. Lieberman

J. Edson Clinton

MASTERING MONEY

How To Create Your Own Financial Plan

MASTERING MONEY

How To Create Your Own Financial Plan

Anne M. Lieberman
J. Edson Clinton

Longman Financial Services Publishing
a division of Longman Financial Services Institute, Inc.

While a great deal of care has been taken to provide accurate and current information, the ideas, suggestions, general principles and conclusions presented in this book are subject to local, state and federal laws and to consult legal counsel regarding any points of law—this publication should not be used as a substitute for competent legal advice.

Sponsoring Editor: Karen Berger
Copy Editor: Jane Johnston
Production Coordinator: Marguerite Duffy
Cover Design: Quarasan
Worksheet Design: Robert Cooley

© 1987 by Longman Group USA Inc.

Published by Longman Financial Services Publishing
a division of Longman Financial Services Institute, Inc.

All rights reserved. The text of this publication, or any
part thereof, may not be reproduced in any manner whatsoever
without written permission from the publisher.

Printed in the United States of America.

87 88 89 10 9 8 7 6 5 4 3 2 1

Library of Congress Cataloging-in-Publication Data

Lieberman, Anne M.
  Mastering money.

  Includes index.
  1. Finance, Personal.   2. Investments. I. Clinton,
James Edson, II. Title.
HG179.L486   1987   332.024   87-3655
ISBN 0-88462-589-3

DEDICATIONS

To the memory of my father, Ralph N. Lieberman, who wanted to be a writer...for helping me to become a person who could fulfill her own dreams...and one of his.

Anne M. Lieberman

To those who will use *Mastering Money* to master their future.

J. Edson Clinton

ACKNOWLEDGMENTS

We would like to thank some of the many individuals who helped take this project from an idea to a finished product:

Thanks to Sponsoring Editor Karen Berger, for grace under fire. This is the second time we have worked with her, and the experience served to increase our appreciation of her clear thinking and editorial skill.

To Ivy Lester of Longman, thank you for the encouraging words and constructive criticism that came at the right times.

Thanks to William E. Horwich and Robert J. Gorlin, of Horwich and Warner in San Francisco, and to Scott Richmon and John Gustafson, for their excellent comments on the chapter on estate planning.

To Susan Beavens, our able researcher, thanks. We are delighted to see people of Susan's caliber preparing themselves for careers in financial planning.

To Reid S. Johnson, Phil Goslawski, and J. Terrence Gallagher, professionals in our field, our gratitude and thanks for being kind enough to review the forms and offer their invaluable suggestions.

For every book that is written, there are people who did not work directly on the manuscript, but who contributed immeasurably to its development.

Anne offers her thanks:

To Douglas Cowley, of Lawrence A. Krause and Associates, a superb financial planner who stepped in to work with my clients while I turned my attention to the manuscript. To Stephen B. Oshry, M.D., who gave immeasurable support on the home front. Few husbands would cook as many meals, do as many dishes or run as many errands; and finally, to Abe and Sylvia Oshry for all of their encouragement and support. I am grateful to all of these.

Jim gives his thanks to:

My dear friends, Fred S. Jahn and Whitney Lyon, who taught me, among many other things, the discipline of numbers.

And to my dear, sweet wife, who patiently gave up those precious weekends needed for me to work on this project.

TABLE OF CONTENTS

Preface		xi
Chapter 1	**Planning to Win**	1
	Does Money Run Your Life?	1
	Planning? Who Needs It?	2
	What Planning Covers	4
	Financial Planning as a Process	4
Chapter 2	**Planning Issues and Strategies**	7
	Finding a Way To Do It All	7
	The Meaning of Money—USA, 1980s	8
	Key Financial Issues and Strategies Vary with Age	9
Chapter 3	**Dreams and Goals: The Foundation of Your Plan**	17
	Starting the Wheels in Motion	17
	Financial Independence Goals/Retirement Goals	23
Chapter 4	**Gathering Information: Your Financial Check-Up**	27
	And Now What?	27
	Working Through the Worksheets	28
Chapter 5	**Basic Investment Concepts**	63
	Managing Investment Risk	63
	Beyond Investment Risk and Diversification—Basic Portfolio Concepts	68
	Analyzing Your Current Portfolio	71
	The Role of Taxes in Investment Decisions	75
	Estimating Your Marginal Tax Bracket	78
	Summary	81
Chapter 6	**Creating Your Portfolio**	83
	A Delicate Balance	83
	Guidelines for Portfolio Structure	84
	The Art of Building Your Portfolio	93
	Restructuring Your Portfolio—Playing on Paper	96
	Monitoring Your Portfolio's Performance	96

Chapter 7	**Managing Risk and Insuring Wisely**	**101**
	Making Wise Insurance Decisions	101
	Protecting Your Property: Homeowner's and Automobile Insurance	103
	Protecting Your Health and Income: Medical and Disability Insurance	110
	Summary	114
Chapter 8	**Estate Planning Strategies: Taking Care of Your Heirs**	**115**
	Estate Planning—Not Just for the Rich	115
	How Your Estate Plan Should Change Over Time	117
	Estimating the Size of Your Estate	121
	Estate Planning 101	124
	Trusts—Keeping Your Wealth Intact	126
	Other Estate Planning Issues	133
	Summary	137
	Life Insurance—Do You Need It?	137
	Life Insurance Options	141
Chapter 9	**Financial Independence**	**145**
	Getting Right on the Money	145
	Managing Your Cash Flow: The Three-Bin System	147
	Accumulating Capital to Meet Goals other than Financial Independence	151
	Accumulating Capital for Financial Independence	153
	What If Your Goals Conflict?	155
	Special Funding Opportunities for Financial Independence/Retirement	156
Chapter 10	**Financing a College Education**	**161**
	The Rising Cost of a College Education	161
	Funding Strategies	163
	Investment Vehicles for College Funding	166
	Summary	168
The Workbook	**Create Your Personal Financial Plan**	**169**
Appendix A	**Where To Go For Additional Help**	**237**
Appendix B	**Calculations and Formulas**	**249**
	Glossary	**257**
	Index	**263**

PREFACE

How much money do you have? If you save as much money in the next ten years as you did in the last ten years, how long will it take before you can be financially independent?

What are your financial goals? How close are you to realizing them?

If you don't know the answers to these questions, you're not alone. If you don't think you make enough money to set some aside for saving, you've got plenty of company.

In fact, if you're like most people, you probably don't know exactly how much money you have, but you want more. You haven't quite figured out what you want to achieve financially. Or, if you have, you don't know how you're going to make your paycheck stretch far enough to pay for all the things on your "wish list."

If we managed our business affairs the way most of us manage our personal finances, we would go bankrupt. And, indeed, the majority of people do end up financially dependent. They end up mastered by money—or, more accurately, by the lack of money.

How would you like to be financially independent? Perhaps retire with a million dollars? What kind of lifestyle would that support? A house in the country? A second career as a novelist? A trip around the world?

There is a price tag to this million-dollar lifestyle, but it's far less than you might imagine. The key is mastering your money. Depending on how early you start and how wisely you invest, you could achieve that million-dollar retirement by saving less than a hundred dollars a month. Start now, and let the planning techniques described in this book, and the effect of compounding interest, work their magic.

Showing you how to achieve financial independence is only one part of *Mastering Money*. You'll learn how to manage your tax strategies, your estate plan, your exposure to risk and a host of other issues that affect the financial well-being of you and your family.

Financial planning encompasses your entire economic situation. Financial planners and their clients know that the key to financial independence is planning *now*. *Mastering Money* shares the strategies and techniques that the authors have learned from working with hundreds of clients from all walks of life. It is our hope that it will be your key to financial freedom.

CHAPTER ONE

PLANNING TO WIN

DOES MONEY RUN YOUR LIFE?

Have you ever felt that money was your master? Have you felt driven by your need for money or baffled by what to do with the money you have? *Mastering Money* is designed to do exactly what its title suggests—make you the master of your financial life. Taking charge of your finances will bring you peace of mind in the short run and financial independence in the long run.

Planning is the key to gaining financial independence, and you are about to find out exactly why there is so much talk about financial planning. With the help of this book, you are going to create your own financial plan.

Thirty years ago it wasn't difficult to find answers to financial questions. You went to a broker for stocks or bonds, an insurance agent for whole life policies and a real estate agent for a home. Your pension was maintained by your company and, if it wasn't, Social Security would always be there.

Did your stockbroker have more than a passing interest in taxes in those days? Did your insurance agent know what a variable annuity was? Did your real estate agent consider the estate implications of how you held title to your property? Probably not. They didn't have to know or consider such things.

Today, the opposite is true. Simple questions and answers have turned into complicated issues with multiple answers. Rapidly changing economic conditions and frequent overhauls of tax laws have added to the complexity. Investment opportunities have grown into a dizzying array of choices. In a world such as this, turning small pieces of your financial life over to your broker, insurance agent, accountant, attorney and others, works about as well as an automobile that needs tuning: the parts don't work together, it drives like a tortoise and sounds like a bucket of bolts.

With so much going on, someone needs to examine your overall financial situation to be sure that each piece fits together into one coordinated whole. That's what makes the engine hum, and that's what all the talk is about.

You may think that financial planning is for the very rich, or that you need professional help. Well, yes—and no. The rich use financial planning, and professional help is available and often recommended. But financial planning is for everyone. This workbook will take you through the same data gathering and analysis that financial planners use to help you evaluate your financial situation. Someone needs to take the time to understand all your financial needs. Because financial planning is for everyone, someone needs to figure out what you want financially and whether you're doing what you need to do to get it. Someone needs to look at every aspect of your situation. Starting now, that person is going to be you.

PLANNING? WHO NEEDS IT?

Passages

In her best-selling book, *Passages,* Gail Sheehy showed a fascinated readership that adult life is not an even landscape, but a series of challenges that occur at predictable times in most of our lives. Before *Passages,* the study of human psychological development usually went only as far as adolescence—as if we were fully formed when we negotiated that threshold. Now we know that adults, like children and adolescents, have their own "developmental tasks." One of these tasks is mastering money.

The earlier and more fully you master money in your life, the more likely you are to achieve what everyone wants: a financially comfortable today and a financially secure tomorrow. Unfortunately, mastering money is not a simple task in our culture. As a society, we have very mixed feelings about money. On one hand, we say, "Money is the root of all evil." On the other hand, we tend to value people by what they earn—doctors more than janitors, lawyers more than clerks. Mastering money is a complex emotional issue as well as a complex rational issue. Making sound financial decisions requires knowledge of investments, taxes, risk management, estate planning, pension benefits, and other areas, coupled with an understanding of how these elements interrelate.

Who masters money? In a lengthy study of Harvard graduates, there was one especially interesting difference between the financially successful and less successful: those more successful were likely to have committed their financial goals to writing. They planned. And they planned *on paper.* Because they were Harvard graduates, probably most used brokers, insurance agents, attorneys and accountants. What we think the "planners" had in addition was a *destination;* they knew what they were trying to accomplish financially. Having such a destination resulted in a more organized and concerted approach toward financial problem-solving. After all, when you don't know where you're going, any path will take you there. When you know your destination, it becomes necessary to select one of the paths that will take you there.

We've just described planning. When you engage a financial planner, he or she will work with you to define what you want to accomplish, where you "want to go." The planner will work with your other advisors to see that you get there. Your chosen destination becomes the focus of all financial planning.

Not for Just the Rich and Famous

First of all, you must erase the notion from your mind that financial planning is just for the rich. The rich may be able to take better advantage of the more interesting financial strategies, but middle income people need planning too. In fact, middle income people may need planning more than the wealthy because every dollar counts.

Who else needs planning? Anyone who wants to get the most for his or her money needs it. Without planning, we make day-to-day decisions as problems arise, which is like sending five people out separately to buy furniture for your living room. The colors and styles would clash, and it would be expensive to sell the "mistakes" and buy coordinated replacements to create a workable and pleasing space. In contrast, if you spend time thinking about color, mood, price range, and available space, you could put together a lovely room at an affordable price, avoiding costly mistakes. That's planning.

Anyone who has not taken a thorough look at the major aspects of his or her financial situation needs planning. If you don't know where you are, how do you know you're headed where you want to go?

Anyone who has taken a thorough look at the major areas of his or her financial life—insurance, investments, tax management, estate planning and capital accumulation—needs planning if he or she isn't sure that all the pieces are working together to produce the best results.

Anyone who feels disorganized about his or her financial life needs planning. If you feel disorganized, you're not on top of things. You need to "mind the store" to be successful financially, or hire someone to do it for you. You will get organized as you use this workbook.

So far we've said that people who are rich need financial planning, and so do people who are not; that people who have looked at their finances need planning, as well as people who have not; that people who want more from their money need planning, and that people who want to get organized need planning. Have we missed anyone? Probably not. We think nearly everyone can benefit from planning.

WHAT PLANNING COVERS

Planning reaches into every part of your financial life—from how you hold title to property to how to reduce your taxes. Financial planners divide their work into these categories:

1. Risk Management or Insurance involves protecting yourself adequately and *economically* against the risks that human beings face: for example, the premature death of a breadwinner or the risk of being sued.
2. Capital Accumulation deals with building net worth. Some people want to accumulate capital for its own sake, but most want to build capital for emergencies, achieve dreams and goals, or meet obligations.
3. Retirement Planning, or what we like to call "financial independence" planning, can make retirement worry-free. Not everyone wants to retire, and few young people think about such a distant goal; however, almost everyone is enthusiastic about financial independence. Financial independence means freedom—freedom to decide whether you want to work or not, freedom to take a lower-paying job because it is more fulfilling in other ways, freedom to live exactly as you wish. Planning for financial independence means finding what you must do today to reap the financial benefits at a point later in your life.
4. Tax Planning means keeping more of what you earn by carefully integrating your investment decisions, for example, with your tax circumstance. Imagine how much better off you would be if you held on to ten percent more of what you earned during your lifetime. That's what tax planning is about.
5. Estate planning is planning for your heirs. It encompasses wills and trusts and the titling of property. It assures you that your money goes where you want it and that the accompanying tax bite is minimized.
6. Investment is probably the most interesting part of planning. It has many facets, from deciding how to structure your portfolio to selecting investments to fit within that structure.

FINANCIAL PLANNING AS A PROCESS

You might be tempted to think that when your financial plan is done, the picture is complete. Not so. Your financial plan is really the beginning—the foundation—of a continuing process. You will grow and change as time passes, and so will your financial goals. The economy will change and, as we know too well, the tax laws will change too. It helps to think of planning as a continuous process—like navigation on the high seas. You must take the wind and weather into account and, if you can be flexibile, your destination may change. Staying on course doesn't require constant attention; it requires periodic monitoring and mid-course corrections according to circumstances.

If planning is like navigation, your first financial plan charts the course. After the plan is laid out, an annual update will keep you on course with additional revisions made as required.

Financial planning starts with getting a clear picture of where you stand today by gathering information and taking stock. The second part of the process involves deciding where you are headed financially. This entails dreaming about what you would like to accomplish in both the short term and the long term.

The third step in the process is acquiring the knowledge you need to map a strategy. When you finally map your own strategy for the first time, you will know where you are headed financially and how to get there.

To goal of this workbook is to get you started on financial planning today. Remember, the earlier you master money, the more successful your financial life will be.

CHAPTER TWO

PLANNING ISSUES AND STRATEGIES

FINDING A WAY TO DO IT ALL

Financial planning is like a balancing act. When you make a mental list of everything you want to do—buy a car, buy a house, help your kids or put them through college, start a new career, help aging parents, get a VCR, upgrade your wardrode, go to Europe, retire comfortably—it's overwhelming. When you think about the cumulative price of all these dreams, you might decide that the only reasonable solution is to buy a hundred lottery tickets and hope for the best or to buy something extravagant so that you can enjoy a momentary feeling of material well-being. Or is it?

Those would be natural reactions in our instant gratification society where "instant on" televisions, microwave ovens and high-speed trains are commonplace. It's hard to accept that when your goals are finally defined you can't reach them immediately. And being in a hurry is just one of many cultural attitudes that keeps people from being successful in their financial lives.

THE MEANINGS OF MONEY—USA, 1980s

Our attitudes toward money often interfere with the accomplishment of our financial goals. Let's take a brief look at the sources of those attitudes and at the key financial issues most people face at particular points in their lives. You can use many of these strategies to become a more effective financial manager regardless of your attitude or life stage.

In today's culture most of us have trouble being rational about money, but by preparing your own financial plan, you can enhance your ability to make rational decisions about money. One of the best ways to become more rational about a subject is to understand why you might be irrational about it.

Money: The Last Taboo

"Filthy lucre" and "the root of all evil" are ways we describe money. At the same time, when you go to a party, people ask you what you do for a living (other cultures consider this quite rude), and you can be fairly sure that your value in their eyes will be linked to the prestige of your job. Prestige often is equated with how much MONEY you make.

"Hello, you're on the air," says Dr. Ruth Westheimer when people call her on television to discuss the intimate details of their personal lives. We never heard anyone mention how much they earn to Dr. Ruth, even when she initiates a conversation about the role of income in the caller's troubled relationship—but no one bats an eyelash when asked to detail their romantic troubles. Americans are more embarrassed to discuss their incomes publicly than their sex lives. Even within families, parents often don't tell their children how much they earn or how the family income is spent.

Such uneven cultural patterns mean that we all grow up confused about money. We're told how bad money is, yet how good we must be to earn a great deal of it. It is okay to earn money, but not to *have* money. We place a veil over the subject that adds to the confusion and makes it difficult for us to make intelligent, informed decisions.

Money is the medium of exchange in our culture, the means we use to satisfy almost every need. Paradoxically, it is even the way that most non-material needs are satisfied. People do not devote themselves to higher intellectual and spiritual pursuits when basic survival needs are not met.

Money means many things to us because it is a medium of exchange, and these meanings make it difficult to make clear-headed decisions about money. To some of us, money means security; to others, it means nurturance. It can mean power, too, and a thousand other things.

The fallout from our mixed messages about money is clear when we look at Charlotte Bartolo. Charlotte was so protective about her money that she kept it all in the bank. That worked reasonably well for her when interest rates were ten percent, but when the rates fell to five percent, her interest income was cut in half and she was uncomfortable. She wanted to become a client, but it was clear that she was so afraid of losing her money that she could not trust any advisor. We recommended that she not become a client because she would pay for services and, unable to follow the advice, she would receive little benefit. Instead, we referred Charlotte to a psychologist who specializes in treating people who have difficulty with money in their lives.

Eric Hilton never made more than $30,000 a year, but he had saved $500,000 by his mid-fifties. Like Charlotte, Hilton put it all into the bank, unable to move even the smallest amount into investments that could help him get ahead financially. Eric was a compulsive saver, sacrificing the basic comforts of life for the sake of that growing pile of cash in the bank.

Larry and Carla Vanowen, on the other hand, were compulsive spenders. The had very high incomes—$250,000 per year—but they were spending $275,000. With that kind of earnings, the Vanowens could have had a comfortable lifestyle and a growing net worth. Instead, they had credit card bills, loans and more. They had to sell Larry's stock options to pay bills and they were still behind in their payments. If you are a compulsive spender, a high income makes it easier to get yourself into big trouble.

Charlotte, Eric, Larry and Carla are extreme examples. Few of us have such obvious problems with money. We share their stories with you to offer insight into how our culture can get in the way of a healthy attitude toward money. Just knowing the roots of our attitudes often allows us to free ourselves from them!

We recommend that you spend some time thinking about what your parents told you about money, and what they failed to tell you. Give some thought to how you feel about money and the way it fits into your life. Some people never have enough money while others can save no matter how much or little comes their way. Some people hardly think about money because it fits so comfortably into their lives that it becomes a non-issue. We hope you find your way into the last category if you're not already there.

KEY FINANCIAL ISSUES AND STRATEGIES VARY WITH AGE

Your goals, your financial situation, and your attitude toward risk will all effect your financial plan. In turn, all these factors will change at different stages in your life. Although each individual's situation is different, the following section highlights some of the issues and strategies that may be influential in structuring your financial plan at different stages in your life.

Early Career to Age 35

Issue: Before age 35, most of us do not give much thought to the future.

The most important things at this stage of life are the establishment of a career and a relationship. The late 20's are usually a heady time of life—our power seems endless and the world seems without limit. We make such great strides in mastery of our lives during this stage that we tend to view life as infinitely "masterable." Along with this sense of power comes an orientation to the present. We don't think much about the future or about balancing what we want today with what we want tomorrow. Tomorrow always seems to take care of itself. Planning for the future takes a backseat for today. We have many unfulfilled material needs because we have just begun to buy cars, furniture, homes and other basics of life in an affluent society.

Issue: Wealth means "income." At this stage of life we tend to equate "wealth" with high income and high spending. The message of the former cover girl who is now a bag lady in San Francisco is wasted on us. We haven't realized yet that, even for high earners, income stops eventually and real wealth comes from whatever they've accumulated in investments. All our material possessions give pleasure, but not financial security.

Strategy: Mastery means learning to balance consuming and saving. The first step in mastering money in your twenties is learning to save. Glitzy ads on television and in magazines entice you to spend. Saving seems like going on a diet. We live in a consuming society that encourages you to spend and makes saving seem like punishment. There is no ad that turns the message around to read: "You don't have to give everything you earn to Macy's or the local theater. You deserve to keep some for yourself."

However, when you begin saving there are suddenly two wage-earners in your family—you and your money. When you earn money and your money also earns money, things begin to get exciting.

Start with a bank account. After you save $1,000, you can begin to think about investing. A growth stock mutual fund is a good beginning. When you read later about Richard and Trish Walter in Chapter 8, you'll see that they saved ten percent of their earnings. They had modest salary growth over their working lives and their investments earned eight percent after tax. At age 56, they had $1 million dollars in investment assets alone. That didn't count their home or retirement benefits. They accumulated that much even though they spent $48,000 puting their kids through college and Trish did not work while the kids were pre-school age!

It's easy to be wealthy if you establish the habit of saving early in life. If you want to accumulate $1 million and you begin at age 25 and can earn a 12 percent rate of return, it will take only $85 per month to do it (Table 2-1). If you wait ten years, you'll have to save three times as much. Wait 20 years and you'll have to save almost 12 times as much. The amount you need to save increases geometrically! Start now, it will never be easier!

Table 2–1 How To Accumulate $1 million by age 65

(Assuming a 12% After-Tax Rate of Return)

Your Age	Monthly Savings
25	$ 85
35	286
45	1,011
55	4,347
64	78,848

If you were offered a terrific job with a great future, would you take a ten percent pay cut to do it? Of course you would. And you'd manage quite well. Think of your ten percent savings goal in the same way; it will give you a greater future than almost any job.

Strategy: Find a way to get yourself excited about investing and develop a system that makes it easy. You'll see in Chapter 5 that if you had put $10,000 in the fiftieth ranked mutual fund ten years ago, you'd have over $40,000 today. If you had picked the top performer for the period, you would have over $180,000! In Chapter 10, you'll also find a discussion of the "three-bin system" that lets you manage your money like a well-run corporation. It will give you a system to make saving easy.

Strategy: If you want to become wealthy, you have to take some risks. Now is the time of life to take risks.

Throughout your twenties and until your mid-thirties, you can afford to take the risk of investing in speculative things—after you have a safety cushion of three month's living expenses in the bank. At this time of life, leveraged real estate and a diversified pool of venture capital investments makes sense in addition to growth stock.

Why leveraged real estate? When you borrow $80,000 and invest $20,000 in a $100,000 piece of real estate, you have used 80 percent leverage. If that piece of property appreciates four percent (a $4,000 increase in value), you receive a $4,000 return on your $20,000 investment—that's a 20 percent return. Leverage magnifies your return, but it magnifies your chance of loss as well. If you have a high mortgage payment, it will be harder to hold onto the property if you have a vacancy or major repairs.

Venture capital involves investing in start-up companies at various stages in their development. It has very high upside potential—ask multimillionaire Steve Jobs, founder of Apple Computer—but also it has greater risk of complete failure.

When you take an aggressive stance in your investing, make sure it is a carefully calculated risk with enough upside potential to make the added risk worthwhile.

Strategy: Although it's hard to think about life's limitations at this stage, make an appointment with yourself to review your whole insurance program and to think about what your will should say. If you don't have a will yet, see an attorney. You don't have to focus on the future, you just need to touch base with the future every year to be sure you are taking care of it.

Strategy: If you have children or plan to, start a college funding program early. With eighteen years to accumulate the money, $25 per month growing at 12 percent will increase to nearly $19,000. Inflation will make it worth less than $19,000, but a small amount set aside early can give you a real beginning.

From Age 35 to Age 50

Issue: You begin to think more about preparing for the future. The greatest hurdle at this time of life is acknowledging and accepting limitations—that's what the midlife crisis is all about. Not all our youthful dreams will be realized, not everything in life can be mended. This period is usually accompanied by an intense reevaluation of lifestyle and values. Many people divorce or change careers, others find more fulfilling ways of doing things they have always done. When the crisis passes, we sense new power in our lives. We often feel as though we're "coming into our own." A broader perspective allows us to navigate life's storms with an ease we didn't know in our twenties.

Issue: The middle-age squeeze. A few years into our middle years, we often feel overburdened. Children are still dependent on us and sometimes our parents are too. Carrying the weight of two generations often seems crushing and, unfortunately, it usually coincides with greater career responsibilities or the time-consuming aspects of career change.

Strategy: Use your sense of limits to motivate you. Systematic planning will help you accomplish as much as you can with your resources and to do it in a way that is in harmony with your values.

Strategy: Early in this period, continue to invest aggressively, but with a smaller proportion of your portfolio. Toward the end of this stage of your life, you should begin to add more deflation hedges—for example, bonds, certificates of deposit, deferred annuities. They offer added safety.

Strategy: Lack of time is your greatest challenge. Make a date with yourself once a year to review your financial situation. Monitor your investments systematically as recommended in Chapter 6. You'll be tempted to let this aspect of your life slide and that can be expensive! Someone has to tend the garden if your financial life is to flourish. If you cannot free the time, hire a professional to do it for you.

Strategy: Think about the use of trusts in your estate plan. Make a phone call to your attorney and review your current financial situation. Ask for guidance as to what events in your life should lead you to call again for further review or change to your estate plan.

Strategy: Your life insurance needs may peak in this period and decline rapidly as your dependents become independent, your net worth grows and you grow older. Dropping unneeded coverage can save you money; just be sure you have analyzed your situation and that you truly do not need it.

From Age 51 to 65

Issue: We worry about our future financial security. At this time of life, people wonder if they are doing what is necessary to be financially secure later. The burdens of midlife are shifting and money is freed-up to invest at a greater pace. Embarking on a major life change—the transition to being a non-working person—can make us fearful and those fears have a focal point—money.

Issue: Conserving what we have becomes more important as we dream about—or even dread—giving up the nine to five work routine. The certainty that, having lost it, we won't be able to regain it gives us a sinking feeling.

Issue: We get seized by the "if only's." We often go through an "If only I had..." period of regret about the way we have conducted our lives. Life never turns out quite the way we think it will—it is usually infinitely more interesting. If we do go through this period of second-guessing ourselves, it can be very painful.

Issue: We begin to think about passing on to others what we've accumulated. You may find yourself becoming a mentor to a younger person at work; you probably become concerned about passing your estate to the next generation.

Strategy: Harness your nervousness about the future and let it work for you. Analyze your retirement income needs every two years. Adjust your savings goal accordingly. This will motivate you and it will set your mind at ease.

Strategy: Your growing conservatism should express itself in the area of investing. Move assets gradually to more conservative positions. Include a larger proportion of investments that expose you to an absolute minimum of risk: losing your money, bank accounts, Treasury Bills, deferred annuities and the like. Shift gradually toward more deflation-hedged investments. Make sure, however, that you still have some inflation hedges to protect your purchasing power as the years go by. (See Chapter 5 for guidelines.) When you reach your mid-forties, it is time to begin to move gradually into more conservative investments.

Strategy: Take a fresh look at your estate planning. Are things arranged as you want? In the event of your premature death, do you feel comfortable that your heirs have the maturity or the support they need to use their inheritances wisely?

Strategy: At this point, your net worth should be nearing a peak. Is your risk management program adequate to protect you? Review your entire insurance program to be sure your assets are adequately protected.

Over Age 65

Issue: Have you arrived at your destination of financial independence and what lifestyle can your assets sustain? Many changes lie ahead as you make the major life transition to becoming a non-working person. Financial concerns are likely to be a focal point—even if you have accumulated several million dollars. This transition is very difficult for many people, but ultimately quite joyful. This time is for you. It is a chance to do what you want to do, and you've *earned* it. You may use your new-found leisure to open new horizons and involve yourself in volunteer activities, new hobbies or travel.

Issue: If you die prematurely, will your heirs be left comfortable; will they handle your wealth responsibly? Passing the torch may become even more important to you than it was before. Your assets are probably nearing their apex and, if you manage correctly, your net worth should grow in the early years of retirement. Will your heirs be equipped to handle them well?

Issue: Health Problems. There are concerns about health and its impact on financial security. Government-sponsored health care is limited in scope; private insurance is expensive. In order to receive broader health coverage under government programs, you may have to be medically indigent—meaning that it will not help you until you have exhausted your net worth.

Strategy: Review your retirement benefits and other assets to analyze the level of purchasing power they will sustain. You do not want a fixed income during retirement, but a fixed level of purchasing power—your income should rise with inflation. It will do that if you strike the right balance between income and growth. Don't plan to spend all your annual income from your portfolio in the early years of retirement. Be sure some is returned to your capital base to grow and compound.

Strategy: If you have accumulated an estate large enough to put you in a financially secure position, consider gifting assets to children or other family members to reduce estate taxes.

Strategy: Position your portfolio to have a strong inflation-hedged component: 40 percent if you can meet your income needs at the same time. You need this to sustain your purchasing power.

Strategy: Review your risk management program. Health care should be a central point. Perhaps you should add a supplement to medicare or nursing home insurance. Magazines such as *Money* evaluate these kinds of policies periodically. Your public library has additional sources of information.

Strategy: If you still carry life insurance, you are unlikely to need it. You are financially independent and, if no one else depends on your ability to earn a living, you don't need life insurance unless you have an estate tax problem. If you need insurance to provide estate liquidity, then maintain the appropriate insurance, consider establishing a life insurance trust or making someone other than yourself the owner of your policy. See your estate planning attorney for advice on how to do this.

CHAPTER THREE

DREAMS AND GOALS: THE FOUNDATION OF YOUR PLAN

STARTING THE WHEELS IN MOTION

This should be the most important chapter of all. It is your chance to think about the important things you want to do with your life. Not only will you think about doing the things you value, but you will also begin the process that seems to separate the financially successful few from their unsuccessful peers. That process consists simply of writing down what you want to accomplish.

It is interesting that some single people and families do so well with their resources while others with the same resources are mired in debt or floundering with lack of purpose. You'll be in the first group if you complete your plan and if you take a flexible approach to planning. Your circumstances will change and your values may change and the economy will change. Think of your plan as dynamic: something that adapts to changes as time passes—just as you do.

Money has different meanings for all of us, as you learned in Chapter 2. Some of us like to spend money, others like to keep it. Some people are comfortable with their lifestyles, others ache to be wealthier. As you define your goals, try to get a clear picture of your own attitudes toward money.

Worksheet 1–Dreams and Obligations

Worksheet 1 asks you to record your dreams and obligations in two different categories: the next five years and five to ten years from now. The worksheet asks you to put your goals in order of importance, but that is a bit tricky when you're just beginning to think things through. To help crystalize your thoughts, list your goals by year on Table 3–1. Fill in your goals, then examine what you want to accomplish each year and make any adjustments you think are appropriate. Then turn to the worksheet at the back of the book and list each item in order of importance, rather than chronologically. This is the beginning of your personal financial plan.

When we want to probe a client's dreams, we have a freewheeling discussion that lasts for two or three hours. It is interesting how we usually get to the meat of the conversation toward the very end. Perhaps that's the nature of the process of discovery of our deepest wishes. Or maybe it just takes a few hours to develop enough trust to reveal such things to a stranger.

We recommend that you go through the same process with yourself or someone close to you. Set aside a block of time to dream about what you want to do financially. If you are married or have a significant other, sit down together where you can be free from distractions and talk at length about where you see yourselves headed. A financial plan for a couple works best when both are committed to it... and therein lies the challenge.

You and your partner may not agree. After reading Chapter 2 about our cultural crossfire with regard to money, you may understand better why money is the main source of conflict in marriages. Going through this process with your mate may uncover conflicts you did not know were there, or magnify ones you did know about. How can you deal with conflict? If one of you talks while the other listens without judgment, you will achieve the most significant step in seeing eye-to-eye about money. Developing a shared view becomes easier when we feel that we have been heard and that our opinion matters.

If you and your mate find that you are polarized about money, try to understand your own and each other's attitudes. Influences from the past may be keeping you from making good decisions today. You'll know that you and your partner are polarized if you each view the other as being on the opposite end of the monetary spectrum: she's the spender, he's the saver, or she won't let him have any fun and he spends it all so there's nothing left for her. When this happens, we intensify conflict. Polarization ends when the spender realizes that part of him or her is a saver, and the saver sees the spender within herself or himself. When this happens, you and your mate will find common ground; the way will be open for meaningful compromise and financial success because both of you will be pulling in the same direction.

Whether you are planning alone or with a partner, your ultimate goal is to have enough money for a comfortable lifestyle throughout your life. You have to maintain your current lifestyle—from feeding the dog to filling the Mercedes—and you'll need to set aside money to meet short-term goals. (The

Table 3-1 Financial Goals

Year	Goal	Dollar Amount
1988	_____	$ _____
	_____	$ _____
	_____	$ _____
1989	_____	$ _____
	_____	$ _____
	_____	$ _____
1990	_____	$ _____
	_____	$ _____
	_____	$ _____
1991	_____	$ _____
	_____	$ _____
	_____	$ _____
1992	_____	$ _____
	_____	$ _____
	_____	$ _____
1993	_____	$ _____
	_____	$ _____
	_____	$ _____
1994	_____	$ _____
	_____	$ _____
	_____	$ _____
1995	_____	$ _____
	_____	$ _____
	_____	$ _____
1996	_____	$ _____
	_____	$ _____
	_____	$ _____
1997	_____	$ _____
	_____	$ _____
	_____	$ _____
1998	_____	$ _____
	_____	$ _____
	_____	$ _____
1999	_____	$ _____
	_____	$ _____
	_____	$ _____
2000	_____	$ _____
	_____	$ _____
	_____	$ _____

WORKSHEET 1   DREAMS AND OBLIGATIONS

1) What are your short-term (next five years) dreams and goals? Write them in the order of importance. Then estimate the amount of money you will need to realize these dreams and when you will need that money.

#	DREAM/GOAL	DOLLARS NEEDED	TIMING
1	Cabin	$5,000	6/89
2	Second Car	$10,000	12/88
3			
4			
5			

2) Now, do the same for your more long-term goals. Start with goals you would like to reach in five to ten years and finish with any goals you have for the distant future (other than financial independence).

#	DREAM/GOAL	DOLLARS NEEDED	TIMING
1	Junior college	$6,000/year $24,000	1994-99
2			
3			
4			
5			

WORKSHEET 1 (Continued)   **DREAMS AND OBLIGATIONS**

1) What are your short-term obligations? Include those obligations that will become due in five years or less.

	OBLIGATION	AMOUNT OF OBLIGATION	TERMS OF PAYMENT	DATE WHEN OBLIGATION WILL BE FULLY PAID
1	Note from Dad	$10,000	interest only at 8%	balloon payment $10,000 9/89
2				
3				
4				
5				
6				
7				
8				
9				
10				
11				
12				
13				
14				
15				
16				
17				
18				
19				
20				

2) What are your long-term obligations? Include those obligations (your mortgage may be one example) that will take more than five years to pay for.

	OBLIGATION	AMOUNT OF OBLIGATION	TERMS OF PAYMENT	DATE WHEN OBLIGATION WILL BE FULLY PAID
1	Mortgage	$75,000	9 3/4 % 25 years $662.96/mo.	4/2012
2				
3				
4				
5				
6				
7				
8				

three-bin system in Chapter 9 can help with this issue.) This is not truly savings, but briefly-postponed spending on vacations, VCRs or big New Year's Eves. You must also consider the big expenditures—buying a home, putting the kids through college, putting yourself through college.

When you have defined your goals, you will be able to fix a price tag to them and figure out how much you need to set aside today to achieve them (Chapter 9). Some things you should think about when you are defining your goals include:

Your Home. Do you own one? Do you want one? Do you plan to purchase a better one or improve the one you have? What would it cost to buy, remodel or replace your home? Think about the cost in today's dollars; we can worry about the rest later. When do you expect to make this expenditure?

You and Your Mate. Do you have educational or other self-improvement objectives? Do you want more schooling, music lessons, attendance at seminars or workshops? What does it cost, in tuition and lost earnings, to acquire that goal? When would you like to do it?

Educating Your Children. Do you want to pay for your children's education? Where do the children go to school—a state college or university, Harvard, a junior college or trade school? Will you be responsible for the complete cost or will you expect them to pay for part of their education? When will you need the money for this?

Do You Own a Car? If not, do you intend to buy one? If so, in what state of repair, or disrepair, is your car today? Will you need major repairs or a new car? What car will you buy and how much does it cost today? When do you expect to make the purchase?

Home Furnishings. Do you have redecorating projects in mind today? Will draperies or furnishings need to be replaced? Do you plan to upgrade the quality of your furnishings? What will it cost and when will you do these things?

Home Entertainment. Is a VCR, new television or stereo on your "want" list? What items do you want and when might you purchase, improve or replace them?

Vacations. Are vacations stay-at-home affairs or do you want to travel? Are you satisfied with the way you spend your vacations now or do you want to change them in some way? How often do you plan to travel? What will the annual expense be for vacations? If you want to plan more than an annual vacation, what would be the cost and when would you go? Do you intend to buy or renovate a recreational vehicle such as a boat or travel trailer? What would you buy and when?

Miscellaneous Expenses. Are there other important goals? Perhaps you want to support your parents, make gifts to your children, pay for your children's weddings, or make other major purchases? Add them to the worksheet.

Setting priorities among these goals may be difficult initially, so enter each item on your "wish list" by year in the space provided on Table 3-1. Then you can sort them into priority order for the worksheet. If your wish list seems too ambitious at first glance, don't worry. Wait until Chapter 9 to see what it will take. You can tell much more clearly whether your list is too ambitious after you have analyzed your goals in Chapter 9.

You have looked at all your goals and attached priorities to them. Now enter them on Worksheet 1 in the appropriate category depending on whether you intend to achieve this goal in the next five years or in five to ten years. There is no category for more than ten years because we find that most people do not have plans beyond ten years other than financial independence. If you are an exception, make a note on the worksheet to remind you to make the appropriate calculation when we get to Chapter 9.

FINANCIAL INDEPENDENCE GOALS/ RETIREMENT GOALS

Financial independence or a secure retirement is the most important goal for most of our clients over 35. Nothing delights us more than to prepare an analysis of what a client needs to do to be financially independent and discover that it is well within his or her reach! The finding usually elicits an audible sigh of relief.

The reason why we like to call this financial independence rather than retirement is that almost everyone—even those who live to work—loves the idea of having economic freedom. If you are financially independent, you can work as long as it pleases you. If it doesn't please you, you don't have to work. If you long for a certain career that would be more fulfilling to you emotionally, spiritually or socially, but does not have a salary comparable to the one you earn today, you can afford to take it if you are financially independent. Money used for consumption can bring you momentary pleasure, or great and lasting pleasure. But material things can also bring a rigidity to your life— you hate to move because you have so many possessions or you can't relocate to change jobs because it is not a good time to sell your house. Capital does just the opposite—it brings flexibility and freedom to your life. However, it does so at some cost. You must set aside money today to accumulate capital for tomorrow.

When would you like to be financially independent? Forget about midnight tonight and think about a realistic answer. When do you expect to retire? What is the minimum income that would satisfy you, and what represents a comfortable lifestyle to you? You expect to have major expenses at the threshold of retirement. We will analyze these figures in Chapter 9 so that you will know what to do to achieve these goals.

Estate Planning Goals

When you think of estate planning, think of what your heirs would need if you were to die today. If you are part of a two-income household, think also of what you would need if your spouse were to die today. Your estate consists of all that you have accumulated. If it is not enough to leave your dependents in a secure financial position, you will need to augment it with the purchase of life insurance. When you are financially independent, your need for insurance will end. One exception to this would be if you have insufficient liquidity in your estate to pay estate taxes. In that case, you may need life insurance.

Factors that affect your need for insurance include whether or not your dependents intend to remain in your current home, the bills that would be paid off, including the mortgage on your home, and whether you want to provide money for your children's education.

Notice that these are goals, not solutions. The means of achieving them will be covered in the analysis chapters, Chapters 5–10.

Conflicting Goals

In Chapter 9 when you analyze the amount you will have to set aside every year to meet your goals, you will know whether or not they conflict. You may be able to achieve them all, or you may have to adjust some of them.

What if you have to make adjustments? You may find it to be painful, or you may take it in stride. We hope you will be philosophical. You have had conflicting goals before, but you didn't know it because you had not articulated nor analyzed them. The only thing that has changed is your level of knowledge. With that knowledge, you can find solutions. Without it—as you were before—you might not have discovered the problem until it was too late to do anything about it.

John and Marjorie Kemp are 42 and 40 years old and have two teenagers, Will and Sandra. Both the Kemps are employed and have good incomes. They live in a lovely home—with a sizeable mortgage. Marjorie works as a freelance computer programmer. Sandra is a good student who just got her driver's license and like most of her age mates, wants a car. Will is especially good at foreign languages and wants to be a foreign exchange student in two years during his junior year in high school.

John and Marjorie made a list of things the family wants to do. They want to buy partial interest—perhaps a time share—in a resort area cabin. Their house needs some sprucing up and the water heater has been hiccoughing lately. The list mounts as the Kemps lay out all their goals in chronological order. Then they set priorities. The cost of all these things makes John gulp.

To do it all, they would have to reduce their lifestyle today to an unacceptable level.

They talk, and decide to put the cabin on hold for a year or two. The children will be leaving home soon and a family vacation spot may not fit with their lifestyle. They have a frank discussion with the kids and make some decisions. Kim says that she can get a summer job and save half of what she needs for a car. Marjorie could take some steps to increase her freelancing income. She's working half-time now, and could increase her hours to three-quarters time. Marjorie plans to employ Will in her business where he can run errands and do office clean-up chores. Will intends to set aside half of what he earns to pay for his year as an exchange student. Marjorie will also set up a retirement plan so that some of what the Kemps need for the future can be set aside this way. Every dollar saved is tax deductible, so the Kemps will be reducing their taxes and making more money available for their own use. John wishes he had started planning earlier so he wouldn't have to ask his family to make these adjustments. On the other hand, the whole family has found a balance between dreams and reality. The children know more about running the family's finances than they ever did, and feel positive about their own ability to contribute.

When goals conflict, you can use any of the techniques the Kemps used and more. You can adjust the timetable, tap unused resources in the family, make your investments work harder, reduce your taxes, decrease your current lifestyle or drop some dreams from your list.

Achieving your goals takes patience and a long view. You will be surprised at what you can accomplish when you begin to plan systematically. We've seen the transformation in many of our client's lives. When people come to us, they may be deficit spending, have credit card debt, and little knowledge of investments. When they begin to plan, things turn around because they make a commitment to taking charge of their financial lives. You will soon find that you have an emergency reserve, back-up liquid investments, a portfolio that works and the flexibility to alter your direction when necessary.

The real dream is not any one thing, but the ability to achieve what is important at any given time. Planning will make you aware of your possibilities and your limitations, and *that* is the secret of achieving your goals.

CHAPTER FOUR

GATHERING INFORMATION: YOUR FINANCIAL CHECK-UP

AND NOW WHAT?

You've already completed the first step in the financial planning process—you have defined where you want to go. The second step is to examine where you are today. Knowing where you are, your long-term destination and some of the stops along the way allows you to plot the best course to take you there.

Gathering data takes time, but it is worth it because you will lay the groundwork for a lifetime of financial success! It often takes six hours to review a client's file completely and to cover the facts. Financial factfinding is time consuming, so set aside blocks of time rather than try to do it all at once.

Assembling the Documents You Need

Most of the financial information you need can be found on various documents in your possession. Perhaps your first session should be devoted solely to sorting out your paperwork. Important papers should be stored in a safe place such as a safe deposit box, so don't put actual documents into your financial plan. Record information from the documents and then return them to their appropriate places.

Gather together the following documents:

bank statements

brokerage statements

detailed information on your stocks and bonds

terms of loans for money you owe and are owed including origination date, ending date, interest rates, monthly payment

information on real estate you own including rent revenue, taxes, insurance, other operating expenses, depreciation

confirmation statements from limited partnerships you own

information on the value of businesses you own

your latest tax return

employee-benefit brochures and retirement plan statements

homeowners, automobile and excess liability policies

disability, medical, and dental insurance policies

life insurance policies

legal agreements such as pre-nuptial agreements, wills and trusts

Getting Organized

We recommend that you take this opportunity to get all your financial documents in order. You may want to include an inventory of the contents of your safe deposit box with your financial plan or you may want to make copies of valuable documents and store them together with your plan.

It is difficult for family members to know where to find important documents and understand your full financial situation if you are suddenly not there. Take this opportunity to gather everything together as your gift to yourself and your family.

WORKING THROUGH THE WORKSHEETS

In this section we will "walk through" all the worksheets you will be using to record your financial information. Some of the analyses will be left to later chapters, some will be explained here.

Title Page

Notice that the title page has room for the initial date and several lines for updates. This is to remind you that your completed plan is a beginning, not a culmination. Your completed plan should be updated at least once a year. You'll find that updating takes only about one-third the time that creating the original plan took.

Worksheet 1–Dreams and Obligations

You filled out Worksheet 1 while reading Chapter 3. Take a second look at it now. Are your priorities the same? Are the dollar amounts still on target?

Worksheet 2–Financial Independence/Retirement

This worksheet asks you to determine when you want to be financially independent and what type of lifestyle you want to lead. Before you answer, think carefully. How old do you want to be when you become financially independent? What time in your life will you want the option of continuing to work or not, or of accepting a lower-paying job if it is more fulfilling? Is your retirement age young or old? What point in your life do you intend to be out of the workforce? Answer these questions *thoughtfully*. Then turn to the other issues presented by this worksheet.

After-tax spendable income should allow for a "no frills" lifestyle at the minimum and the desired income a comfortable lifestyle. Be realistic. When thinking about major expenditures, analyze what things might require a major commitment of assets and could not be paid from your normal cash flow. Educational expenses will be considered separately, so think in terms of money to capitalize a new business, a car if you'll need to pay cash for it or other big expenses.

In setting financial independence goals, bear in mind that the earlier you want to retire, the more of today's income you must set aside for tomorrow. It is generally unrealistic to aim for a retirement lifestyle that is better than the one you have today. You'd have to save so much money that it would probably reduce your current lifestyle more than you would like. What you want is to balance today's lifestyle with tomorrow's.

Worksheet 3–Estate Planning Questions and Considerations

The answers you give to the questions on Worksheet 3 will help you evaluate your existing will. If you do not have a will, it will prepare you to have one drafted because these are the questions a lawyer will ask you. Let's touch on some of the trickier questions.

Question four on revocable living trusts may be puzzling because we have not covered the subject yet. A brief explanation will help. A revocable living trust is a device to avoid probate, but not to avoid estate taxes. During your life, your assets are titled to the trust and you manage them exactly as if they were titled in your name. Most people establish living trusts with themselves as trustees. Most married couples name themselves as co-trustees.

If you have made any gifts in excess of $10,000, or if you and your spouse have made joint gifts in excess of $20,000, you have used up some of your estate transfer credit, and you should have filed a gift tax return. Enter the amount in question seven.

FINANCIAL PLAN FOR:

NAME: *Richard and Trish Walters*

DATE OF INITIAL PLAN: *10/10/87*

UPDATES: _____

WORKSHEET 2   **FINANCIAL INDEPENDENCE AND RETIREMENT**

1) At what age do you wish to be financially independent? _____60_____

2) At what age do you expect to retire? _____65_____

3) What is the annual income you will need
   at retirement in today's dollars?

   Minimum $ _36,000_   Desired $ _48,000_

4) Do you anticipate any extraordinary major expenditures? ___yes___

PURPOSE OF EXPENDITURE	AMOUNT	APPROXIMATE DATE
1 Money to start antique business	$20,000	at age 65
2		
3		
4		

5) What kind of lifestyle would you select for yourself at retirement or if (and when)
   you are financially independent and are no longer required to work for an income?

_____
_____
_____
_____
_____
_____
_____

WORKSHEET 3 — ESTATE DISPOSITION QUESTIONS

1. Do you or your spouse expect to inherit a substantial amount of property? Indicate estimated amounts and sources.

    spouse $70,000 from mother now age 80

2. Do your children have substantial estates in their own right and income from salary or investments, etc.?

    no

3. Do you and your spouse have wills? When were they last revised?

    Wills done 7/8/83

4. If a revocable living trust is appropriate for you, who would you select as Trustees and successor Trustees?

    Myself

5. Do you plan to leave substantial gifts to charity at your or your spouse's death? Indicate any intended charities and approximate amounts.

    Want to give $10,000 to college when second of us dies

6. Would you be willing to make outright gifts to your children and grandchildren or other relatives at this time if there were estate and income tax advantages to be gained?

    yes

7. Have you used any Estate Transfer Credit in making gifts? If so, how much has been used up?

    no

8. Are you contributing to the support of any parent, relative or in-law? Indicate any such person, relationship and annual amount. Might any of the above depend on you for financial support in the future?

    no. Father may need support. Not likely for five years, not likely to be more than $100/mo.

WORSHEET 3 (Part Two)   **ESTATE CONSIDERATIONS**

Please answer the following questions for the adults
in your household—whether or not they are employed outside the home.
Note any relevant comments in the space provided.

	IF HUSBAND DIES	IF WIFE DIES
1. What would your family's minimum after-tax monthly income requirement be in today's dollars?	3,000	3,000
2. To what degree is the surviving spouse capable of handling financial affairs?	completely	completely
3. Would the surviving spouse obtain or continue employment?	yes	yes
4. What would the estimated pre-tax monthly income of the spouse be?	1,500	2,500
5. Would the surviving spouse continue to live in your present home?	yes	yes
6. Should the home mortgage be paid off?	yes	yes

7. Estate Planning Objectives (Select one from each category):

   - [X] Maximize Assets Available to Spouse
   - [ ] Maximize Assets Available to Children
   - [ ] Simplicity and Flexibility
   - [X] Maximize Estate Tax Savings

8. Are there any assets you would not consider liquidating upon a death
   to provide for your family's monthly income needs?
   yes
   Comments: Keep mountain cabin so children can inherit.

WORKSHEET 4   EDUCATIONAL GOALS

	CHILD'S NAME	Peter				
1	YEARS UNTIL COLLEGE	5				
2	COST PER YEAR	17,000				
3	NUMBER OF YEARS	4				
4	TOTAL COST	68,000				
5	PERCENT YOU WILL PAY	80%				
6	FUNDS NEEDED	54,400				

The estate considerations section asks what your family would need in the event of your death. If your spouse works, the same questions need to be answered about family income needs in the event of his or her death. You'll use this information later to estimate your need for life insurance.

Educational Goals

Worksheet 4 asks several questions relating to children's educational goals and the extent that you wish to fund those goals. As you think about this the key question is where Junior wants to go to school. If it is too soon to tell, the question then becomes what kind of school should you plan for your child to attend? Do you want to be able to send your son or daughter to an Ivy League school, a less expensive private college, a state university or a community college?

Educational expenses have been rising faster than inflation. Between academic years 1986/1987 and 1987/1988 when we were experiencing inflation of approximately 4 percent, tuition at a University of California campus rose 9.1 percent, Stanford's tuition rose 6 percent and tuition at a private religious university, University of San Francisco rose 9.9 percent.

Tuition, room and board at a top private college costs approximately $17,000 per year. This does not include travel to campus and back or pocket money. The cost for a state college or university is approximately $6,000 per year. Living at home and going to a local junior college for two years and then to a state college would probably cost $1,000 a year for the first two years for tuition, books and increased transportation costs. The total price tag would be $14,000 for four years of higher education. Keep these approximate costs in mind as you fill out the worksheet. Remember, if you save for college educations and the children don't go, or go to less expensive schools, the funds accumulated will be available to achieve your other goals. This will be true unless you choose a college funding strategy that involves making outright gifts or establishing certain trusts for your children (see Chapter 10). Chapter 10 will describe some planning opportunities that will help you realize them.

Worksheet 5–General Statistics

Use the general statistics page to record basic information about you and your family. This includes income information and summary information from your latest tax return.

Estimate your income for the current year using the estimated incomes section. The Latest Tax Return Section is designed to build awareness about your payment of taxes. When we asked Jerry and Leslie Snyder how much they paid in taxes last year, they said "We got a refund." On closer examination, the Snyders paid $15,000 in federal and state taxes and $6,000 in social security taxes (FICA). Perhaps the psychological mechanism that leads us to block memories of other painful things does the same when it comes to

WORKSHEET 5 **GENERAL STATISTICS**

PERSONS

1	HEAD OF HOUSEHOLD	Jon Smith	DATE OF BIRTH	8/29/42	AGE	45
2	SPOUSE	Ellyn	DATE OF BIRTH	6/13/46	AGE	41
3	CHILDREN: NAMES & AGES	Peter 16	Liza 14			

ESTIMATED INCOMES 19 —

	DESCRIPTION	HEAD OF HOUSEHOLD		SPOUSE		COMBINED	
		MONTHLY	ANNUAL	MONTHLY	ANNUAL	MONTHLY	ANNUAL
4	SALARY	3,000	36,000	1,500	18,000	4,500	54,000
5	PROFESSIONAL INCOME						
6	ALIMONY	0					
7	INCOME FROM ANNUITIES	0					
8	PENSION	0					
9	PENSION	0					
10	SOCIAL SECURITY	0					
11	OTHER	0					
12	INVESTMENTS					100	1,200
13	TOTAL					4,600	55,200

CASH FLOW FOR LAST YEAR

14	INCOME FROM ALL SOURCES		55,200
15	LESS: FEDERAL TAXES	(	8,840)
16	STATE TAXES	(	1,650)
17	FICA*	(	3,851)
18	LOCAL TAXES	(	0)
19	AFTER-TAX CASH FLOW		40,859
20	LESS: LIVING EXPENSES	(	32,000)
21	DISCRETIONARY INCOME		8,859

*1986 FICA: 7.15% of earnings to a maximum of $42,000 in earnings. Maximum Tax = $3,003.
For self-employed: 12.3% to a maximum tax of $5,166.
1987 FICA: 7.15% of earnings up to $43,800. Maximum tax is $3,131.70.
For self-employed: 12.3%, maximum tax is $5,387.40.

WORKSHEET 6 — ESTIMATED LIVING EXPENSES FOR 19 _____

COMMITTED EXPENSES		MONTHLY	OR	ANNUAL
Residence:				
Rent or Mortgage Payment		840		
Interest rate	9.5			
Original balance	100,000			
Origination date	2/81			
Term of loan	30 years			
Current balance	93,940			
Property tax		—		1,250
Household garden help		—		
Water/trash		20		
TV Cable		20		
Other housing costs		50		
Automobile:				
Payments		—		
Interest rate				
Original balance				
Origination date				
Term of loan				
Current balance				
Gas/oil		100		
Maintenance/repairs				600
Parking		25		
Other transportation/commuting costs				
Insurance:				
Homeowners/renters insurance		256		
Life		670		
Medical		employer		
Disability		"		
Personal liability		125		
Auto insurance		450		
Other				
Household/Personal Expenses:				
Utilities/fuel				1,500
Telephone		50		
Groceries/liquor		400		
Clothes/dry cleaning		100		
Personal care		25		
Medical/dental care		25		
Prescription drugs		0		
Miscellaneous:				
Alimony		0		
Support of relatives		0		
Education		0		
TOTAL		3,156		3,350

WORKSHEET 6 (Continued) ESTIMATED LIVING EXPENSES FOR 19 _____

DISCRETIONARY EXPENSES	MONTHLY	OR	ANNUAL
Residence:			
Home improvements			1,200
Furniture/linens/etc.			600
Entertainment:			
Dining out	150		
Recreation	100		
Vacations			2,000
Babysitters	0		
Memberships/clubs			150
Hobbies			500
Miscellaneous:			
Charitable contributions			1,000
Gifts/holiday gifts			1,200
Work-related expenses			600
Lunches	100		
Books/periodicals			200
Legal/accounting/financial services			850
Other Tax Deductible:			
Other non-deductible:			
TOTALS	350		8,300
Total living expenses: (Committed and Discretionary)	3,532		11,650

Are you planning any major purchases or expecting any unusual fluctuations in these amounts?

Will need to purchase a new car next year

tax liability! It is important, however, to know how much of your income goes to taxes.

All the entries in the Latest Tax Return section come directly from your tax return except Income for All Sources. Why? Luckily, not all the income we receive is subject to tax. So, rather than using your tax return to develop this number, look at your actual cash flow. If you have only salaries, it will be simple. If you have municipal bonds or other tax-exempt securities, be sure to count them. Some investments that have negative taxable income may provide you with positive cash flow. Real estate is an example of this.

Remember, all of the information in this section refers to last year. Taking a backward look allows you to work with complete information.

Worksheet 6–Living Expenses

This is the fun part! And it also can be a very revealing exercise—an opportunity to see where your money goes. The easiest way to complete this projection of your living expenses for the current year is to go over 90 days of your check ledger, your credit card statements and other expenditure records. Use them as a basis to estimate annual expenditures. Make adjustments for non-recurring expenses and expenses that occur less than monthly: for example, holiday gift expenses, auto insurance premiums and the like. Infrequent expenses may be overrepresented or underrepresented in the 90-day period that your check ledger covers.

Worksheet 7–Casualty and Liability Insurance

The next three worksheets address insurance issues. You'll need your automobile, homeowner's, excess liability, disability, medical, dental and life insurances. The last four types of insurance may be described in your employee benefits brochure.

You should find all the information you need on the Declarations Page of your automobile policy for Worksheet 7. Enter the make and model of each car on the top line and the coverages that apply to them in the spaces below. If your coverage reads "Bodily Injury 300/500," that's insurance-ese for $300,000 coverage per person for bodily injury liability and $500,000 per accident. You may have two different deductibles, one for collision and one for other occurrences, for example fire and theft. This is usually called comprehensive coverage. On the line labeled "Collision" or "Comprehensive" note whether you have such coverage. Then, note the amount of the deductible in the space provided.

As with your automobile policy, the declarations page of your tenant's, condo or homeowner's policy should have all the information you need about your home. Note the location that is insured on the top line of the home section of Worksheet 7, and all coverages pertaining to that property below. If you have a condo or tenant's policy you will have no dwelling coverage. The condo

WORKSHEET 7 — RISK MANAGEMENT: CASUALTY AND LIABILITY

AUTO INSURANCE	AUTO 1	AUTO 2	AUTO 3	Note any changes needed in any of the preceding policies or provisions (See Chapter 7)
Make and model	'85 Mazda			
Bodily injury liability	100/300			
Property damage liability	25,000			too low, raise to at least $50,000
Medical payments	5,000			
Underinsured motorists	15/30			too low, raise to at least 100/300
Collision (yes/no)	Yes			
Collision deductible	100			increase if premium goes down enough
Comprehensive (yes/no)	Yes			
Comprehensive deductible	100			
Company	ABC			
Premium and frequency	400/yr.			

WORKSHEET 7 (continued) — RISK MANAGEMENT: CASUALTY AND LIABILITY

Homeowner's Insurance	Primary Residence	Second Home	Rental Property	Other	Note Needed Changes
Location	472 Shady Ln.				
Market value	170,000				
Dwelling	135,000				
Appurtenant structures	13,500				
Unscheduled property	40,000				
Living expenses	10,000				
Personal liability	100,000				
Medical payments (per person and per occurence)	5,000				
Deductible	100				increase if premiums reduced enough
Scheduled property	none				
Inflation guard	Yes				
Replacement value	No				obtain
Burglar/smoke alarm	Yes				
Earthquake/flood	Yes				
Company	ABC				
Premium and frequency	250/yr.				

Umbrella Coverage (yes/no) __Yes__ Coverage Amount __$1 million__

Required Underlying Coverage: Automobile __100/300__ Homeowners __100,000__

Premium and Frequency: __125/yr__ Company __ABC__

WORKSHEET 8   RISK MANAGEMENT: MEDICAL AND DISABILITY

I. DISABILITY INCOME INSURANCE

	POLICY 1	POLICY 2	POLICY 3	POLICY 4
Insurance company and policy number	Employer			
Who is insured on this policy?	Bill			
Amount of monthly benefit	1,000			
Length of time before benefits begin	90 days			
Length of benefits A. For illness:	65			
B. For accident:	65			
Premiums and frequency	paid by employer			
Definition of disability (own occupation, any occupation, or split definition)	split (2 years, own)			
Other notes about policy				

WORKSHEET 8 (Continued)   RISK MANAGEMENT: MEDICAL AND DISABILITY

2. MEDICAL INSURANCE (If your medical care is provided through an HMO, note that information here.)

	POLICY 1	POLICY 2	POLICY 3	POLICY 4
Insurance company and policy number	ABC 123456			
Who is insured on this policy?	Bill Sally Children			
Premiums and frequency	150/mo.			
Deductible	$100 per person	$400 per family		
Coinsurance (percent you must pay)	20%			
Stop loss (maximum amount you are liable for each year)	200			
Major medical limit	$1 million			
Other notes about policy	covers prescriptions			

3. DENTAL INSURANCE

	POLICY 1	POLICY 2
Insurance company and policy number	Employer	
Who is insured?	family	
Premiums and frequency	employer paid	
Deductible	$50	
Coinsurance percent	0% cleaning 20% fillings	
Annual limit	1,000	
Other provisions or notes	only $1,500 life time orthodontal	

master policy or your landlord's policy should insure the dwelling itself. "Scheduled Property" refers to high value items that have been appraised and insured separately. "Inflation Guard" refers to the policy feature that automatically adjusts your dwelling coverage to changes in the cost of construction. Enter "yes" or "no" in this box to indicate whether or not you have such coverage. "Replacement Value" is a special endorsement or rider on most policies which insures the contents of your home for replacement cost. If your policy says ACV or actual cash value, put "no" in this box.

Worksheet 7 provides space for you to note whether or not you have appropriate coverage. In Chapter 7 you'll be analyzing your policies and making the appropriate notations.

Umbrella or Excess Liability policies have coverages that start at $1 million and require certain bodily injury and property damage liability limits on auto and homeowner's policies. This information can be found on the declarations page of the policy. The homeowner's limit may be listed as CPL or comprehensive personal liability. Note the required amounts and look above to see if you have those amounts on your auto and homeowner's policies. If you don't, make a note to change the coverage on your automobile and homeowner's policies to meet the requirements of the umbrella policy.

Worksheet 8–Medical and Disability Insurance

Read your disability policy provisions and note the amount of monthly benefit—sometimes stated as a dollar amount, sometimes as a percentage of your base salary or total compensation. Length of time before benefits begin may be called the elimination period. Length of benefits may be stated as "to age 65" or "65/life." If 65/life or 5 years/life is shown, the first number applies to disabilities caused by illness, the second to disabilities caused by accident.

The policy usually highlights the definition of disability in some way, so it should be easy to find. Some employee benefit brochures, however, do not cover this important aspect. You may have to check with your employee benefits department.

Disability may be defined as inability to perform the duties of your *own* occupation; of *any* occupation for which you are suited by training and education; or of *any* occupation whatsoever (this is the strictest occupation defined). It may also have a split definition such as *own* occupation for two years of disability and any occupation thereafter.

Medical policies are probably the most difficult to read. Look carefully at information regarding deductibles, the percentage you must pay and the maximum out-of-pocket cost per year. Look over the schedule of benefits also, and try to judge whether or not it will meet most of your health care needs. If you are of child-bearing age, for example, it is important that maternity benefits be covered. The more comprehensive policies we have reviewed include substance abuse treatment, psychological care—although both are subject to limits—and prescriptions.

WORKSHEET 9

LIFE INSURANCE

	A	B	C	D	E	F	G	H	I	J	K	L
	INSURANCE COMPANY	POLICY NUMBER	INSURED	OWNER	BENEFICIARY	TYPE OF POLICY[1]	FACE VALUE	ANNUAL PREMIUMS	CASH VALUE BEFORE LOANS[2]	POLICY LOANS	NET CASH VALUE (I-J)	NET INSURANCE PROTECTION (G-J)
1	ABC	JX-743	Tom	Tom	Ellen	T	100,000	$175	—	—	—	—
2	ABC	JX-744	Tom	Tom	Ellen	Wh	$50,000	250	5,000	3,000	2,000	47,000
3												
4												
5												
6												
7												
8												
9												
10												
TOTAL												

[1]Term, Whole or Ordinary, Universal, Single Premium Whole Life or Other
[2]Tables provided in your policy will show estimated cash value. This will not include accumulated dividends.

If you are fortunate enough to have dental coverage (it is generally available only as an employee benefit), note the same factors as you noted for health coverage: the deductible, the amount you pay for certain procedures and the maximum annual benefit. There may be no maximum amount for which you are liable (your out-of-pocket cost). The policy is more likely to be written in a way that limits the insurance company's liability, not yours.

Worksheet 9–Life Insurance

Worksheet 9 is for recording information regarding your life insurance policies. When filling the "Owner" column, be aware that most policies are owned by the insured—but not all. In fact, some estate planning benefits come from having someone other than the insured own the policy. If someone else owns the policy, it is not part of the insured's taxable estate, subject to some limitations.

Note the column labeled "Net Insurance Protection." Many people do not know that if you have a cash value loan, you must subtract it from the face amount to determine death benefit. For example, if you have $100,000 worth of coverage and a cash value loan of $25,000 your beneficiary will receive only $75,000 at your death.

You can estimate cash value from tables in the policy. They will never be completely accurate because they do not include accumulated dividends that the insurance company cannot predict. Write to the insurance company for accurate cash value information. Don't forget to include your policy number in all correspondence.

Worksheet 10–Disability Income Needs

You've worked your way through all the insurance facts and defined your life insurance needs in the estate planning section. Let's turn now to disability needs. Answer these questions for you, or for you and your spouse. Some parents feel that, even if they become disabled, they want to pay for their children's college educations. Others do not. To maintain the same educational standard, disability coverage needs to be increased if the children will not be financially responsible for their own college.

Worksheet 11–Cash and Equivalents

Cash and equivalent investments include savings accounts, life insurance cash values, deferred annuities, and credit union, bank, and savings and loan deposits. Also include Treasury Bills, money market accounts and the like. The maturity date is important for certificates of deposit, Treasury Bills and deferred annuities. Yield is simply the interest rate paid. Multiply the yield times the amount on deposit to arrive at the estimated income.

WORKSHEET 10 **DISABILITY INCOME NEEDS**

	IF HUSBAND WERE DISABLED	IF WIFE WERE DISABLED
What would be your family's after-tax minimum monthly income requirements?	3,000	3,000
Would your spouse obtain or continue employment?	Yes	Yes
Estimated pre-tax monthly income of spouse	1,500	2,500
Anticipated retirement date	2,007	2,007
Would your family's educational objectives change?	no	no
Comments		

DISABILITY NEEDS ANALYSIS

		IF HUSBAND WERE DISABLED	IF WIFE WERE DISABLED
Family Income Need		3,000	3,000
Less:	Spouse's income	1,500	2,500
	Disability benefits	0	0
	Social security disability	0	0
	Portfolio income (6% of working assets)	1,250	1,250
	Adjustment for taxes	450	565
Disability Insurance Needed		−700	185

WORKSHEET 11

CASH AND EQUIVALENTS

A REGISTRATION	B DATE DEPOSITED	C DESCRIPTION	D MATURITY DATE	E CURRENT VALUE	F YIELD (PERCENT)	G INCOME (E × F)	H REMARKS
1 JT	3/84	ABC Savings CD	3/87	10,000	8%	800	
2							
3							
4							
5							
6							
7							
8							
9							
10							
11							
12							
13							
14							
15							
16							
17							
18							
19							
20							
TOTAL							

Gathering Information: Your Financial Check-Up

WORKSHEET 12   **FIXED INCOME SECURITIES (Bills, Notes, Bonds and Preferred Stock)**

	A	B	C	D	E	F	G	H	I	J	K	L
	REGISTRATION	PURCHASE DATE	NUMBER OF BONDS	DESCRIPTION	COUPON OR DIVIDEND	MATURITY DATE	COST PER UNIT	PRESENT PRICE PER UNIT	MARKET VALUE (C × H)	CURRENT YIELD	ANNUAL INCOME	CAPITAL GAIN OR LOSS (I - C x G)
1	JT	5/87	5	ABC Water District	6.5	3/7/05	4,892	5,000	25,000	6.5	1,625	540
2												
3	JT	6/82	1	ABC Corp	8%	5/10/05	1000	925	925	8.6	80	(75)
4												
5												
6												
7												
8												
9												
10												
11												
12												
13												
14												
15												
16												
17												
18												
19												
20												
TOTAL												

WORKSHEET 13

NOTES RECEIVABLES (Mortgages/Loans)

	REGISTRATION	DESCRIPTION	ORIGINAL AMOUNT	YEAR OF ORIGINATION	INTEREST RATE	ANNUAL PAYMENTS RECEIVED	MATURITY DATE	BALLOON PAYMENT	BALANCE
1	H	2nd Mortgage Phelps	10,000	3/84	9%	900	3/89	$10,000	10,000
2									
3	JT	Loan to Susie	5,000	3/87	8%	1,252	3/92	0	4,061
4									
5									
6									
7									
8									
9									
10									
11									
12									
13									
14									
15									
16									
17									
18									
19									
20									
TOTAL									

WORKSHEET 14

COMMON STOCK

	REGISTRATION	PURCHASE DATE	NUMBER OF SHARES	DESCRIPTION	TOTAL COST	PRICE PER SHARE	$ PRESENT MARKET VALUE	PER SHARE INCOME	ANNUAL INCOME	DIVIDEND YIELD (PERCENT)	CAPITAL GAIN OR LOSS
1	JT	11/82	100	ABC Corp	1,750	21 1/4	2125	1.00	100	4.7	375
2											
3	I	6/86	200	XYZ Corp	5,000	17 1/8	3425	0	0	0	(1,575)
4											
5											
6											
7											
8											
9											
10											
11											
12											
13											
14											
15											
16											
17											
18											
19											
20											
TOTAL											

Worksheet 12–Fixed-Income Securities

When entering fixed income securities, enter information on what you originally paid for the investment and its current market value. The difference between them is your capital gain or loss if you elect to sell the bond. Bond prices are sometimes hard to come by. You might be able to find a broker to look up this information for you. If not, leave it blank.

Worksheet 13–Notes Receivable

Enter personal notes, unsecured loans, mortgages and similar investments on this worksheet. These are notes and deeds that bring you income, not ones on which you make payments to others. Include the payor, the amount the note was originally written for, the annual income, date of the final payment and any balloon payments that will come due. Finally, enter the remaining balance.

Worksheet 14–Common Stock

It will be easy to find current market values for most of your stocks. If your local paper does not have good listings, pick up the *Wall Street Journal.* As with bonds, note what you paid for the stock and its current market value. Calculate the capital gain or loss you would incur if you sold it today.

Worksheet 15–Mutual Funds

The basic items on the mutual funds worksheet are the same as the common stock worksheet. We have not asked you to compute your capital gain on your mutual fund because it can be very difficult. If you sell it, however, you will have to figure this information. Tax accounting for your fund is difficult because you paid taxes on the capital gains in the fund as you went along; consequently, your cost has to be adjusted to reflect that you have met your tax liability to some extent. To make this computation, you need a complete history of fund transactions. A word to the wise: Keep your year-end mutual fund statements every year as a permanent record. To give you a special challenge, your state's tax treatment of the mutual fund may be different from the federal.

Worksheets 16, 17 and 18–Real Property

If you have ever wondered how your rental real estate has performed, you will love the next three worksheets. They will put your finger on the pulse! Worksheet 16 asks for basic information on the current value, mortgage balance and original cost, as well as capital gain. Use it as a summary page. Worksheets 17 and 18 allow you to look at your property in two ways: You

WORKSHEET 15

MUTUAL FUNDS

REGISTRATION	NAME OF FUND	PRESENT NUMBER OF SHARES	CURRENT DOLLARS PER SHARE	CURRENT VALUE	DIVIDEND PER SHARE	ANNUAL INCOME	CURRENT YIELD	LATEST CAPITAL GAINS DISTRIBUTION DOLLAR PER SHARE	LATEST CAPITAL GAINS DISTRIBUTION DOLLAR AMOUNT	ORIGINAL PURCHASE DATE	ORIGINAL COST
1 JT	ABC Growth	182.581	9.86	1,800	.19	$35	2%	$1.00	182.58	4/83	440
2											
3											
4											
5											
6											
7											
8											
9											
10											
11											
12											
13											
14											
15											
16											
17											
18											
19											
20											
TOTAL											

WORKSHEET 16

REAL PROPERTY

A REGISTRATION	B DESCRIPTION	C ESTIMATED MARKET VALUE	D BALANCE ON MORTGAGE	E ESTIMATED NET EQUITY (C-D)	F ORIGINAL COST	G YEARS HELD	H CAPITAL GAIN OR LOSS
1 JT	duplex 132 Elm Street	$100,000	75,000	25,000	95,000	3	5,000
2 JT	lot 16 Mariner	4,500	-0-	4,500	10,000	8	(5,400)
3							
4							
5							
SUBTOTAL							
TOTAL							

Gathering Information: Your Financial Check-Up 55

WORKSHEET 17   **RENTAL UNIT ANALYSIS: Income and Cash Flow**

Name of property: _814 Shady Lane_

Current year: _19 X X_

TAXABLE INCOME

Gross Rents		12,000
Subtract Cash Expenses:	Property taxes	(1,000)
	Insurance	(300)
	Miscellaneous expenses	(800)
	Interest on mortgage	(6,000)
	Depreciation	(3,200)
Taxable Gain or Loss		$700

CASH FLOW BEFORE AND AFTER TAX

Gross Rents		12,000
Subtract:	Cash Expenses (property taxes, insurance and miscellaneous expenses)	(2,100)
	Mortgage payments	(7,400)
Pre-Tax Cash Flow		2,500
Add Back:	Taxes Saved on Loss (loss multiplied by your marginal tax bracket)*	
OR		
Subtract:	Taxes Paid on Gain (gain multiplied by your marginal tax bracket)*	(217)

*700 x 31% = $217

After-Tax Cash Flow   2,283

*Assumes 31% Combined State and Federal Bracket

WORKSHEET 18 RENTAL UNIT ANALYSIS: Estimated Return on Investment

Name of property: __814 Shady Lane__

TAXABLE GAIN OR LOSS

Market Value			100,000
Subtract:	Real Estate Commission (6%)	(	6,000)
	Purchase price	(	75,000)
	Improvements	(	5,000)
Add:	Accumulated depreciation	+	19,200
Unrealized Gain (Loss)			33,200

CASH TO YOU UPON SALE

Market Value			100,000
Subtract:	6% Commission	(	6,000)
	Mortgage balance	(	60,000)
Subtotal:	Pre-tax equity		34,000
Subtract:	Deferred capital gains tax* (unrealized gain or loss multiplied by marginal tax bracket)	(	10,292)

After-Tax Equity $23,708

After-Tax Yield on After-Tax Equity   2283 ÷ 23460 = 9.7%
(after-tax cash flow from Worksheet 17
divided by after-tax equity)

Appreciation   25,000
(subtract purchase price from current market value)

Purchase Date __1/81__

Average Annual Appreciation   4%
(appreciation divided by years you have held property.
See Appendix B to calculate compound rate of appreciation.)

*Assume 31% Combined marginal bracket

can examine income and cash flow on Worksheet 17 and compute the return on your investment on Worksheet 18. Use both worksheets to analyze each piece of income property.

Many individuals buy a piece of real estate and hold it forever. Just as with any other investment, real estate has a life cycle and there is a peak time to sell it. This may be when the tax benefits are greatly reduced, when the appreciation curve flattens, when maintenance problems threaten to overwhelm you or when some other event occurs than you had in mind when you purchased the property.

Worksheet 17 is divided into two sections. One looks at real estate as you account for it on your tax return. This computation is important because it allows you to take the tax benefits or tax cost of the investment into account when you compute cash flow. That figure tells you exactly what the real estate is yielding on an after-tax basis. The bottom line on this half of the analysis is your taxable gain or loss. You'll need to complete this worksheet after you compute your marginal bracket in Chapter 5. After you make that computation, follow the instructions in the lower half of the analysis. Meanwhile, fill in all of the elements you can. Although you will be looking backwards, we recommend that you draw these figures from last year's tax return. Actual operating data for this year may be hard to project due to unexpected vacancies or repairs. Repeat this analysis every year after your tax return is complete. It will allow you to track performance and give you better judgment about when to sell.

Worksheet 18 will help you analyze your total return on investments. Total return on a piece of real estate comes from operating income, or after-tax cash flow, and appreciation. To complete Worksheet 18, you need to know your marginal bracket. Fill in the worksheet as completely as possible and finish the computation after you read Chapter 5.

Worksheet 19–Energy

If your energy investment is in the form of oil company stocks, enter it on Worksheet 14. Investments that we classify as true energy investments come in the form of ownership interest—such as units in a limited partnership or a percentage ownership in a working interest. Estimate the value at the original purchase price unless other information is available.

Worksheet 20–Exotics

Use this worksheet to record ownership of precious metals, including gold stock mutual funds, precious gems and collectibles. It may be difficult to assess the value of some assets in this category. When no organized market can assist you in valuation, make the best estimate you can; but try to err on the side of conservatism.

WORKSHEET 19

ENERGY

	REGISTRATION	DESCRIPTION	PURCHASE DATE	PERCENT OWNED OR NUMBER OF UNITS	COST PER UNIT	ESTIMATED VALUE	ANNUAL INCOME	YIELD	PRESENT ESTIMATED GAIN OR LOSS
1	JT	ABC Oil Income	4/85	20	500	$10,000	$1,025	10.3%	Unk
2									
3									
4									
5									
6									
7									
8									
9									
10									
11									
12									
13									
14									
15									
16									
17									
18									
19									
20									
TOTAL									

WORKSHEET 20

EXOTICS: Gold funds, Precious Metals, Precious Stones, Art, Stamps, Etc.

	REGISTRATION	PURCHASE DATE	DESCRIPTION	QUANTITY	TOTAL COST	ESTIMATED PRESENT DOLLARS			YIELD	ESTIMATED CAPITAL GAIN OR LOSS
						PER SHARE OR UNIT VALUE	TOTAL VALUE	ANNUAL INCOME		
1	JT	various	Maple Leaf	12	$4,800	$380	$4,560	0	0	(240)
2										
3	I	various	ABC Gold Mutual Fund	185	1,665	$9.50	$1,757	$70	4	92
4										
5										
6										
7										
8										
9										
10										
11										
12										
13										
14										
15										
16										
17										
18										
19										
20										
TOTAL										

Worksheet 21–Business

If you own a business, enter the owner's name, the form of ownership and the value of the business. Write yourself a few notes on how you derived the value of the business. If the business has been valued recently, note the date. Business valuation is tricky and, as we advised you in the exotics section, you should err on the side of conservatism by undervaluing your business.

Worksheet 22–Other Investments

Use this "other" category for anything not yet entered—for example, tax shelters such as cattle breeding, solar energy and cable TV. Value partnership interests at what you paid for them unless you have a way to update the value—say, an independent appraisal or offer to buy your units.

Worksheets 23 through 33

The remaining worksheets are part of the analysis of your financial situation, rather than the data-gathering phase. They will be covered in the following chapters.

Congratulations on having finished the data-gathering phase. Now, let's find out what all the data means.

WORKSHEET 21   **BUSINESS**

Owner's name ___Sam_____

How is the business registered? Sole proprietor ____X_____

                                 Partnership   _____

                                 Corporation   _____

Percent of business owned ___100%_____ %

Approximate value of business (100%) ___20,000_____

Value of your share of the business ___20,000_____

How did you arrive at the total value of your business?

Based on furniture and inventory. Business's value is almost completely dependent on Sam's special skills. Would have little or no value to someone else.

WORKSHEET 22

OTHER INVESTMENTS

	REGISTRATION	PURCHASE DATE	DESCRIPTION	NO. OF UNITS	TOTAL COST	$ ESTIMATED PRESENT			YIELD	PRESENT ESTIMATED GAIN (LOSS)
						PER UNIT VALUE	TOTAL VALUE	ANNUAL INCOME		
1	JT	8/84	Venture Capital Partnership	20	5,000	250	5,000	0	0	link
2										
3										
4										
5										
6										
7										
8										
9										
10										
11										
12										
13										
14										
15										
16										
17										
18										
19										
20										
TOTAL										

CHAPTER FIVE

BASIC INVESTMENT CONCEPTS

MANAGING INVESTMENT RISK

The Risk Spectrum

As we discussed general concerns and investment strategies for various ages, the term "risk" appeared several times. *Every* investment has risk as Figure 5–1 illustrates.

We all know that high risk often accompanies the prospect of high reward. When you buy a lottery ticket, you have a high risk of losing your investment. In return, there is the remote possibility of earning a high reward. What most of us don't realize is that low-reward investments, like bank accounts, carry a high level of risk. Even federally-insured bank accounts carry an element of risk. This is because there are actually two kinds of risk: the risk of losing your capital and the risk of losing your purchasing power. Bank accounts, to use our example, are usually viewed as very low risk, but they nearly maximize one form of investment risk: it is very unlikely that, on an after-tax basis, the money you take out of the bank will have the same purchasing power as when you put it into the bank. Bank accounts—second only to money under the mattress—maximize the risk that you will lose your purchasing power.

You can see how this works by looking at the investment performance in

Figure 5-1 Risk Curve

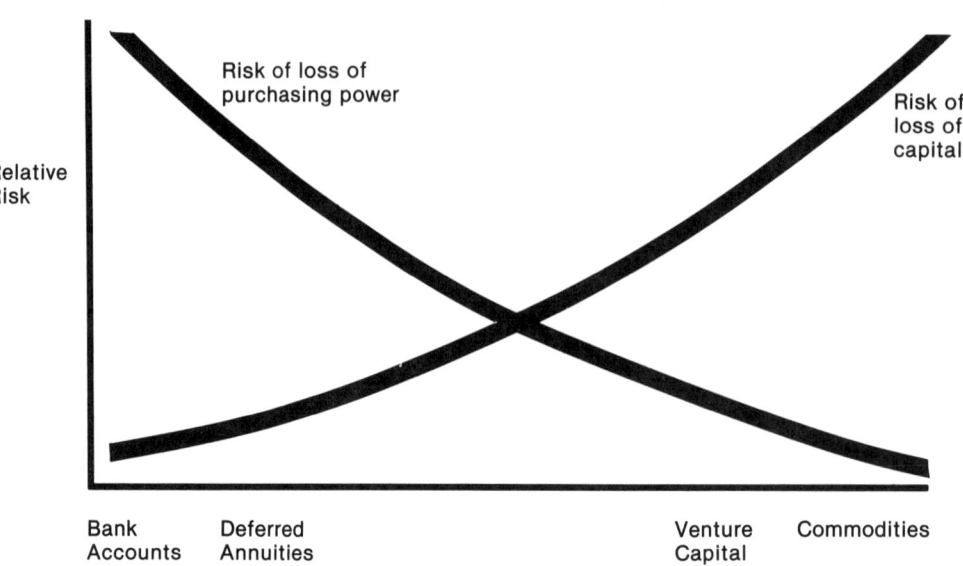

the United States economy over the long run. Between 1926 and 1985, bank deposits averaged a 3.2 percent yield while inflation averaged 3.1 percent. If you had been in an average 25 percent marginal tax bracket during that period, your after-tax yield would have been 2.4 percent. That's a 0.7 percent spread between the after-tax bank rate and inflation. If you had $1,000 in the bank for five years it would grow to $1,125. Unfortunately, you would need $1,165 just to stay even! In real terms, you lost money in your "insured" bank account. So, although bank accounts minimize the risk of losing capital, they nearly maximize the risk of losing purchasing power. You can be reasonably sure that you will get the same number of dollars out of the bank. But remember: bank accounts tend to lag behind inflation on an after-tax basis, and your dollars will almost certainly be worth less.

Speculative investments such as growth stocks, venture capital and real estate are riskier. You could lose your money. If, however, they are successful, they can provide substantial yields that will protect your purchasing power. During the same period noted above, 1926 to 1985, common stocks averaged 9.8 percent and small company stocks averaged 12.6 percent compound annual returns. Even on an after-tax basis, these should have produced a yield in excess of inflation for most investors. Remember, inflation averaged 3.1 percent during that period.

Before leaving the subject of the risk of loss of capital, we should examine it more closely. There are really three components of risk that make up capital risk: financial risk, market risk and interest rate risk.

Financial Risk. This is the risk you face that the issuer of an investment will not fulfill a promise. For bondholders, it is the risk that the municipality or corporation won't be able to pay outstanding debts. Before the United States government decided to bail out New York City and Chrysler, the bondholders of those organizations were acutely aware of the nature of financial risk. Stockholders face this same kind of risk.

Market Risk. This risk expresses itself in market price fluctuations. When the Federal Reserve announces a change in the discount rate, the stock market reacts. If you hold stock in a company that is financially sound, has a good earnings record and just announced an outstanding new product, the value may still go down with market fluctuations. The stock market is not the only "market," nor are stocks the only investments with market risk. A market can be stocks or bonds or real estate; it can also be high technology stocks or other sub-sections of a market.

Interest Rate Risk. This risk is found in investments that respond to changes in the general rate of interest in the economy. Bonds are the best example of investments of this type. Generally, a rise in interest rates causes a decline in market value of bonds and a decline in interest rates causes an increase in market values. Let's say you bought a bond which paid six percent interest and that you purchased it at par, or $1,000. The bond pays you $60 a year in interest. A few years later, economic factors in the economy drive interest rates up to the point where investors in the bond market will not settle for less than an eight percent yield. For the $60 your bond is paying to represent an eight percent return to an investor, he or she would have to purchase the bond for $750. A $60 annual interest payment on a bond you paid $750 for is an eight percent yield. Interest rate risk, fortunately, works in the other direction as well. Assume that rates in the market are eight percent today and you buy a six percent bond at a discount—you purchase a $1,000 bond for $750—to obtain your eight percent yield. Interest rates trend downward and bond investors will settle for a six percent yield. Your bond should sell at par and you have made a $250 profit plus whatever interest you made while holding the bond.

We are not suggesting that you should avoid banks. Bank accounts have a place in your portfolio and we would not suggest putting all your capital in small company stocks, despite excellent performance records. Just be aware that what looks safe may not be, and that every investment has positive and negative sides.

Furthermore, investors can afford to take different amounts of each kind of risk at different stages of life. At 65, when you leave the work force, it makes sense to forego some of the upside potential that investments like small company stocks and real estate offer. In exchange, you take greater risk of loss of purchasing power in order to receive greater protection from loss of capital that bank accounts and similar investments offer.

The Role of Diversification

Because it is impossible to avoid investment risk, you must seek to minimize it through diversification. To a certain extent, the economy will always dictate the investments you should make. When interest rates are rising, you'll want to avoid the bond market, for example. Bonds are interest-sensitive investments that lose value when interest rates rise.

When interest rates are declining, you'll want to be in bonds and common stock while reducing your holdings of bank deposits and treasury bills. Bank and treasury bill rates decline with interest rates in general in the economy—ask anyone who had a 14 percent certificate of deposit that matured in 1987 and could be reinvested at six percent, not 14 percent.

Unfortunately, none of us know the future direction of the economy, so we hedge our bets by diversifying. Rather than try to guess the economy's future direction, it makes sense to have a portfolio "for all seasons" that requires only minor adjustments for economic changes.

Some investments—inflation hedges such as real estate and growth stock—perform especially well if we have high or increasing inflation. Other investments—deflation hedges such as bonds—do best when inflation is decreasing or when there is actual deflation. Other investments such as gold may be a hedge against severe economic disruption. Gold acts as both an inflation and deflation hedge.

When we talk about diversification, we mean that the portfolio should be structured so that there are both inflation and deflation hedges in it. The proportion should change over time. When you are young and portfolio growth is your most important concern, your investments should be heavily slanted toward inflation hedges. As you enter mid-life, you should begin a gradual shift toward deflation hedges because they are more conservative and because they provide income, which you will need as you move into retirement. Table 5-1 illustrates the risk characteristics of various investment vehicles.

Table 5-1 Risk Characteristics of Investment Vehicles

Type	Loss of Capital Risk			Purchasing Power Risk
	Financial Risk	Market Risk	Interest Rate Risk	
Savings Accounts	Low	Low	Low	High
High Grade Bonds	Low	Moderate	High	High
Long-Term Bonds	Low	High	High	High
Blue Chip Stocks	Low	Moderate	Moderate	Low
Small Company Stocks	High	Moderate	Low	Low

Managing Risk Along the Spectrum

The way to handle risk as a portfolio concept is to diversify across economic markets, striving for an appropriate mix of stocks, bonds, real estate, venture capital, precious metals, and other investments. This is the best strategy for minimizing overall portfolio risk. It is important, however, to minimize risk in your selection of individual investments and to minimize risk by the way you invest in individual economic markets.

At every point along the risk spectrum, there are more risky and less risky ways to invest. Let's assume that in putting together your portfolio, you have $10,000 dollars to invest in the stock market. You could invest all $10,000 in a small company and have a highly risky stock market investment. It would be risky on several counts. First, your entire stock portfolio would rise and fall with that one company's fortunes. Second, it is a small company and small companies have shown higher failure rates and greater fluctuations in value along the way to success.

As another alternative for your $10,000 stock market investment, you might elect to purchase a diversified portfolio of individual stocks. This is less risky than the first alternative because you would have stocks of at least ten companies in your portfolio, and they could be invested in various economic sectors to reduce the risk. Unfortunately, if you don't want to become an expert in the market, you will be flying blind without a basic strategy for management of the portfolio. How will you decide what to pick and when to buy and sell each stock? Going on tips from friends or what is written in the business paper this week is not a sound approach to portfolio management.

A third alternative would be to invest $10,000 in a growth stock mutual fund with a ten-year track record of good performance through good and bad markets. Assuming the manager who made the track record is at the helm, you have some assurance—although no guarantee—that the same successful principles that led to earlier success will lead to continuing success. In addition, you would have purchased shares in a larger, more diversified portfolio than you could have acquired on your own and this would also reduce the risk compared to the other two methods.

Each of these three examples could represent your stock market investment and each one has a distinctly different level of risk.

Consider venture capital investing—definitely among the riskier forms of investing—and look at how you might reduce the risk. If you had $10,000 to invest in this market, you could give all $10,000 to your brother-in-law who has what sounds like a great idea. It's a device for measuring the flow of liquids without interrupting the flow. To hear him talk, the applications are infinite. The gadget could be used in any setting where liquids are delivered—hospitals, refineries, restaurants. There seems to be an endless list of users. What are the risks of investing now? You might find that the idea can't be translated into a workable invention. Or perhaps your brother-in-law will lose his enthusiasm—after he spends your money. Or, suffering from a Gauguin fantasy, he could go off to Tahiti to paint the natives.

If that sounds too risky for you, you do have other options. You could wait until he has other sources of financing and a fully developed idea ready for production. To attract financing, there should be a business plan that you could review for soundness. When the idea is ready for production, you need a tested prototype, rather than just an idea that may or may not be translatable into a working device. This would be a safer investment.

Alternatively, you could forget about your brother-in-law and purchase a limited partnership interest in a venture capital pool. The manager of the pool would be knowledgeable in selecting companies and might select eight or ten, rather than one, for you and your fellow investors to support. The companies selected would be in various stages of development—some in the riskier initial stages, some in later stages. Of the three alternatives, this would be the least risky because of the diversification and professional management selected on the basis of past track record.

The lesson to be learned from these examples is that there are ways to reduce the risks of even the riskiest investments and ways to make sound investments highly risky. As you structure your portfolio, pay attention to minimizing the risk of each investment choice and of the overall portfolio. Diversification and careful evaluation of the history of each investment are musts.

BEYOND INVESTMENT RISK AND DIVERSIFICATION— BASIC PORTFOLIO CONCEPTS

In the previous sections we discussed investment risk and the use of diversification and careful selection to hedge that risk. There are other important considerations to keep in mind when making portfolio decisions. Should you manage your own investments or hire a "pro"? Should you focus on what an investment earned or on what you get to keep? How do you bring balance to your portfolio?

Go It Alone or Hire a "Pro?"

If your portfolio is properly diversified, you will have gold, stock, bonds, real estate, natural resources; perhaps equipment leasing and collectibles; possibly treasury bills and notes receivables; and you'll be open to the new possibilities that arise regularly. Face it, you can't understand all these investments well enough to manage perfectly. This is where professionally-managed investments, such as mutual funds and limited partnerships, can relieve you of some of the day-to-day headaches of managing your money.

If you select a stock mutual fund, all you need to do is research the fund itself. When you are satisfied with its performance history, invest in the fund and continue to track its performance. That's much easier than the alternative, which is to research every stock that is a candidate for your portfolio, make your own decisions about the right timing of buying and selling, and follow the economic trends and indicators that effect the market. Whew! If you had to do all this for each of the areas you invest in, you would not have time to sleep.

You can obtain low-cost professional management for your portfolio by selecting, for example, mutual funds and limited partnerships. You will compensate the management for services through fees and commissions, often called "loads." What you are counting on is that, given the manager's skill and purchasing power, you can share some of your investment return and still come out ahead.

If you are a do-it-yourselfer and you want to take a more active role, pick your territory. Start with one area in which you are or would like to become expert.

We have clients, for example, who are skilled in selecting real estate—but they leave the management of their stocks, bonds and gold to mutual funds. When they purchase real estate, it is generally single-family residences or small commercial buildings in the local market. There are advantages to managing your own investments. You have the benefit of control of the asset, as well as that "hands on" feeling that is so satisfying. There are disadvantages too. Consider the example of investing in real estate on your own and compare it with a limited partnership. With its economic power, a partnership can retain experts, shop in a national market, diversify by investing in several properties and purchase office buildings, apartment complexes or industrial property. Making the right trade off between doing it on your own and hiring a professional is an individual decision. Carefully evaluate the pros and cons and limit your investment management to one area where your special interests and capabilities reside.

Pay Attention to What You Keep

A second important investment principle is to focus on the "Keep Factor." This concept applies to two separate issues: investment expenses and after-tax yields. Valerie Johnson's broker suggested that she purchase units in a real estate limited partnership. Valerie was very reluctant to invest in it, although the investments within the partnerships looked good and the general partner's credentials and track record were excellent. What stopped her was an eight percent commission and another ten percent in organizational expenses. Valerie declined and elected to purchase a growth stock mutual fund instead. After five years of operation, that partnership returned just over 35 percent compound annual return on the whole amount invested, not just the amount invested less the commission. This was a far better return than the one that Valerie achieved in the free investment—the mutual fund earned a respectable 16 percent compound annual return during the same period. Valerie's $5,000 would have grown to $15,258 in the real estate partnership; in the mutual fund, it grew to $10,501.

Knowing what an investment will cost you is very important and you should be clear about the exact dollar amounts or percentages. However, what it costs is far less important than what it will return to you.

The other dimension to looking at what you keep has to do with taxes. How much of an investment's return is yours to keep after taxes are paid? Later in this chapter, we will show you how to calculate whether you would be better off with a taxable bond paying 9.5 percent or a tax-exempt bond paying eight percent. The after-tax rate of return on an investment is an issue you should keep in mind with every portfolio decision you make.

Investment Types and Characteristics

We discussed the need to diversify and hedge your portfolio earlier in this chapter when we covered the concept of the risk spectrum. Now let's take a closer look at the building blocks of your portfolio. When you analyze your investments in the next section, you'll need to be aware of these categories.

We divide assets into seven major categories. Three of these are deflation hedges and five offer inflationary protection. The first deflation hedge consists of cash and its equivalents, including bank savings, credit union accounts, savings and loan accounts, time deposits, treasury bills, insurance cash values and deferred annuities. The next category are bonds—tax exempt, corporate or federal. The third deflationary hedge category is notes and deeds of trust, or mortgages. All of these retain an increase in value when prices and interest rates are falling.

Inflation hedges are common stock, real estate, energy, venture capital—or research and development—and exotics. The primary inflation hedges are, of course, real estate and common stock, while less emphasis is placed on energy and still less on exotics. This last category includes precious stones, art, stamps and other collectibles, and gold: either gold stocks or mutual funds and gold itself as coins, ingots or bars. Although gold is in this category, it can act as a deflation hedge too.

Common stocks may be purchased to fit almost any investment objective. Mutual funds of common stocks also offer a broad array and give the benefits of greater diversification and professional management. A utility stock mutual fund may be appropriate for a retired couple while an aggressive growth fund might be a good choice for younger investors. Although you could purchase a position in energy via common stock in oil companies, for example, we show energy as a separate category. Energy stocks behave like stocks. Direct ownership of energy resources is important enough to classify it as a separate category.

All of the above investment categories can be classified into liquid and illiquid. The illiquid investments are notes, deeds, real estate and venture capital.

Liquid assets include those which are truly liquid—you can sell them and realize your original investment plus accrued interest—and those that are marketable. Marketable assets can be readily converted to cash, but you may suffer a loss or realize a gain in the process. Adequate liquid assets for emergencies is a vital part of a well-constructed portfolio. When you have enough liquidity for unforseen problems—or opportunities—you protect yourself from having to dip into marketable assets when the market is not good.

Many of these investments have a place in every portfolio, but the appropriate structure for any particular investment may vary from portfolio to portfolio. Take oil and gas investing. Petroleum is a precious natural resource, and domestic supply sources are dwindling due to recent drastic price declines. If you have a contrarian's instinct, this looks like a great time to invest in oil and gas.

If you are young, can afford to assume some risk and could use some tax write-offs, you might want to have direct ownership and drill for oil. To benefit from one of the new tax shelters left, you will have to be at risk in this investment—if something goes wrong and more money is needed, you are on the hook.

On the other hand, if you are older and looking for income, rather than undertaking the risk of drilling for oil and finding a dry hole, you might want to become a limited partner in a partnership that will acquire producing wells. Although the amount of oil in the ground in any given well may be difficult to estimate, the over- and under-estimates by geologists will tend to average out over many wells. The most conservative way to invest directly in oil and gas might be to invest with an experienced general partner who has a good track record. The program should contain several wells for added safety and should focus on acquiring existing wells, not on drilling for oil.

Finally, you could chose to buy stock in oil companies. Remember, these will tend to behave more like stocks than like direct ownership of energy investments.

Earlier in this chapter we discussed how to maximize or minimize the risk of any particular investment, using the stock market and venture capital as examples. The same principle applies here. There are many ways to invest in every economic sector. The way you choose to invest in one should suit your age, financial circumstances and your tolerance for risk.

ANALYZING YOUR CURRENT PORTFOLIO

As you worked through Chapter 4, you collected complete information on all your assets. Turn now to Worksheet 23, Summary of Assets and Income. Transfer the totals from the individual investment sheets to the worksheet to create a picture of your portfolio. Estimate the average annual appreciation you have achieved on each investment. For an example of how to calculate, see Appendix B. Fill in lines 16, 17 and 18 only if you are depending on your portfolio for current income.

As we go through Worksheets 24 and 25, you should focus on the assets you have today that can be repositioned into other investments. You'll be looking primarily at the Working Assets section of the Summary of Assets and Income; however, if you have investment discretion over your pension plan assets in the Reverse Assets section, you should evaluate and consider alter-

WORKSHEET 23 — SUMMARY OF ASSETS AND INCOME

RESERVE ASSETS

	DESCRIPTION	NET VALUE
1	LIFE INSURANCE PROTECTION	$100,000
2	HOME EQUITY (Current Market Value Less Mortgage Balance(s))	75,000
3	BUSINESS, PENSION AND PROFIT-SHARING BENEFITS	35,000
4	TOTAL RESERVE ASSETS	$210,000

	WORKING ASSETS	NET VALUE	DOLLAR INCOME	PERCENT YIELD	PERCENT OF WORKING ASSETS	ESTIMATED APPRECIATION
5	SAVINGS TYPE ACCOUNTS	47,930	2,636	5.5	30.9%	0
6	BILLS, BONDS, NOTES AND PREFERREDS	36,112	2,889	8.0	23.3%	0
7	NOTES AND RECEIVABLES*					
8	COMMON STOCK					
9	MUTUAL FUNDS	20,250	608	3.0	13.0%	9.0%
10	REAL ESTATE	—				
11	ENERGY	—				
12	EXOTICS	—				
13	OTHER *Retirement Plan*	50,465	1,552		32.6%	8.7
14	TOTAL WORKING ASSETS	154,757	7,685	5.0	100%	4.0%
15	TOTAL ESTATE VALUE	364,757				

			REMARKS:
16	MONTHLY INCOME		
17	MONTHLY COST OF LIVING		
18	SURPLUS OR (DEFICIT)		

* Borrower may default

WORSHEET 24 **CAPITAL ANALYSIS: Present Portfolio**

Note: Perform this analysis for only those investments that can be repositioned.

Present Portfolio

	DESCRIPTION	AMOUNT	PERCENT OF WORKING ASSETS	INCOME	YIELD	AMOUNT TAXABLE	TAXES*	EXPECTED APPRECIATION	NET AFTER TAXES
1	SAVINGS-TYPE ACCOUNTS	47,930	30.9%	2,636	5.5	100%	817	0	$1,819
2	BILLS, NOTES, BONDS AND PREFERRED STOCK	36,112	23.3	2,889	8.0	100%	895	0	1,994
3	COMMON STOCK	—	—	—	—	—	—	—	—
4	MUTUAL FUNDS	20,250	13.0	608	3.0	100%	188	9% / 1,822	420
5	REAL ESTATE	—	—	—	—	—	—	—	—
6	ENERGY	—	—	—	—	—	—	—	—
7	EXOTICS	—	—	—	—	—	—	—	—
8	OTHER *Ret. Plan*	50,465	32.6	1,552	3.1%	0	0	8.7 / 4,390	1,552
9	TOTAL	154,757		7,685	5.0%		1,900	4.0 / 6,212	5,785

* 31% Combined Marginal bracket

WORKSHEET 25 — CAPITAL ANALYSIS: Proposed Portfolio

Proposed Portfolio

	DESCRIPTION	AMOUNT	PERCENT OF WORKING ASSETS	INCOME	YIELD	AMOUNT TAXABLE	TAXES	NET AFTER TAXES	EXPECTED APPRECIATION
1	SAVINGS-TYPE ACCOUNTS	12,930	6.9	711	5.5	100%	220	491	0
2	BILLS, NOTES, BONDS AND PREFERRED STOCK	36,112	19.2	2,166	6.0	0	0	2,166	0
3	COMMON STOCK								
4	MUTUAL FUNDS	30,250	16.1	907	3.0	100%	281	626	9% / 2,772
5	REAL ESTATE	10,000	5.3	600	6.0	0	0	600	6% / 600
6	ENERGY	10,000	5.3	1,000	10.0	20%	62	938	0
7	EXOTICS	5,000	2.6	150	3	100%	46	104	6% / 300
8	OTHER *Retirement Plan*	50,465	26.9	3,078	6.1	0	0	3,078	8.7% / 4,390
9	TOTAL	154,757		8,612	5.6			8,003	5.2% / 8,062

Comparing Portfolio Performance Before and After Adjustment

	DESCRIPTION	INCOME	YIELD	NET AFTER TAXES	EXPECTED APPRECIATION
1	BEFORE ADJUSTMENTS	7,685	5%	5,785	6,212
2	AFTER ADJUSTMENTS	8,612	5.6%	8,003	8,062
3	DOLLAR DIFFERENCE	927	—	2,218	1,850
4	PERCENTAGE DIFFERENCE	.6%	—	1.4%	1.2%

natives for these as well. If your portfolio is small or non-existent, stick with us, we'll help you create a model portfolio for the future in Chapter 6.

The purpose of evaluating your portfolio is two-fold. First, you want to judge whether or not your portfolio is adequately diversified and appropriately balanced. If not, you will need to shift some of your investments into other investments or make additions over time to correct the balance. Second, you want to know how each individual investment is performing. And you'll want to evaluate that performance against other alternatives. Use the Appendix A, "Where to Go for Additional Help," to assist you in identifying alternatives and investigating their performance against what you already own.

When you look at some published investment evaluations, you will see only statistics. Other investment analysis publications, such as the *Mutual Fund Forecaster,* will give recommendations to buy, sell, or hold. At the Institute for Certified Financial Planners' annual meeting in 1987, portfolio managers from three mutual funds suggested that individual investors limit their criteria to "buy" and "sell" only. What they meant was that, unless you would now repurchase an investment for your portfolio at today's price and in today's market, you probably should not be holding it. This was an excellent piece of advice for Jason and Emily Price, a retired couple who had held AT&T stock at the time of the divestiture. They received shares of stock in the "Baby Bells," as all AT&T shareholders did. In an environment of declining interest rates, utility stocks usually do very well—they are interest-sensitive just as bonds are. The stocks appreciated and split, and did so well that they soon represented over one-third of the Price's portfolio. That large a proportion of stocks in a single economic sector was imprudently high—especially for people in their retirement years. Unfortunately, the Price's became very attached to the stock due to its fine past performance and high dividends. They did not want to sell it; however, when they asked themselves if they would buy that much of those stocks at today's market price, the answer was a clear "no." They sold one-half of their holdings. Now the proportion is still high, but not glaringly so. And no matter how the stock performs in the future, the Price's have locked in some of their gain.

As you look at each investment in your portfolio ask yourself if you would buy it in today's market. Mark it as a candidate for repositioning if the answer is no and research it against the available alternatives.

THE ROLE OF TAXES IN INVESTMENT DECISIONS

Tax Management

The role of taxes in investments changed radically when the Tax Reform Act of 1986 was passed. Before that time, there were a host of investments—from equipment leasing to research and development—that investors could use to generate tax losses and reduce taxable income. Congress did away with much of this type of activity in the hope of accomplishing two things. One of Congress's objectives was to make the system more fair—the public perception being that the rich could invest to avoid paying their fair share. The other objective was to have investors make their investment decisions based on the economics of an investment, not on its tax benefits. In the opinion of many in Congress and the Treasury, great economic inefficiencies—overbuilding of real estate, for example—were the result of tax-driven investment decisions.

Whatever your opinion of the most revolutionary tax reform since World War II, one thing is certain: Individuals who invest with tax reduction as their primary goal have undermined the growth of their net worth in the past. And you could still do so today, but to a lesser degree now that many tax-reduction strategies are no longer open to you.

Our first advice about tax management is let it take a back seat to the more important goal of increasing your net worth—just as John Caulfield did. With proceeds from the sale of a piece of real estate, we developed two portfolios for John Caulfield after the Tax Reform Act 1986. One had a tax-advantaged emphasis—municipal bonds, tax-deferred annuities, a tax-exempt money market fund and tax-sheltered cash flow from equipment leasing. The other portfolio had an emphasis on taxable investments—corporate and government bonds and a taxable money market fund. We looked at what John would keep in each case. Although the taxable investments would result in a higher tax, they also resulted in a higher after-tax cash flow. It was an awakening for John because it had not occurred to him that it was sometimes better to pay more taxes. Be single-minded about the growth of your net worth and use tax-management strategies to support that goal. When tax reduction becomes your goal, it can cost you a lot of money. It would have cost John $1,462 per year in spendable income if he had implemented the tax-exempt portfolio (Table 5–2).

Table 5–2 John Caulfield—Cash Flow

	Tax-Exempt Emphasis	Taxable Emphasis
Salary	$45,900	$45,900
Interest	16,901	19,261
Dividends	4,350	4,350
Partnership Cash Flow	5,900	5,900
	$73,051	$75,411
Less Taxes		
(Federal, State, FICA)	(2,923)	(3,821)
	$70,128	$71,590

Difference $1,462

One of the most radical changes in the Tax Reform Act of 1986 was the division of income into three distinct categories—earned income, passive income and portfolio income. Passive income is income from passive activities such as limited partnerships and from rental real estate activities. Portfolio income is interest and dividend income. Most tax shelters will end up on the passive income side of the ledger—an exception being working interests in oil and gas properties where the taxpayer's form of ownership does not limit liability.

Passive losses may offset passive income, but may not longer be used to offset earned or portfolio income. Unused losses are "suspended" and may be used when the taxpayer disposes of a passive asset. Then passive losses may offset earned and portfolio income if the asset is sold at a loss. Suspended losses may offset the gain if the asset is sold at a gain.

Although the 1986 Tax Reform Act may render the term "tax shelter" obsolete, investments in what used to be called tax shelters will still be available and will still make sense. Their structures will have changed and investors may have to wait to take advantage of the tax benefits they once received "up front." The net effect of this will be just what Congress wanted—a more serious evaluation of the basic economics of an investment.

Tax management strategies are divided between procedural strategies and investment strategies. The best way to avoid taxes has always been through the use of tax procedures. Procedural solutions always involve lower risk. Only after you have exhausted the possibilities of procedural strategies should you look elsewhere. Tax procedures include such things as claiming all of the deductions and exemptions you are entitled to. IRAs and Keoghs and corporate pension plans are procedures along with shifting income from higher to lower bracket years. Shifting income from high-bracket family members to lower-bracket family members, a much-restricted strategy since the 1986 Tax Reform Act, is also a procedural strategy. The procedures are too numerous to cover here, but this list should give you the picture.

Tax shelters include such things as personally-owned investment real estate, and investments that generate passive income and passive losses. Historically, investments that had tax benefits associated with them also had a higher level of risk. As a matter of public policy, tax incentives were created to attract more investment into sectors of the economy that were too risky to attract sufficient investment capital unless the pot was sweetened with tax benefits. Ultimately as you know, Congress felt that the pot had been overly-sweetened. These kinds of investments—oil and gas, real estate, equipment leasing and the like—are still available. With the exception of real estate, these investments will provide tax-sheltered cash flow now rather than tax losses to offset earned income or income from other-than-passive investments. Real estate losses will be available to offset earned income and portfolio income to the extent of $25,000 per year. If you are a high-income taxpayer, the available loss will be phased out when your adjusted gross income reaches $100,000 before the real estate loss. The $25,000 write-off will be phased out at the rate of one dollar for every two dollars of earnings. When your income reaches $150,000 you will not be able to take advantage of any real estate losses.

Tax-advantaged investments is a more inclusive category of investments than tax shelters. It includes such things as municipal bonds, single-premium deferred annuities, variable annuities, tax-exempt money market funds, treasury securities and the like.

How can you tell if you would be better off in a taxable or tax exempt security? A very simple calculation will show you:

$$\text{Taxable Equivalent Yield} = \frac{\text{Tax Exempt Yield}}{\text{Your Marginal Bracket}}$$

If, for example, you could invest in a tax-exempt money market fund paying 4.05 percent and be in a 28 percent marginal bracket this year, the formula would look like this:

$$\text{Taxable Equivalent Yield} = \frac{.0405}{1-.28} = .05625 = 5.62\%$$

What it means is that 4.05 percent after-tax income has the same value to you as 5.62 percent subject to tax. Right now, taxable money market funds are paying about 5.2 percent, so you would be almost one half of one percentage point better off in the tax-exempt fund.

The hardest part of this equation is knowing your marginal bracket. We will get to that in the next section. For now, be aware that your marginal bracket means the amount of tax you would pay on the next dollar you would earn. Effective tax rate, on the other hand, is the percentage of your total income that you paid out in taxes. Marginal brackets are always used to make decisions between investments. This is because when you consider one investment versus another, you are looking at adding a few more dollars to the income you already have, so you must look at how additional dollars will be taxed.

When you know your marginal bracket and use it to choose investments that allow you to keep more of your investment return, you must continue to monitor the situation. Your marginal bracket may change and so may the spread between taxable and tax-exempt investments. Now that you are in the business of planning, you should be able to estimate your tax circumstances early in the year. Then you will have the information you need to determine whether taxable or tax-advantaged investments will maximize what you keep.

ESTIMATING YOUR MARGINAL TAX BRACKET

One of the changes made by the Tax Reform Act was to reduce the number of marginal tax brackets. It is now much easier to estimate your federal marginal bracket, so it will not be necessary for us to drag you through the process of preparing a tax estimate. However, if you are interested in doing so, or if your tax situation is extremely complicated, we encourage you to estimate your taxes. It is easiest to estimate your taxes by using your last completed tax return as a basis for estimating what this year will look like. Will your income be higher or lower, will itemized deductions go up or down? (The appendix has a worksheet to assist you in the process.) If you take this approach, you will be able to estimate your marginal bracket and also the tax you will owe. If you know your earnings, your taxes and your living expenses, you will also know your annual surplus that is available for investment. For less stalwart souls, we recommend you estimate your marginal federal bracket based on Table 5-3:

Table 5-3
Married Filing Jointly—1988

If Taxable Income is		Then Tax is		
More Than	But Not More Than	This	Plus This %	Of Amount More Than
$ 0	$ 29,750	$ 0	15%	$ 0
29,750	71,900	4,463	28	29,750
71,900	149,250	16,265	33	71,900
$149,250		$41,790	28*	$149,250

Single Taxpayer—1988

If Taxable Income is		Then Tax is		
More Than	But Not More Than	This	Plus This %	Of Amount More Than
$ 0	$ 17,850	$ 0	15%	$ 0
17,850	43,150	2,686	28	17,850
43,150	89,560	9,762	33	43,150
$89,560		$25,077	28†	$89,560

*There is a 5 percent exemption surcharge that effectively removes the benefit of personal exemptions for taxpayers with income over $149,250. The maximum surcharge is based on the number of exemptions claimed, and the amount is $546 per exemption.

†There is a 5 percent surcharge that effectively removes the benefit of personal exemptions for taxpayers with incomes over $89,560. The maximum surcharge is based on the number of exemptions claimed, and the amount is $546 per exemption.

Now that you have the wherewithal to estimate your federal marginal bracket, there is one more wrinkle in this game—your state taxes. For this estimate, check your last year's state tax return and the tax tables for your state. Some states have you use your federal adjusted gross income or taxable income with minor adjustments. When adjusted, you apply a percentage to it. That percentage is your marginal bracket. Other states have tax codes that vary greatly from the IRS code. If you are in one of these states, look at your latest tax return, make adjustments to reflect this year's differences, recalculate and check the table. The percentage you apply to amounts in excess of a particular number is your marginal bracket.

Finally, as soon as you know your state and federal marginal bracket, you can calculate your combined marginal bracket—a very important number. You can't simply add the two together because your state tax is deductible from your federal tax, so, in a sense, the federal government is paying part of your state tax. The proper formula for calculating your combined bracket is as follows:

Combined Marginal Bracket = Federal Marginal Bracket + State Marginal Bracket − [Federal Marginal Bracket × State Marginal Bracket]

In this formula, the expression in parentheses is there to take into account the fact the money you save on federal taxes by being able to deduct your state taxes.

Let's say that you are a Californian in a 28 percent federal marginal bracket and an 11 percent state marginal bracket. Your calculation looks like this:

Combined Marginal Bracket = .28 + .11 − [.28 × .11]
.3592 = .28 + .11 − .0308

Going back to our money market fund example, assume that we had a choice between a taxable money market fund paying 5.2 percent, a federally tax-exempt money fund paying 4.08 percent and a Federally and State tax-exempt money fund paying 3.9 percent. Which one would be better?

Taxable yield   5.2%

Federally Tax-Exempt:
Taxable Equivalent Yield = $\frac{4.08}{1-.28}$ = 5.66

Federal and State Tax Exempt:
Taxable Equivalent Yield = $\frac{3.9}{1-.3592}$ = 6.08

We translated three investments with three different tax treatments into comparable numbers. If an investment is only Federally tax exempt, then your Federal marginal bracket is used in the computation. If it is doubly tax exempt, use your combined marginal bracket. The three figures are comparable because they are all adjusted to reveal the taxable equivalent yield. The doubly tax exempt fund will give the highest yield to the taxpayer in question.

SUMMARY

This chapter covers basic investment concepts—the nature of investment risk; the importance of evaluating what an investment returns, rather than what it costs; investment types and characteristics; and the role of taxes in portfolio decisions. In Chapter 6, we will complete the picture by looking at how to restructure—or structure if you are just beginning a portfolio—your portfolio taking taxes into account. It will present guidelines to reach the right kind of balance for your age and circumstances.

CHAPTER SIX

CREATING YOUR PORTFOLIO

A DELICATE BALANCE

Portfolio construction is an art, not a science. There are nearly as many ways to create a sound portfolio as there are arrangements of notes to create melodies. Asset allocation models have been designed to allocate monies across investments to achieve various objectives. They are valuable, but they miss one thing: portfolios are created for people, not computers, and each portfolio reflects both economic conditions and the preferences and risk tolerance of the portfolio's owners.

As you design your portfolio, you will be striving to accomplish these four things:

- adequate diversification within each investment grouping (enough different stocks or bonds to provide a diversified portfolio of them)
- appropriate proportions of investment groups (the right mix of stocks, bonds, real estate, cash, etc.)
- the right balance between deflation hedges and inflation hedges and the right balance between liquidity and illiquidity
- maximization of your total return in keeping with the objectives of diversification, proportion and balance.

The process may seem overwhelming at first blush, but if you return to Worksheet 24, Capital Analysis, it will become clearer. Remember this is a summary of all relevant data for *investments that could be repositioned*. Illiquid investments, or investments that cannot be changed, were not included in this analysis. The purpose of looking at this part of your portfolio alone is to be able to judge the impact you have made by changing investments. If you included all investments in this analysis, the investments which remain the same would dilute the impact of the changes. In a later exhibit we will look at the total portfolio. Ultimately, you are striving to correct (or create) a proper balance for the whole.

GUIDELINES FOR PORTFOLIO STRUCTURE

Cash and Equivalents

As a general guideline, we recommend keeping three month's living expenses in the form of cash. This is an emergency reserve and the recommended amount recognizes, among other things, that most disability policies have a 90-day elimination period before benefits begin. If your disability policy has a longer elimination period, we recommend a back-up of liquid assets such as stocks and bonds, rather than more cash. Too much cash means too great a sacrifice in return on your investment.

If you are just beginning to save, it seems to take an infuriatingly long time to build such a reserve, and building cash is not as motivational as "really investing." If this describes your situation, consider putting half of the funds available for savings into some form of cash account and the other into a "real" investment such as a good growth stock mutual fund—something you can get excited about. There are exciting possibilities among mutual funds—several have averaged more than 20 percent compound annual rate of return over the last ten years! Appendix A gives you sources of information for researching stock mutual funds. Do this "50/50 split" until you have accumulated your three month's reserve.

If you are accustomed to having more than three month's living expenses in cash, you should evaluate that strategy. Cash balances drag down your portfolio because they cannot compete with other investments in their rate of return—there is a penalty in portfolio performance that you pay whenever you keep excess cash. There are three exceptions to this general rule of limiting cash and equivalents to three month's living expenses:

1. If the cash is set aside for a near-term expenditure—for example, paying taxes in April or a down payment on a home—it should remain in cash and equivalent investments. Short-term cash balances should not be placed at market risk in stock or bonds. There is too great a chance that the market will take a downturn just when you need to

pull out your cash. Then, instead of being able to ride out a down cycle, you will have to realize a loss. Therefore, only money that you intend to leave for three to seven years should be put into stocks, bonds and other investments. Long-term investment in these vehicles gives you a chance to overcome the constant ups and downs of the market and to take advantage of the longer-term uptrends that effective management can create.

This is a lesson that Justin and Sarah Levin learned the hard way. They had been saving for a down payment on a house and decided that growth stock mutual funds were the place to accumulate it. They purchased the fund when shares were in an upward trend, and that trend continued for some time after they invested. Eighteen months after their investment, the Levins were ready to make an offer on a house. They needed to take money out of the fund, but the market had taken a downturn and they lost $2,500. The Levins were able to purchase their home; the fund recovered and increased in value well beyond what it was when Justin and Sarah invested. The Levins were in a fund that performed well, yet they lost money because they had to move out of the fund at the wrong time. Protect yourself from Justin and Sarah's experience by investing in the market only with money that you intend to invest for the longer run.

2. If you are retired, we recommend that you maintain a higher proportion of cash and equivalents. We think it is important to build a portion of your portfolio in investments that do not expose you to market risk. One way to do this without making the usual sacrifice in yield is to purchase a single premium deferred annuity. This insurance product behaves much like a bank CD and falls into the category of cash and equivalents. It has a stated interest rate for a stated period of time and penalties for early withdrawal. Unlike a bank CD, a deferred annuity is not subject to tax currently. If you select carefully, you will find annuities that have consistently yielded a higher percentage than you could have earned on $100,000 negotiable certificates of deposit. And the earnings are tax deferred.

Larger cash balances do make sense when you're retired not only because they protect a portion of your portfolio from market risk, but also because cash may be needed for medical emergencies or other unexpected events.

3. If you cannot sleep at night without more than three month's cash reserve, then have more than three month's reserve. One of the most important investment principles is the "sleep-at-night" factor. It doesn't matter how well your portfolio does: If you don't have peace of mind, it is not worth investing. But—there's *always* a "but"—if your comfort zone is so narrow that you feel comfortable only with bank accounts or equally conservative investments, you are unlikely to advance financially. We recommend education as an antidote to

this problem. When you understand investments, you will become more comfortable with the sound ones and more nervous about the ones that are not.

Whatever your age, consider the following vehicles for your cash balances: bank market rate accounts, money market mutual funds, treasury bills, deferred annuities, credit union, savings and loan, or mutual savings bank accounts and the like. Remember that there are money market funds that invest in short-term municipal securities and, therefore, are tax exempt. Compare yields to find the alternative that gives you the greatest "keep factor." Remember that treasury bills are exempt from state income taxes. Compare taxable and tax-exempt alternatives periodically because the spreads between taxable and tax-exempt investments change. Make a new comparison if your marginal tax bracket changes, and shift your money to the investment that provides the greatest after-tax rate of return.

Cash and equivalents are liquid investments. How much liquidity should you have? As much as you need. We recommend at least three month's cash reserve and up to 33 percent both in stocks and bonds. These will be the primary liquid assets.

If greater liquidity is needed to fulfill your goal — liquid assets for a college fund, for example — then greater liquidity is appropriate. Adjust your investments to suit your particular needs.

Liquid investments tend to give lower returns than illiquid ones and are less risky. Therefore, the proportion of illiquid investments should decline as you grow older. This is in the interest of greater safety.

Bonds

As you know from Chapter 5, we recommend that you invest in bond mutual funds, or engage the services of a portfolio manager, rather than invest in individual bonds. Follow that advice unless you are already an expert in the bond market and have the time and temperament to manage a portfolio.

If you are young, we recommend that you minimize your position in bonds because they are deflation-hedges, and inflation hedges—also called growth investments—should be your emphasis. As a general guideline, we recommend one percent in deflation hedges for every two years of your life until age 40, then one percent from age 40 to 50 and two percent per year to age 65. This percentage is in addition to your three month's cash reserve (Table 6–1).

If, at 65, you can live on that cash flow from a portfolio that is 40 percent invested in growth, we recommend you leave the proportion at that level for the rest of your life. It is the growth portion of your portfolio that will help you maintain your purchasing power as the years go by.

Table 6-1 Inflation and Deflation Hedges in Your Portfolio

Your Age	% Deflation Hedges	% Inflation Hedges
20	10	90
25	12.5	87.5
30	15	85
35	17.5	82.5
40	20	80
45	25	75
50	30	70
55	40	65
60	50	50
65	60	40

Notes and Deeds

As are bonds, notes and deeds are deflation hedges. As such, they should represent a small portion of your portfolio early in your investment career, and an increasing one as the years pass. To many investors, notes and deeds mean second mortgages on residential property. This is not an ideal investment, but attractive because of the relatively high yields. Invest carefully because mortgage investing can be a better deal for the borrower than for the lender. Rates usually are fixed throughout the life of the mortgage. The nature of mortgages leaves little room to maneuver if interest rates in the economy go up. Mortgages are usually illiquid unless you want to sell them at a discount. You assume considerable risk in the event of a default because a second mortgage has a junior claim to the asset pledged as collateral. If the property is not worth enough to pay the first mortgage holder and the second mortgage holder, you lose. When you're a mortgage holder, the best that can happen is that you get your money back. No upside potential will compensate you for the risk of default and the illiquidity.

As you can tell, we are lukewarm on the subject of second mortgages. An alternative to investing in second mortgages is investing in a mortgage pool. These are usually limited partnerships, and your units represent your share in a pool of mortgages. If pools meet your investment objectives, we recommend you choose one that invests in first and wraparound mortgages. In the event of default you will be paid first because they put you in a senior position. Also, look for a program with an **equity kicker** that allows you to participate in the appreciation of the property. This is also called a **participating mortgage** and it gives you some upside potential to compensate for the downside risk. Finally, if you select a program where the pool's manager is also experienced in managing real estate, the risk of default might turn out to be a lemon turned into lemonade. If an exceptional real estate manager successfully manages a piece of property due to a default, the mortgage holders may have an unexpected equity windfall.

Common Stock

Unless you are a stock market expert with the time, temperament and skill to manage your own stock, we recommend you seek professional management for your stock investment. You can do this by engaging a portfolio manager. The disadvantage, for most of us, is that portfolio managers often require that you have at least $250,000 to invest in stocks and bonds. Another option is to acquire professional management through mutual funds.

There are many mutual funds with many investment objectives: aggressive growth funds, growth funds, balanced funds, total return funds and others. Hundreds of established funds exist and new funds open every day. In Appendix A you'll find references to research mutual funds. Look at long-term and short-run performance, performance in good and bad markets and at whether the team that set a stellar track record is still managing the fund. Write or call for the prospectus and carefully review it. But be aware that it is often hard to get a clear picture about fund performance from the prospectus. Ironic, isn't it? The prospectus may show a few years' dividends and capital gains dollars per share. But it rarely translates those figures into percentages, and it never compares performance with other funds. We recommend you consult sources that are easier to use and also provide comparison information.

A carefully selected mutual fund, or several of them, will be one of the real workhorses of your portfolio. In the top 50 mutual funds in the ten-year period ending January 31, 1987, the worst performer would have taken a $10,000 investment and increased it to $41,523. That is a compound annual return of 15.3 percent. The best performer increased at 34.2 percent. If you had started with $10,000, you would have had $189,463 ten years later, assuming that all dividends and capital gains would be reinvested. Although the top performer would have been preferred, even the 50th best growth mutual fund would have netted a very respectable return!

Always beware of last year's number one fund. If you always invest in last year's top fund probably you will not do well in the market. Instead look for a multi-year stellar performer with a solid history during both good and bad markets. Your position in stocks should not exceed one-third of your portfolio, and we recommend that one of your stock mutual funds invests some assets in foreign economies. As good as the U.S. economy is, between 1970 and 1980 the U.S. ranked 15th in growth of the 18 major equity markets in the world. More recent statistics confirm that pattern. Other economies in the world have more spunk! International investing also offers diversification and a chance to profit—or lose—from fluctuations in the relative value of currencies.

For your international investment, we prefer global funds rather than ones that specialize in a geographic area. Such investments are limiting. The fund must invest in the Pacific Basin, for example, even if other world economies are more appealing at that time. They are like sector funds that invest only in technology, say, and must continue investing in technology even when that sector of the economy is not faring well.

Stock ownership is generally viewed as an inflation hedge; however, some stock funds are structured so that they have deflation protection too. Thus, your position in the stock market may remain relatively constant, but the nature of that investment may change. For example, you might invest your entire stock position in foreign and domestic growth funds until you reach your mid-50s, when you might shift to a fund that moves among stocks and bonds and cash. Such a fully-managed fund can take a defensive posture by moving into cash when the market is slipping downward or, better yet, before the downward trend begins. You might also add a utilities fund. Utilities, with their relative safety and higher yield are one of the classic "widows and orphans" investments.

Real Estate

We recommend that you not hold more than one-third of your portfolio in real estate, and that you continue to hold it no matter what your age. You might want to select and manage your own real estate. Personally-owned real estate that is actively managed is one of the few tax shelters left. If your adjusted gross income is under $100,000, you can write off as much as $25,000 in losses from real estate. These losses may come from depreciation, interest expense and the operating expenses inherent in the ongoing management of property. When your income reaches the $100,000 mark, one dollar of that loss is phased out for every two dollars of earned income. When your income reaches $150,000, you may not take advantage of any losses. If you want to purchase a piece of property, use the two rental analysis exhibits, Worksheets 17 and 18, to examine the property on paper. Compare the real estate to municipal bonds. Ask yourself how much appreciation you would have to achieve to exceed the same after-tax return as you could earn on the bonds. Demand that the real estate provide a considerably greater return to compensate for the greater risk and the illiquidity. If it will not, look for another piece of real estate or consider another type of real estate investment.

You can also invest in real estate through REITs, real estate investment trusts. REITs have shares that can be freely traded so they represent a method of real estate investment that allows the investor to have liquidity. REITs may be involved in development, lending and acquistion.

Limited partnerships offer another method of investing in real estate. As with REITs, limited partnerships offer the opportunity to diversify, but limited partnerships are illiquid and partnerships can have many different structures.

You might want to purchase a partnership that uses leverage if you are young, although leverage is a two-edged sword. Leverage exposes you to more risk because, when you borrow money to purchase rental property and rental income declines, you may have difficulty paying a substantial mortgage. Leverage is appealing because it allows you to take greater advantage of the appreciation potential. John and Rosalyn Henderson purchased a $100,000 property with a $20,000 down payment. By the time they sold it, their equity in the property had risen to $25,000 from mortgage payments and improvements. The property had risen in value to $150,000. When the property was sold and all expenses were paid, the Hendersons had $139,500 left or a 39.5 percent increase in the value of the property. This is a 158 percent increase in the Hendersons' $25,000 in equity! That's leverage. The value of the entire property increased 39.5 percent, representing a 158 percent increase on the amount John and Rosalyn had invested.

Energy

Energy resources are basic commodities in short supply, which is the best formula for investment opportunity. The oil and gas industry is very cyclical and, since OPEC's coming of age, a painfully complicating factor has been introduced into the oil and gas markets. At this writing, oil prices are the lowest they have been in years but, unfortunately, low prices may be sowing the seeds of OPEC's return to dominance. Domestic exploration is at a nadir and 98 percent of domestic supplies are being used. In 1958 the United States was able to meet all oil needs from domestic supplies. We currently produce only 60 percent of what we consume and, in the future, with today's reduced domestic exploration we are likely to produce an even smaller percentage of what we need.

You can invest in oil and gas by purchasing oil company stocks, through limited partnerships or by purchasing working interests in oil and gas. The last alternative is one of the few tax shelters that survived the Tax Reform Act of 1986. If your working interest does not limit your liability, you can deduct oil write-offs—principally intangible drilling cost—from your other income.

Oil company and gas stocks have some disadvantages. They are indirect investments that may behave more as stock does than as oil and gas. They provide minimal diversification of your overall portfolio, although they may serve to diversify your stock holdings. Your dividends are taxed doubly—once as earnings to the corporation and secondly as dividends to you. Finally, oil and gas stocks do not allow you to take advantage of depletion allowances that shelter your cash flow from tax.

On the positive side, stocks are liquid and information is readily available on the company and on the stock's historical performance. Finally, unlike working interests, stocks limit your liability.

Limited partnerships are a direct investment in oil and gas. Because limited partnerships in drilling limit your liability, the tax benefits associated with them in the past no longer exist. With the tax incentive gone, the incentive to take the economic risks of drilling is also gone. More appealing are income programs that buy producing wells and whose income will be partially sheltered by the depletion allowance. These programs purchase producing wells based on the value of the reserves and their level of income. These investments are safest when the program purchases a number of wells. The law of averages says that the geologist's estimate of what is in the ground—your partnership pays for the wells on this basis—will become more accurate as the number of wells increases so that under- and over-estimates cancel each other out.

As currently structured, working interests are not appropriate for most individual investors. With marginal brackets declining, the tax benefits shrink and the investor has a greater proportion of his own capital at risk. In the past, a 50 percent taxpayer had only 50 percent of his own capital at risk in many oil programs. With the maximum marginal tax bracket at 28 percent, even the highest-bracket taxpayer will have 72 percent of his own capital at risk.

Investment markets do respond to tax law changes and, in the future sound—but still speculative due to the legal requirement that you be at risk—investments may exist that have good balance between risk and reward for those who wish to invest in working interests.

Energy investment makes sense in nearly every portfolio, and should be in the range of 10 percent to 25 percent of the total. You may want to decrease the amount as you grow older, when you may want to change the way you invest.

Exotics

As you know from Chapter 4, exotics include precious metals and other tangibles such as gold, silver, diamonds, art and other collectibles. Exotics can make good investments while providing something of beauty or pride to the investor.

Gold

We recommend gold in almost every portfolio, not as a vehicle for speculation, but because of its unique characteristics and impact on your portfolio. Gold is an insurance policy. It is the investment that rises in value when everything else fails. Gold is both a deflation hedge and an inflation hedge. When we have inflation, or the threat of it, gold increases in value. In times of economic stability, it declines or flattens. People turn to gold in times of depression and the increasing demand drives the price up. Thus gold is a paradoxical commodity. It is volatile itself, but because its value changes in a pattern that is different from most other investments, gold can reduce the overall volatility of your portfolio. Less volatility means less risk.

To invest in gold, you could purchase shares of gold mining companies or a mutual fund that invests in such shares. We prefer mutual funds to individual stocks and to holding the gold itself. Gold, like money under the mattress, does not pay dividends. Gold mining shares do, and they tend to move with gold price movements, giving the same sort of "portfolio insurance" as gold does.

You can also invest in bullion or coins. Bullion ownership has costs associated with it, including costs for storage and/or assaying costs when you wish to sell it. Coins are a reasonable compromise because they do not have to be assayed and carry a relatively small premium over the value of the gold. Like other forms of gold itself, however, they pay no dividends.

Maintain approximately 3 percent to 5 percent of your portfolio in gold. Accumulate your position gradually to avoid the risk of investing in this volatile commodity at the wrong time. If, for example, you wish to invest $10,000 in gold, begin with a $5,000 investment and add another $500 each month until you accumulate your initial position. Then add more as your portfolio grows, keeping your gold position at the appropriate percentage.

Silver

Silver is not on our list of important elements in your portfolio. Silver's track record for growth has been poor over the past ten years and negative for the last five years. Silver does not play the same vital role in a portfolio as gold does. Perhaps that is because it is significantly affected by industrial demand, making the political and hedging aspect — so important to gold — a less important factor.

Opportunities to buy silver are limited primarily to junk coins—those minted before copper was substituted for silver—silver bars and uncirculated silver dollars.

Precious Gems

Diamonds are the most popular of precious gems. Diamonds have appreciated at approximately 10 percent per year over the past ten years, according to Sotheby's. In addition to their value as investments, precious gems are beautiful and can give great pleasure to the owner.

You have probably seen many ads that promote the ownership of diamond jewelry and jewelry containing other precious gems as "investments." Investment grade diamonds and gems, however, are not the same as jewelry grade. The considerations are the same—clarity, cut, carat weight and color—but special expertise is required in the selection of investment gems.

It is important to work with a reputable gem dealer. There is much more uncertainty to investing in gems than in stocks or bonds. There is no organized exchange such as the stock exchange for trading, so you may be unable to find a buyer when you want one. Valuation is much more subjective, and specialized expertise is the primary ingredient for successful investing.

Collectibles

Investment-grade collectibles include scarce and historically significant items such as carousel animals, folk art, comic books, scrimshaw and at least a thousand other categories. Just as with precious gems, there is no organized market for collectibles, so finding a buyer or something to buy is often a challenge. Even more than stocks, successful investing in collectibles requires knowledge plus the right temperament.

Collectibles have another pitfall. Collectors generally collect things that fascinate them, making it hard to part with what they acquire even when the assets have matured. Bill and Jessica Martin collect carousel animals. They have some real beauties decorating their home. Perhaps if they are desperate somewhere down the road, they will sell them; but what began as an investment has become a group of prized possessions. We can hardly blame them. Walking into their living room with its carousel horse and carousel cat takes us back to childhood and kindles a sense of play.

THE ART OF BUILDING YOUR PORTFOLIO

This chapter painted the world of investments with a broad brush. The seven categories we discussed do not include a number of investments: venture capital (described in Chapter 5), equipment leasing, commodities, options, cable TV and the like. Instead, we concentrated on the basic building blocks of your portfolio. We recommend that you explore in depth all the areas we covered. As you become a more sophisticated investor, we recommend that you explore the rest.

Sample Portfolios

It will be hard to go from the descriptions and guidelines above to a finished portfolio, so we will provide you with samples of the art of portfolio construction and accompany them with a few comments.

Portfolio 1—Brad and Laura. Brad and Laura are 28 and 26 years old. They have accumulated $10,000 that is in a bank certificate of deposit. They want to invest it at maturity. They can save $400 per month, and their living expenses are $1,500 per month.

Although Brad and Laura should build a $4,500 cash reserve, we recommend that they start with a smaller amount and build from there. Although they can not deduct their IRAs because their combined income is more than $50,000, we recommend that they establish IRAs because they will gain many years of tax-deferred compounding. We would recommend that they follow this pattern for one year. If they can increase their savings rate, we might advise them to accumulate a lump sum for investing in real estate through a limited partnership. Their financial circumstances make direct ownership of income property less appealing. It would be difficult for them to "feed" a property if it were vacant or needed major repairs.

Investment for $10,000

Cash and Equivalents (Tax Exempt Money Market Fund)	$ 3,000
Growth Stock Fund (Domestic)	5,000
Growth Stock Fund (Foreign)	2,000
	$10,000

Investment for $400/month

Add to Cash	$ 68
Domestic Stock Fund (Brad's IRA)	166
Foreign Stock Fund (Laura's IRA)	166
	$400

Portfolio 2—Leslie. 37 years old with a $100,000 inheritance to invest, Leslie's monthly expenses are $3,000 and she can save $600 per month.

Investment for $100,000

Cash and Equivalents (Tax-Exempt Money Fund)	$ 10,000
Growth Stock Fund (Domestic)	30,000
Growth Stock Fund (Foreign)	15,000
Leveraged Real Estate	25,000
Venture Capital	15,000
Gold	5,000
	$100,000

Investment for $600/month Savings

Cash (Accumulate for Lump Sum Investments)	$375
Add to Domestic Stock	150
Add to Foreign Stock	50
Add to Gold	25
	$600

Leslie wants part of her portfolio to be more speculative, so we have recommended some venture capital. Lest you think this is a highly risky investment, we should tell you that most pension plan trustees allocate 10 percent to venture capital in the pension plans they manage. If this were not prudent, they would have been taken to task long ago. We've been a bit more aggressive by placing 15 percent in venture capital. Leslie is at the point in her investment life when she can think about accumulating lump sums for making larger investments—additional real estate, for example. She is considering buying a house, so this money will be set aside until she decides one way or another. If she decides not to buy a home, additional real estate investment might be a good choice for her lump sum. The rest of her portfolio will be growing in the meantime so that an additional real estate investment could be made without driving the percentage above one-third.

Portfolio 3—John and Thelma. John and Thelma are 60 years old and have $200,000 to invest. John intends to work for five more years and his pension benefits will be enough to support him and Thelma without additional income from their portfolio. This situation will continue for several years until inflation increases their need for spendable income. Their living expenses are $3,000 per month and they are able to save $1,000.

Investment for $200,000

Cash and Equivalents:	
Bank Market Rate Account	$ 10,000
Single Premium Deferred Annuity	25,000
Growth Stock Mutual Fund (Domestic)	35,000
Growth Stock Mutual Fund (Foreign)	15,000
Utilities Stock Fund	20,000
Corporate Bond/Government Bond Funds	60,000
Real Estate (Low-Leveraged and Mortgage Pool)	30,000
Gold	5,000
	$200,000

Investment for $1,000/month Surplus

Add to Cash	$250
Add to Bonds	500
Add to Growth Stock	150
Add to Foreign Stock	50
Add to Gold	50
	$1,000

John and Thelma can probably go for another eight years without touching the income from their portfolio. That allows sufficient time to profit from additional growth opportunities, so we have left a substantial growth position—the domestic and foreign stock funds are growth-oriented and the utilities and the real estate partnership combine income and growth. Cash and equivalent investments are a larger part of this portfolio than of the other two. This gives the added stability that comes from positioning some of the portfolio to avoid market risk. It does, however add safety at the expense of total return.

RESTRUCTURING YOUR PORTFOLIO— PLAYING ON PAPER

By now, you should have researched some investment alternatives and you should have data on expected cash flow and appreciation. Be sure you have completed Worksheets 23 and 24 regarding your current portfolio. Now you can begin to identify weaknesses in balance or performance and determine steps you could take to correct them. Worksheets 25 and 26 will enable you to structure a trial portfolio using the above guidelines. Test your new portfolio on paper to see whether you are better off in terms of balance and overall return. These worksheets also allow you to test your current portfolio performance against your proposed portfolio. If you have not begun to invest, you can test two proposed portfolios using the same worksheets.

If restructuring your portfolio will involve selling some assets, use Worksheet 32 to keep track of transactions.

MONITORING YOUR PORTFOLIO'S PERFORMANCE

If you have followed our advice in selecting professionally managed investments rather than individual securities, monitoring and tracking will be much simpler. Follow your statements and check the paper periodically for the latest data. If you observe downturns in stock and bond funds, for example, it may be nothing to worry about. Watch for notices that the fund's investment strategies or portfolio managers have changed. If you have carefully selected a fund and the management remains in place, you should be able to remain in the fund indefinitely.

If you have selected individual securities, you should have set an objective for each one at the time you bought it so that you can sell it when it achieves the price or if the dividend declines—whatever criteria you have established. Watch your securities daily if they are stocks or corporate bonds. It is difficult to get daily values on municipal bonds, so check these periodically with your broker and pay attention to interest rate fluctuations!

If you own your own real estate, it will "mature" just as any stock or bond will. Analyze your properties annually. When you have achieved your objectives, sell them. If investments of lower risk will give you equal return, sell the real estate. It is not compensating you for the additional risk.

Whatever your approach, take a systematic look at your portfolio. Someone has to mind the store. Use Worksheet 31 to track your portfolio's performance. It provides space to show updated market values and annual cash flow from investments.

Creating Your Portfolio

WORKSHEET 26   **COMPARING NET INCOME, BALANCING AND LIQUIDITY FACTORS**

Note: The difference between this form and the preceding one is that you now can look at your portfolio as an entirety.

ESTIMATED INVESTMENT INCOME AND TAXES

DESCRIPTION	INVESTMENT INCOME	TAXES	NET INCOME AFTER TAXES
CURRENT PORTFOLIO	$ 7,685	$ 1,900	$ 5,785
PROPOSED PORTFOLIO	$ 8,612	$ 609	$ 8,003

YIELD

DOLLAR DIFFERENCE	$ 927	$ 1,291	$ 2,218
PERCENTAGE DIFFERENCE	.6 %	%	

APPRECIATION

DOLLAR DIFFERENCE	$ 1,850	
PERCENTAGE DIFFERENCE	1.2 %	

BALANCING FACTOR

CURRENT PORTFOLIO			PROPOSED PORTFOLIO		
DEFLATION HEDGES	$ 109,274	70 %	48 %	$ 74,274	DEFLATION HEDGES
INFLATION HEDGES	$ 45,483	30 %	52 %	$ 80,453	INFLATION HEDGES
TOTAL	$ 154,757	100 %	100 %	$ 154,757	TOTAL

LIQUIDITY FACTOR

CURRENT PORTFOLIO			PROPOSED PORTFOLIO		
LIQUID	$ 104,292	67 %	54 %	$ 84,292	LIQUID
NONLIQUID	$ 50,465	33 %	46 %	$ 70,465	NONLIQUID
TOTAL	$ 154,757	100 %	100 %	$ 154,757	TOTAL

Remarks on Total Portfolio:

If assets from Worksheet 23 were not repositioned (excluded from Worksheets 24 and 25), be sure to include them on this worksheet

WORKSHEET 31 — RUNNING BALANCE SHEET AND CASH-FLOW STATEMENT

DATES REVIEWED:	DATE: 5/87		DATE: 5/88		DATE: 5/89		DATE: 5/90	

WORKING ASSETS

DESCRIPTION	$	%	$	%	$	%	$	%
SAVINGS-TYPE ACCOUNTS	8,000	16	9,000	16	10,000	15		
BILLS, NOTES, BONDS AND PREFERRED STOCKS	10,000	20	12,000	21	14,000	21		
MORTGAGES AND NOTES	—		—		—			
COMMON STOCK	20,000	40	25,000	43	28,000	43		
REAL ESTATE	10,000	20	11,000	19	12,000	18		
EXOTICS	2,000	4	1,000	2	1,500	2		
OTHER	—		—					
SUB-TOTAL								
TOTAL WORKING ASSETS	50,000		58,000*		65,500*			

RESERVE ASSETS

	$		$		$		$	
INSURANCE PROTECTION	100,000		100,000		100,000			
HOME EQUITY	50,000		52,000		55,000			
BUSINESS NET WORTH	—							
TOTAL RESERVE ASSETS	150,000		152,000		155,000			
TOTAL ESTATE VALUE	200,000		210,000		220,500			

INCOME AND LIVING EXPENSES

INVESTMENTS	2,500		2,900		3,275			
SALARY	36,000		37,800		39,690			
PENSIONS	—		—		—			
SOCIAL SECURITY	—		—		—			
TOTAL INCOME (pre-tax)	38,500		40,700		42,695			
TOTAL LIVING EXPENSES	24,000		26,000		27,000			

*doesn't add up to 100% because of rounding

WORKSHEET 32 — SUMMARY OF SALES FOR CALENDAR YEAR

Creating Your Portfolio — 99

		PURCHASED						SOLD			CAPITAL GAIN (LOSS)		$ INCOME
REGISTRA-TION	DATE	NUMBER OF SHARES, UNITS OR % OF OWNERSHIP	DESCRIPTION	TOTAL COST	DEPRECIA-TION, PROFIT EXEMPTION & OTHER ADJUSTMENTS	TOTAL ADJUSTED COST	DATE	NUMBER OF SHARES, UNITS OR % OF OWNERSHIP	$ PER SHARE, UNIT, % OWNER-SHIP	$ PROCEEDS	SHORT-TERM	LONG-TERM	CURRENT NET TO SALE DATE
1. JT	9/85	100 shs.	ABC Corp	1,000	—	1,000	9/87	100	15	1,500		500	
2.													
3.													
4.													
5.													
6.													
7.													
8.													
9.													
10.													
11.													
12.													
13.													
14.													
15.													
16.													
17.													
18.													
19.													

CHAPTER SEVEN

MANAGING RISK AND INSURING WISELY

MAKING WISE INSURANCE DECISIONS

When financial planners use the term **risk management,** generally they are talking about insurance of all kinds: property, casualty, liability, medical and disability. Life insurance, on the other hand, is often considered along with estate planning. This is called risk management rather than insurance for an important reason. Risk management means using any of several ways to deal with risk. You can deal with risk by avoiding it, retaining it or transferring it. For example, driving your car to work exposes you to risk. You could run over a pedestrian or get involved in a fender-bender. You could be at fault or not. The risk exposure varies: You could be stuck replacing a broken headlight or be involved in a million dollar liability suit. If you want to avoid the risk inherent in your automobile, you can simply refuse to own one. If you want to retain the risk of automobile ownership, you should keep $1 million in the bank that isn't needed for your own financial security because six-figure liability judgments are common. If, on the other hand, you want to transfer the risk, you should purchase automobile insurance. The insurer creates a pool of people exposed to automobile risk. Not everyone will make a claim, but everyone pays into the pool. If everything works out, the pool will have enough money to pay claims and leave a profit for the company.

As you can see, risk management is not the same as insurance, although you can deal with many risks by buying insurance.

If you wonder why your automobile insurance, for example, is important to your financial plan, think of this: If you do not protect the financial resources you own today, an accident, sickness or casualty could render your financial plan useless. Such events undo the best-laid plans because they consume cash flow or force you to liquidate assets. Furthermore, we live in the most lawsuit-happy society on the planet. Six-figure settlements are not uncommon in personal injury suits. If you were on the losing end of such a suit and were not adequately insured, it could deprive you of any hope of future financial security.

Anyone can be sued. And the circumstances can sometimes be nothing short of absurd. In a recent case that made headlines, a burglar was injured by a faulty roof in the process of breaking into a building. His response? To sue the owner! Win or lose, a lawsuit is costly in time, lawyer's fees and emotional trauma. Although the burglar's suit was found to be without merit, the building owner would have had to pay the enormous cost of defending himself if he had not been insured. When an insurance company is on the hook because you have transferred risk to them, they can bring their full economic power to your defense.

Have you ever considered how many risks you face every day? The list is long and intimidating: health expenses, lost of earning power, casualty losses such as auto or home damage, liability for injury to others such as bodily injury or property damage and death. When you manage these risks prudently, you should have peace of mind as well as the ability to minimize actual losses. You should also feel more freedom to invest for the future without worrying about unexpected financial calamities.

One common insurance mistake is to establish your insurance with low deductibles—typically $100 for homeowners or auto policies—and relatively low limits on property damage and bodily injury liability. This contradicts the most important principle of risk management. When you buy automobile insurance, what are you protecting yourself against—$250 in damages to your headlight or a $1 million liability suit? In allocating the money you spend on insurance, you should "retain" responsiblity for the frequent, small losses that are costly to insure. You can pay easily for such minor casualties out-of-pocket without compromising your financial security. "Transfer" the big risks that would devastate you financially to an insurance company. To put it simply, raise your deductibles and choose the highest liability limits you can obtain. Save money by handling the small losses yourself, and let the insurance company take the big ones.

We should remind you also that if you pay too much for insurance or if you overinsure, it may interfere with other financial goals by making you "insurance poor." The art of risk management means that you insure where you need to, shop carefully for adequate coverage at reasonable cost and retain or avoid risks whenever you can. Risks are part of living and our aim is to make sure the obvious—and most financially devastating—risks are covered, wherever possible. Shifting risks to insurers often is not feasible or is prohibitively expensive. In short, managing risk means buying adequate protection, and buying it at reasonable cost.

This section should give you a basic education on the ins and outs of insurance. It will guide you through a thorough insurance check-up and help you formulate questions for your insurance agent.

This section will also introduce you to the basics of property, casualty and liability insurance, and to health and disability insurance. As you read, refer to Worksheets 7 and 8 and compare the recommendations with what you have. Identify areas that need changing, make notes on the worksheets and discuss them with your agent.

We think risk management is the least exciting part of planning, but the most important. It is the foundation that protects what you have and assures you that unexpected events, such as lawsuits or serious property damage, will not undo what you have planned.

PROTECTING YOUR PROPERTY: HOMEOWNER'S AND AUTOMOBILE INSURANCE

Homeowner's, Condominium and Tenant's Insurance

Homeowner's, condominium and tenant's policies all offer two categories of coverage: they cover your property and they cover your liability for injury to others. The property section covers the dwelling if you are a homeowner. If you own a condo, you may have dwelling coverage. Personal property is also covered in this section.

You Need Broad Coverage

You may have an all-risk policy that covers everything except specifically excluded risks such as earthquake, flood or nuclear war. Or you may have a named-risk policy that covers only risks named in the policy. As its name implies, the all-risk coverage is broader in what it covers; however, even all-risk policies have certain exclusions, such as those mentioned above. If you have a named-risk policy, consider upgrading it to an all-risk policy. Also, you may want to augment your all-risk policy with earthquake or flood coverage.

Adequate Dwelling Coverage

Dwelling coverage should be adequate to replace your home or those areas of a condominium that are your responsibility. If you check your home's value on your balance sheet, and compare it to the dwelling coverage on your insurance, you'll probably find a large gap. This may or may not be cause for alarm. The value of your home includes the value of the location, the land and the foundation. If your home or condo is severely damaged, you won't have to pay for the value of the location, land or, in most cases, the foundation. If you doubt the adequacy of your coverage, however, call your insurance agent. He or she can tell you what it would cost to replace your home after asking a few questions about your home's location, construction style and square footage. It is important that your coverage be adequate to rebuild your home in the event of total loss. Most insurers will pay you the replacement cost or the coverage limit. They will pay you whichever is less. Remember: If you don't have enough coverage, you will have to pay the difference.

For More Assurance, Add Features to Dwelling Coverage. Many insurers offer two features that guarantee adequate coverage that is kept up to date. Dwelling coverage that contains a **cost-of-construction adjustment** will increase coverage automatically as the cost of rebuilding increases. A **guaranteed replacement cost endorsement** will provide full coverage for the cost of replacing your home, even if the cost is more than the amount of coverage stated on the policy.

Conditions for obtaining a guaranteed replacement cost endorsement may vary from insurer to insurer. Generally, the dwelling must be insured initially for 100 percent of the replacement cost, and the insurance company must be notified of major additions or improvements to the structures. The additional premium for this coverage is less than $10 with carriers we have seen; but, if you do purchase it, be sure you understand and meet the requirements to keep it in force.

If Your Home Is Unique. If you own a one-of-a-kind house or if it has expensive interior or exterior features, you might want to hire an appraiser to estimate the cost of replacing it. An estimate by an insurance agent, based on location and square footage multiplied by the standard construction-cost-per-square-foot, may be too low. Below you will find a recommendation for a written and photographic inventory of the contents of your home. If your home is unique, extend your inventory to include the house's special structural and interior features.

Inadequate Personal Property Coverage. Personal property coverage should be at a level high enough to replace the contents of your home in the event of total loss. It sounds reasonable enough but fixing the value of your personal property is not an easy task.

Close your eyes and imagine your living room. If you had been burglarized, would you be able to name every item that should be there and identify what is missing? To avoid such a situation, prepare a written and photographic inventory of your home. It will help you judge the contents coverage clearly and could help you substantiate claims later. Great loss often occurs simply because people cannot remember everything that has been lost. Your inventory will fill that need too.

To be sure your inventory is complete, take photographs of all rooms, closets and the insides of cupboards. Lay small items such as jewelry out on tables or other furniture in groups and photograph them. After you begin the inventory, add all new purchases to it. Just take a photo of your new acquisition and add it to your written inventory list. Store the inventory is a safe place away from your home, perhaps at your office or in your safe deposit box.

Most contents coverage is written for **actual cash value** or ACV. This equals the depreciated value of your household goods. If you bought a $700 refrigerator today and sold it in one month, you might get $350: it would be, after all, a used refrigerator. Household goods depreciate quickly and, in the event of a major loss, the difference between the actual cash value covered by insurance and what it will cost to replace your household goods may be very great. Protect yourself by acquiring replacement cost coverage. A replacement cost endorsement generally adds 10 percent to 15 percent to the basic homeowner's premium. In our opinion, it is worth it.

You should understand the overall coverage limits on the contents of your home, but you should also know that special limits apply to certain types of property. Coins and currency, including loss of cash, for example, are often covered only up to $100 or $500. Special limits often are placed on jewelry, furs and watches, goldware and silverware, precious gems or metals and the like. Limits of $500 to $2,000 are common on such property.

If you own high-value items, you may want to add **scheduled property coverage**. Base your coverage on appraisals that are updated at least every five years.

High-value property is one area where you could consider retaining the risk, as we discussed at the beginning of the chapter, rather than turning it over to an insurance company. You could move infrequently-worn pieces of jewelry, for example, to a safe deposit box. If the property is irreplaceable or valuable for sentimental reasons, you might decide not to insure. Compensation for loss would not make you feel any better about the loss. In that case, you could use the item and enjoy it with the knowledge that if it is lost, it cannot be replaced.

Savvy Risk Management

You probably know that raising deductibles can be a good way to reduce premiums. But did you know that not all insurers give you a reasonable premium reduction in exchange for assuming the larger risk? Think about how large a deductible you could easily pay—perhaps $500 or $1,000—and call your agent to see what premium reduction would result from raising it. These first few dollars of insurance are the most expensive and, although many of us pay them, we often don't use them for fear a series of small claims will bring a boost in premiums. Don't pay for what you won't use and remember the basic principle of risk management: Retain the small losses and transfer the big ones.

Liability Is Your Greatest Risk Exposure

Homeowner's, condo and tenant's policies provide **comprehensive personal liability**, or CPL, coverage to cover losses you are obligated to pay legally because of bodily injury or property damage to others. In some cases, legal obligation is not required and personal activities are covered in your home as well as away from your home.

Because we live in a sue-conscious society, we recommend that comprehensive personal liability limits be set as high as your insurer will allow—often $300,000 per person and $500,000 per accident. In many instances, this is not enough and it should be augmented by an excess or umbrella liability policy, described below. Increasing your liability coverage may be very inexpensive—as little as $12 per year for an additional $100,000 of coverage—and it could save you a lot.

You will also find **medical payments coverage** and **guest property damage coverage** in the same section of your insurance policy. Limits are usually set at low levels—such as $1,000 or $5,000 because such claims are considered **goodwill payments** designed to avoid lawsuits for minor expenses. If either limit is exhausted, you would be held legally liable for the injured party to receive additional payments, or your insurance company would have to agree to settle out of court. Under such circumstances, your liability coverage would pay up to the liability limits shown on your policy. Because of the way these goodwill payments work, the generally low limit does not concern us.

Who Is Covered? You should know who is covered on your policy. Usually a policy covers the **named insured, resident spouse,** and anyone under age 21 in the care of any person named. We recommend that both spouses be named insureds to avoid any ambiguity regarding resident spouse in the event of a separation or divorce. Insurance is about providing protection from all the things we hope never happen. Call your agent and have the policy issued in both names.

If you live with a roommate and he or she is not named on the policy, check with your agent about adding the name. Although your roommate may not be concerned about insuring his or her personal property, no one should be without liability coverage.

Condos Have Special Complications. Condominium coverage follows the same general outlines given above, but has a few special considerations. These arise from the nature of condo living where some things are owned by the individual unit owner and some are owned in common, and from the relationship between the individual condo policy and the master policy held by the condo association. If you own a condo, you should discuss the master policy with the appropriate member of the association board.

The key issues with condominium coverage are what you own and what is insured under the master policy. Sometimes, the individual owns only the **air space**; inner walls, built-in appliances, carpeting and cabinetry are jointly owned. Other condominiums dictate that everything beyond the bare walls—paint, wallpaper, appliances and so on—is owned by each unit owner. To further complicate the picture, the condo master policy may insure some or all jointly-owned property and some individually-owned property. You need to determine what you own and what is not insured under the master policy so that you can be sure there are no gaps. You need enough dwelling coverage for all the property that is your responsibility that is not covered by the master policy.

The deductible on the master policy also is important. If, for example, the master policy has a $5,000 deductible and yours is the only unit damaged, you may have to pay the entire deductible. Your policy should have **unit owner's building items coverage** equal to the deductible on the master policy.

Every condominium policy should also have **loss assessment coverage**. This coverage serves two purposes. If you are a member of the condo association board, it provides you with director's and officer's liability coverage as long as you are elected to serve without pay. Many courts have held directors and officers liable for wrongful acts, including errors, omissions and misstatements, and this coverage will handle such a loss. The second purpose of loss assessment coverage is that it covers you if the condominium assocation suffers a direct loss and must assess members for a share of that loss. This coverage comes into play only if the loss is associated with a peril that is covered under the policy. For example, if the damage is caused by an earthquake, and the master policy and unit-owner policy do not cover earthquake damage, then your policy will not pay for the assessment.

Should You Have Flood and/or Earthquake Coverage? Before leaving the subject of homeowner's condo/and/tenant's coverage, we want to be sure that you know that two important perils are not covered by standard policies—flood and earthquake. If you live in areas vulnerable to these problems, you can buy flood coverage through a federal government program by contacting your insurer. Most insurers also can provide earthquake coverage.

Automobile Insurance

The structure of an automobile policy is similar to a homeowner's policy in that there is a section covering your own property and a section covering your liability for bodily injury or property damage to another individual.

If Your Automobile Is Damaged

Auto damage coverage will pay you in the event of a collision or for events other than collision, such as theft and vandalism. You will be paid only for the automobile's repair cost or actual cash value (ACV), whichever is less. Actual cash value is the auto's depreciated value before the damage, not its replacement value. Unfortunately, there may be a big gap between the depreciated value of your car and its "use" value to its owner. Ask Mary Williams who was unemployed when she was involved in an accident. The car would cost $3,000 to repair, but it's depreciated value was only $1,800. Guess which amount her insurer agreed to pay?

Because of low residual value of older cars, many advisors recommend that you drop collision and comprehensive coverage on cars more than a few years old. The premium is high in relation to the benefit that would be paid. Check with your agent about what would be paid for your car and compare that to the portion of your premium that pays for such coverages. If it seems worth it, continue the coverage. If not, consider dropping them.

Your policy may have two different deductibles, one for collision and one for events other than collision. As we mentioned in the discussion of homeowners' policies, higher deductibles may reduce premiums. Increase your deductibles if your insurer will give you a reasonable premium reduction for doing so.

Automobile Liability: Your Greatest Risk Exposure

The liability section of your insurance policy covers injury to others and property damage, medical payments, and uninsured or underinsured motorist's* coverage. The policy may have a single limit or a split limit. With split limits, the first amount is coverage per person, the second is per accident and the third amount is property damage. We recommend that these liability limits be as high as your insurer will allow. As you will see below, we often recommend that they be augmented by additional coverage.

Medical payments coverage usually is set at a relatively low figure—$5,000 is typical. This will pay each person in an accident for medical expenses *without* regard to legal liability. This limit may seem low compared to other limits; however, these payments are considered **goodwill payments** and their purpose is to avoid lawsuits over minor expenses. If this limit is exhausted, you will be held legally liable for the injured party to receive additional payments, or your insurer will have to have agreed to settle out of court.

---

*Insurance policies in no-fault states will differ with the general outline given above. If you live in a no-fault state, call your agent to discuss how the principles discussed in this section apply to insurance in your state. At that time, the liability coverage will be triggered and will pay up to the liability limits shown on the policy.

Uninsured/underinsured motorist coverage is particularly important if you are injured by an uninsured/underinsured driver and lose time from work. This means it will pay for pain, suffering and loss of income, so choose the highest limits possible for this coverage. People often make the mistake of choosing limits of $15,000 per person and $30,000 per accident for this coverage. $15,000 will not replace a year's income for many of us. You need better protection.

Who Is Covered? Like the homeowner's policy, the auto policy covers the named insured and resident spouse, among others. Again, we recommend that both spouses be named on the policy to avoid ambiguity regarding a resident spouse.

If you have a roommate who uses your car more than infrequently, call your agent. You and your roommate may need to add endorsements to your policies to be sure you are covered when driving each other's cars.

The Perils of Children Who Drive. If you have adult children—over 18 years of age in some states—who drive your automobile, don't skip this section. If you don't have kids who drive, skip to the discussion of excess liability coverage.

In our opinion, one of a parent's highest risk exposures occurs every time his or her child drives the family car. The highest accident rates are among young drivers, but when accidents happen, the auto's owner may have legal liability, not the driver. If an accident occurs, the injured party usually will sue the person with the most assets—and, almost without exception, that is mom or dad.

There are two ways to reduce this risk — aside from withdrawing the use of the car. The first is to raise liability limits with an excess liability policy, as discussed below. The second is available only for legally adult children. It involves gifting and retitling the automobile to the child, and acquiring a separate insurance policy in the child's name. This solution requires parting with an asset of value, and is pricey because a family policy with multiple-car discounts is less expensive than separate policies. However, it is an effective risk avoidance strategy. If this is an affordable solution, we recommend you discuss these alternatives with your insurance agent.

Excess Liability Insurance

An **umbrella policy** or **excess liability policy** provides higher payment limits than automobile and homeowner's policies. It also covers risks not otherwise covered such as libel, slander, invasion of privacy and other non-physical injuries. Coverage limits start at $1,000,000. Cost ranges from $75 to $125 per year for the first million dollars of coverage. Premiums are higher if you have many pieces of property.

Who Needs Such High Coverage?

Given today's litigious society and large lawsuit settlements, many people need this type of insurance to protect their substantial net worth or because they are highly visible in their community. People who live a life that conveys wealth—drive expensive cars and live in high-income neighborhoods—need this kind of coverage. Those with visibility—such as doctors, attorneys or politicians — also need it. More and more we recommend excess liability coverage in routine financial planning, rather than only under special circumstances. There is a trend in today's society to solve our differences in the courtroom so that awards seem to grow higher and higher. More of us are vulnerable and need greater insurance protection.

It Must Be Coordinated With Your Homeowner's and Auto Coverages

An umbrella policy requires that you carry specific liability limits on your underlying auto and homeowner's policies. If you are liable for damages, the underlying auto or homeowner's policy will pay first, then the umbrella policy will pay up to its limit.

If you do not have an umbrella liability policy, be sure to integrate it properly with your other policies when you acquire it. If you do have one, congratulations. Check to see that your underlying policies carry the right amount of coverage.

Who Is Insured?

Like other policies, the umbrella policy protects the named insured, resident spouse, and resident relatives. Be aware that auto liability extends to resident relatives only if they have permission to use the auto and use it on an infrequent basis. If you are married, both spouses should be named insureds to avoid any ambiguity regarding resident spouse. If you are single and have a roommate, check with your agent about steps you can take to make sure he or she is covered.

PROTECTING YOUR HEALTH AND INCOME: MEDICAL AND DISABILITY INSURANCE

Disability Income

Unless you are already financially independent, your most valuable asset is your ability to earn an income. Even if you have accumulated a substantial net worth, you would be likely to exhaust your assets if you had to liquidate them to meet current living expenses during an extended disability.

Is There a Hole in Your Insurance Program?

When we review clients' risk management programs, they nearly always have insurance on their home, auto and lives, but they don't always insure their earning ability. Table 7-1 illustrates some interesting statistics that will give you insight about the importance of disability insurance. It seems apparent that adequate disability protection is vital to your financial life.

Table 7-1   Disability Insurance

If your age is:	The chance that you will be disabled for 90 days or longer is this many times as likely as the chance that you will die this year:
22	7½
32	6½
37	5½
42	4
47	3½
52	2½
62	2

Don't Count on Social Security Disability

Disability coverage is available through Social Security and may be available through a program in your state. It is important when you review your disability coverages that you look at how disability is defined. Under Social Security the definition of disability is very restrictive. Even if you are disabled, you may not meet this restrictive definition and, therefore, you may not be eligible for benefits.

Employer-Sponsored Programs

Another common source of disability coverage is group plans through employers or through professional or trade associations. Such coverage is usually not ideal, but may offer a reasonable trade-off between coverage and price. We feel that the best disability coverage should compensate you if you cannot meet the duties of your *own* occupation. If you are a surgeon who can no longer perform surgery, you should receive disability benefits. When disability coverage has a less favorable definition of disability, our surgeon might be refused benefits if he is able to do *any* other job. Most employee benefit and association policies have "own occupation" disability definitions for two years and revert to an "any occupation" disability definition after that.

Although most employee benefit policies are not the best, you cannot opt out of them. If you are insured already, a private insurer probably won't underwrite you. Sounds like a Catch-22, doesn't it? You may not be able to do anything about the situation except be aware that you have only two years of high-quality coverage. If you become disabled and could be rehabilitated, you would need to think about retraining yourself as quickly as possible.

What Is a Good Policy?

To evaluate the quality of your disability coverage, we recommend that you look at five factors: the elimination period—the length of time between the onset of disability and the payment of benefits; the benefit period—how long the benefits last; the monthly benefit—the dollar amounts you would receive; the definition of disability; and the renewal provision.

Elimination Period. The elimination period in disability policies is like the deductible in automobile and homeowners' policies. It allows you to **self insure** for those first and most expensive dollars of coverage. The longer the elimination period, the less the premium cost. Generally, we recommend 90-day elimination periods. However, if you have a 90-day cash reserve and other liquid investments as a back up, you may want to price a 180-day elimination period to see if the insurer will give you a reasonable premium reduction for assuming the additional risk.

Benefit Period. We suggest that you choose a policy that provides benefits to age 65, or for life. If your current net worth is sufficient to make you financially independent at age 65, and your disability benefits will be enough to keep you from dipping into your nest egg, then benefits that last to age 65 will be adequate for you.

Monthly Benefit. The maximum monthly benefit that the insurance company will allow is often two-thirds of your income. After all, the company wants to provide an incentive for you to return to work! However, in deciding how much disability coverage you need, you should look at your living expenses rather than your income. If you live well within your income, there is no need to pay premiums to replace the income. Instead, you should buy enough disability coverage to cover your living expenses. One tax tip: Under present law, if you pay your own disability premiums, your disability benefits will not be subject to tax. If your employer pays, the benefits will be subject to tax.

Definition of Disability. We introduced the concept of the definition of "disability" above. There are many definitions and they range from the most liberal "own occupation" to the most restrictive "any occupation." An **own occupation definition** means that benefits will be paid as long as you are unable to perform the material duties of your own occupation. Obviously, this is the preferred definition for anyone who has achieved professional success and who would not want to engage in less rewarding work.

Policies with "any occupation" definitions are less desirable and open to interpretation and dispute. **Any occupation** definitions may be restrictively defined as the inability to engage in *any* gainful employment. This is the definition that Social Security uses. The term is also commonly defined as the inability to engage in any occupation for which the insured is, or may become, suited by education and training.

Renewal Provisions. There are many types of renewal provisions and, obviously, they do not usually apply to employee benefit policies that are renewed as long as you remain with your employer. The most desirable is a **noncancellable policy**. This policy cannot be cancelled and the premium cannot be increased regardless of change in your occupation, earnings, health or number of claims.

A **guaranteed renewable policy** also cannot be cancelled; however, the premium may be increased for specific groups of policyholders. It cannot be increased only for specific individuals.

Finally, many policies are renewable only at the option of the insurance company. Do not purchase this kind of policy. The risk is too great that you will be cancelled.

Medical

There are several types of medical insurance plans. Some provide service benefits—for example, Blue Cross-Blue Shield; some provide reimbursement—typically insurance company plans; and others are considered pre-paid plans where minimal charges are assessed for services such as **Health Maintenance Organizations (HMOs)**—for example Kaiser-Permanente. HMOs have a unique characteristic. As their name implies, they maintain your health. Thus, preventive and routine care that is not ordinarily covered by other types of insurance is covered by HMOs. In contrast, service benefit and reimbursement plans cover you for illness or injury, not for routine or preventive health care.

Methods of Compensation

A **service benefit plan** normally provides benefits as "services to be rendered," including a particular number of days of semi-private care in a member hospital. With some exceptions, the insured receives his or her service benefits without additional cost. Under **reimbursement plans,** expenses are reimbursed up to a specified maximum. If actual charges exceed this, the insured must pay the difference. With HMOs, various services are provided by the HMO itself, although patients may be able to use other facilities on a pre-approved basis, and services are considered prepaid. Nominal charges—say, $5.00 for an office visit to a physician—may be assessed for certain services or certain types of coverage.

With an HMO, the key issues are accessibility and the range of services covered. Because you must use an HMO facility under most circumstances, the location of the nearest facility is important. Carefully review the benefits provided to assess whether most of your health care needs will be met within the policy.

Evaluating the quality of other medical plans involves looking at a few key areas: lifetime—or annual—reimbursement limits, co-insurance provisions, deductibles and the schedule of benefits and premiums.

Lifetime Limit. We recommend a limit of at least $500,000 or the equivalent in service benefits. Six-figure medical bills are not uncommon, making this level of insurance a reasonable lifetime limit.

What Will You Have to Pay? Co-insurance means that the insurer will pay 80 percent, for example, of normal and customary charges and you pay the remainder. It is important that this co-insurance provision is capped by a stop-loss provision. A **stop-loss provision** says that, when your out-of-pocket costs exceed a particular amount, the insurer will pay 100 percent of normal and customary charges. When you review this part of your policy, add the deductible and the dollar amount you must pay before the stop-loss provision takes effect. Be sure that amount is one that you can handle. You could, of course, shave this amount to nothing, but your premiums would be very high. Look at this as you do your auto and homeowner's deductibles and strike the right balance between the amount of risk you can afford to retain—$500, $1,000, $2,000 per year?—and the cost of coverage.

Schedule of Benefits. The schedule of benefits is an important part of your insurance coverage because it defines what will be covered. Hospital room and board and hospital expenses such as diagnostic services, operating room, drugs, equipment and supplies must be provided. If you are in your childbearing years, be sure that reasonable maternity benefits are provided. Treatment for substance abuse or for psychiatric care are often provided to a set limit. These are valuable benefits, but not as critical as the basics. Coverage for physician's visits is especially important if you have small children.

SUMMARY

By now, you should feel like an insurance expert. We've covered basic principles of risk management and the important aspects of insurance of various types. If you have found areas of your coverage that do not measure up, we suggest you take care of them immediately. All the property and casualty insurance issues can probably be handled by a phone call to your agent.

If you have no disability coverage, we suggest you see a general agent who represents several companies and can shop for the best combination of quality and price.

The only area of risk management not covered here, life insurance, will be covered along with estate planning.

CHAPTER EIGHT

ESTATE PLANNING STRATEGIES: TAKING CARE OF YOUR HEIRS

ESTATE PLANNING—NOT JUST FOR THE RICH

Imagine that it's Friday evening and you're relaxed, looking forward to a leisurely weekend. The doorbell rings. "Hi," says a neatly dressed civil servant. "I'm from your state and I've come to give you your wills. We use them for everyone. I'm sure you'll find them quite satisfactory."

Can you believe it? This man knows nothing about you, yet he claims to know how you want your assets distributed when you die. How can this be? How can the state know what you want? Come to think of it, the state hasn't done anything right for you lately, has it?

This isn't as far-fetched as it seems. You might inadvertently empower a civil servant from the state to distribute your assets as he sees fit. Anyone who doesn't have a will leaves the disposition of his estate up to the state where he or she lives. Each state has **laws of intestate succession.** These specify exactly how your wealth will be distributed.

Now you know why we say that estate planning is not just for the rich. Everyone has an estate, and almost everyone who takes a moment to consider it has definite feelings about who should benefit from that estate. We doubt that the state's one-size-fits-all-estate-plan would really be in accord with most people's wishes.

It's not only a question of who gets what, but also of what happens along the way. In the absence of estate planning, everything you have spent your lifetime doing may be undone. Estate planning can save your heirs estate taxes and the delays, publicity and expense of probate.

If You Don't Have a Will

If having a will is such a good thing, why is it that most Americans don't have wills—much less sophisticated estate plans? The cost of having a simple will prepared is relatively low—$100 or so—or you can write your own will. The time commitment also is not great—perhaps an hour with yourself and the same with a lawyer. It is pretty straightforward, and pretty easy. Why, then, don't most people have wills? We guess that it's not the time nor the money, but the difficulty of facing your own demise. It might also be because you feel that you don't need a will—everything is owned jointly with your spouse, or you're single, or you're not wealthy. None of these is justification for dying intestate. You *do* need a will.

Many of our clients sit bolt upright when we tell them about the estate plan that the state of California—like many states—will provide if they don't provide one of their own. The worst case is for married people with at least two children where the spouses have some separate property. Under those circumstances two-thirds of the estate goes to the children, and one-third goes to the surviving spouse. The surviving spouse—while trying to get by on a diminished net worth—will also have to report to the court every year to account for expenditures on behalf of the children. And, ready or not, the children will receive their entire inheritance at the age of majority—as low as 18 years of age in many states.

Further, if you have children and you and your spouse both die, you are trusting the state to find a guardian to provide a loving home—and you've missed a chance to talk to the guardian about what is important to you. Don't let that happen.

If You Do Have a Will—
Congratulations

If you have a will already—congratulations! You are ahead of most people, but you should be aware that major changes in the estate laws have taken place during the last five years and it may be necessary to revise your will if it was drafted before late 1981. You may also need a revision if your personal circumstances have changed. Any of the following events should prompt you to call your attorney to see if your will needs revisions: your net worth now tops $1.2 million; you have married, divorced, moved in with someone, had children; one of your executors, trustees or guardians is now unwilling or unable to serve; one of your heirs has died. Any of these things could affect your will and should be checked with your lawyer.

Creating or Updating Your Will/Estate Plan

If you have a will, this chapter will help you understand its implications. If you don't have a will, it will help you structure one. It will also outline some key estate planning strategies that you can use to reduce the tax bite and insure that your wishes are carried out. We'll begin by introducing you to Richard Walter who will provide an example of how estate planning needs change during each person's lifetime. As we follow Richard through thirty years of his life, don't expect to understand all the terms that are used. Focus on his life circumstances—on the need—rather than on the estate planning technique that fills that need. By the time you finish the chapter, all the terms will be clear to you.

After we look at Richard's situation, we'll look at available estate planning techniques. The estimate you made regarding the size of your estate, or estates, the answers you gave to the estate planning questions and your current estate plan will all help to select the strategies that are appropriate for you.

Working With an Attorney

Estate planning is one of the most important parts of every financial plan. Estate planning can mean the difference between preserving the estate you worked so hard to build or letting it be destroyed in years of legal battles or by the burden of estate taxes. An estate plan will serve you well if it is drafted carefully in light of the laws of your state and the federal estate tax law.

We recommend that you consult a good estate-planning attorney to draft your estate documents. Use the contents of this chapter to formulate your estate goals, to analyze your current plan—if you have one—and to educate yourself about estate planning techniques. When you sit down with your lawyer, bring the forms that show what you own and how it is titled. With the data you have gathered and organized, and with your own clear-headed approach to what you need, you and your lawyer can form a partnership that will result in a better estate plan and, we hope, a less expensive one. Because you'll be organized and well-informed, you should be able to reduce the amount of time the attorney must spend.

HOW YOUR ESTATE PLAN SHOULD CHANGE OVER TIME

Richard Walter is 26 years old and single. He's been doing his own financial planning since he started his engineering career four years ago at a salary of $25,000 per year. He has consistently met his savings goal of 10 percent and has saved $10,775. He has a money market fund and two growth stock mutual funds. The $10,775 investment has already grown to $12,800! In addition, Richard has a $7,000 profit-sharing plan with his employer and some life insurance equal to twice his annual salary, which is now $30,000 a year. Richard has no will. If he died today, his estate—$12,800 in cash and investments, $7,000 in profit-sharing and $60,000 life insurance for a total of $79,800—would go to his mother and father because Richard is a resident of the state of California. The senior Walters are comfortable financially and, if Richard stopped to think about it, he would rather give some of his estate to the suicide prevention organization he volunteers for regularly and to his best friend, Tom Tigerman. The two have been buddies since grade school and it hasn't been as easy financially for Tom as it has been for Richard. It's hard for Richard to even think about dying; but if he did, it would make him feel great to do something for Tom. He also has a couple of prized possessions that he would want Tom to have—his snow skis and the transferrable portion of his health club membership.

Richard also has a special woman in his life, Trish. He would want to give Trish two items in his apartment that she has admired—a print and the antique oak desk that Richard and Trish spent several days converting from a spray-painted disaster to a lovely piece of furniture.

Richard's situation is straightforward. Without a will, however, all of his property would go to his parents, who do not need it. Richard needs a simple will with some specific bequests to his parents, the suicide prevention organization, Tom and Trish. Richard will need to name an executor to handle his estate and a successor executor in case the executor cannot serve. Before meeting his attorney, Richard should select the executor and successor from among his friends, relatives or trusted advisors. He should be sure that they are willing to serve. When he visits the attorney, he should also bring a list of his assets and liabilities.

Three years later Richard and Trish, both 29, are about to get married. It's time to update the wills. Richard's salary has been increasing at an average of five percent each year and he has continued to meet his savings goal. In the past three years, he has added another $9,500. With a continuing eight percent return, he now has $25,000 in investments. His profit-sharing plan balance has increased to $14,000. Now that he is earning $35,000, his life insurance coverage is $70,000. Trish also has assets—she's a member of the "ten percent club" and her earnings as a computer programmer have been similar to Richard's.

The Walters-to-be live in a community property state and have been advised to keep the property they own as separate property, rather than to commingle it or place it in joint ownership. (More on this later.) Because of this decision, it's especially important that they have wills. If either were to die, the separate property would be divided between the surviving spouse and the decedent's parents. Richard and Trish want to be sure that everything each has goes to the other. Later in life, when Richard and Trish's estates have grown enough to promise financial security to the surviving spouse, special requests to friends and charities will probably find their way back into the wills. For now, they want everything to go to the surviving spouse.

Richard and Trish need simple wills. These are often referred to as **"I love you" wills** because they usually say, "...to my beloved husband, _____ ..."

Five years later Richard and Trish, now 34, have two children and a home. They also have a number of assets that they own jointly. Through thick and thin, they kept their promise to themselves to save ten percent and, when they bought their home a few years ago with $30,000 from their savings, their attorney advised them to title it and other appreciating assets as community property rather than in joint tenancy. Community property has some special tax advantages if the surviving spouse sells an asset that has appreciated.

Richard and Trish sat at home one evening and talked about who should raise their children if Richard and Trish both died. They were about to leave on their first vacation without the children. Choosing the right person or people was very hard. Their best friends, Alison and George, would be wonderful substitute parents and would get along great with the children. But Alison and George couldn't hold onto a nickel. The Walters worried about how their friends would manage the children's assets. The Butlers, on the other hand, were financially astute, but lacked the acceptance and warmth that Alison and George could provide.

Richard and Trish need to revise their wills again. The most important consideration is to provide a guardian for their minor children, and the solution is simpler than you might think. They could name Alison and George as guardians of their children's "persons," and the Butlers as trustees of their assets. It would be important to let the Butlers and Alison and George know their wishes about money, the children and other important issues.

Knowing the pressure two additional children would place on Alison and George's resources, Richard and Trish decided to state in their wills that if physical space were a problem, the trustees of the children's assets should provide the guardians with enough money to make an addition to their home or assistance to buy a larger home. Richard and Trish also selected successor guardians for the children.

The trust the Walters established for their children provided that the assets would be held in trust for them until age 21 and distributed outright at that time.

In addition to the issue of a guardian, Richard and Trish discussed the idea of a living trust with their attorney. A **living trust** operates during your lifetime, as opposed to a **testamentary trust,** which takes effect when you die. Living trusts don't reduce estate taxes, but they reduce the cost of estate settlement. By avoiding probate, living trusts reduce the costs, the publicity and the delays involved in the probate process. Their attorney advised the Walters to structure a living trust. To do this, they had the appropriate legal papers drawn up and they retitled their assets to the name of the trust.

Fifteen years later the Walters have accumulated a substantial estate through their conscientious approach to savings. Their children are approaching college age. At 49, Richard and Trish are taking stock of where they are financially. Trish went back to work when her youngest child was school age. She has earned about 75 percent of what Richard earns. Their ten percent annual savings has grown to more than $500,000, and that does not include their home! Between their investments, the equity in their home, life insurance and retirement benefits, their estate would exceed $800,000 if both died! Looking over their wills, they gasp at the prospect that, if something happened to both of them, each of their children would receive $400,000 outright at age 21! Visions of Ferraris dance in their heads. They can't imagine that the children would make wise decisions with $400,000 burning holes in their pockets.

The Walters decide to change their wills to instruct the trustee of the children's assets to give the children income from the assets and to invade the principal as necessary for their care, maintenance, education or support. At age 25—no longer 21—one-third, instead of all, of the assets will be distributed to each child, half of the remainder will be distributed at age 30 and the remainder at age 35. Not only will their children be older, but by making partial distributions, Richard and Trish are giving their children a chance to make mistakes with a portion of their inheritance so they can become wiser before the next portion is distributed.

Another 11 years have gone by, and Richard and Trish are ready for their financial independence years. They have accumulated enough net worth to supplement their incomes and provide a comfortable lifestyle. Their ten percent savings habit bought them a home, four years of college for each of the children and was still worth $1 million when they were 65!

Both of the Walters have established successful careers—Richard in engineering and Trish in business. Both could continue to work, they could even find part-time consulting assignments. What delights them both is that they can take, or leave, these assignments because they have economic freedom. If they continued to work it would be because the work was something they wanted to do, not because of necessity.

Because their net worth is so large, the Walters should be thinking about trusts that will save estate taxes. Current federal estate laws provide for unlimited tax-free transfer of property between spouses. Unfortunately, when their estate is of sufficient size—some attorneys look at $1.2 million as the appropriate point; others recommend it when your estate is $600,000 and growing—using the unlimited marital deduction may ultimately result in a greater estate tax because the surviving spouse's entire estate will be subject to tax. Other strategies will allow the Walters to pay no estate taxes on the first death and reduce taxes on the death of the second spouse. These involve establishing trusts that will take effect at the death of the first spouse.

In the years to come, with Richard and Trish's continuing rosy financial outlook, they may want to give gifts to their children as a way to reduce the size of their estates. At present, the lowest marginal estate tax bracket is 37 percent. That means that the Walters could give their children one dollar today; or they could leave it in their estate and, after taxes were paid, it would yield only 63 cents to the children. Richard and Trish do not want to start a gifting program that would compromise their own financial security; however, with their high degree of security, gifting might serve to put more of their wealth in their children's hands and less in the U.S. Treasury.

ESTIMATING THE SIZE OF YOUR ESTATE

Worksheet 27 will guide you through the process of estimating the size of your estate. If you are single, the process is a simple matter of transferring the value of various assets from the other worksheets to this one and adding them up. If you are married, you need to compute the size of two estates and the question of "who owns what" becomes an issue. The footnotes give you some guidance on this matter. If property is jointly owned, the presumption is that each spouse owns 50 percent of the asset. If, however, you and your spouse can prove that the ownership percentage is different, enter the correct amount in each column.

Be aware that assets that are separately titled may not be separate property in the eyes of the law. In California, a community property state, assets purchased from the earnings of either spouse are community assets. IRAs and other pension assets are usually titled separately, but would be community property unless the money placed in them were separate property assets or income from separate property assets.

The value of your estate is an issue in overall estate planning strategy. This is because every person has what is called a **unified credit** that can be applied against federal gift taxes and estate taxes. In 1987, the unified credit rose to $192,800. This credit is enough to offset the federal tax on an estate of $600,000. If your estate is worth less than $600,000, it will pass to any heir free of estate tax. Transfers between spouses, no matter how large the amount, are not subject to federal estate taxes. State estate taxes vary from state to state and you should discuss these with your attorney. To estimate your estate tax, complete Worksheet 27 and use Table 8–1. The size of the surviving spouse's estate will usually be the combined total.

We noted above that the unified credit may be used for lifetime gifts or for estate taxes. There are no gift taxes on gifts up to $10,000 made by one donor to one recipient in any given year. Gifts of $10,000 or less are covered by an **annual exclusion** and therefore do not use up any of the unified credit of the individual who gives the gift. Larger gifts are subject to tax, but no actual cash will be required to pay the gift tax. The tax simply will serve to reduce the unified credit available at the donor's death.

WORKSHEET 27 — ESTIMATING THE SIZE OF YOUR ESTATE

DESCRIPTION	HUSBAND	PERCENT OF TOTAL ESTATE	WIFE	PERCENT OF TOTAL ESTATE	COMBINED TOTAL	COMBINED PERCENT OF TOTAL ESTATE
LIFE INSURANCE PROTECTION[1]	200,000	62.3	100,000	48.5	300,000	57
RESIDENCE (NET EQUITY)[2]	50,000	15.6	50,000	24.3	100,000	19
BUSINESS, PENSION, AND PROFIT-SHARING PLAN[3]	12,000	3.7	12,000	5.8	24,000	4.6
SAVINGS-TYPE ACCOUNTS	6,000	1.9	6,000	2.9	12,000	2.3
BILLS, NOTES, BONDS, AND PREFERRED STOCKS	15,000	4.6	15,000	7.3	30,000	5.7
MORTGAGES AND LOANS *owed to you*	3,000	.9	3,000	1.5	6,000	1.0
COMMON STOCK	20,000	6.2	20,000	9.7	40,000	7.6
MUTUAL FUNDS	15,000	4.6	0	0	15,000	2.9
REAL ESTATE	—		—		—	
ENERGY	—		—		—	
EXOTICS	—		—		—	
OTHER	—		—		—	
TOTAL	321,000		206,000		527,000	

[1] Life insurance will be part of the estate of the "owner" of the policy.

[2] If property is jointly owned, the presumption will be that 50% of the value is owned by each spouse.

[3] Although assets may be titled separately, in the eyes of the law, they may be jointly owned. Unless you are sure that the property is jointly owned or sure that a particular percentage is owned by each spouse, assume 50% is attributable to each estate.

Table 8-1 Estate Tax Table

Federal Estate Tax Work Sheet

	Sample Estate	Your Estate
Gross Estate	$1,100,000	$
Less Liabilities	− 30,000	
Adjusted Gross Estate	1,070,000	
Less Marital Deduction	−300,000	
Less Charitable Contribution Deduction	− 20,000	
Taxable Estate*	750,000	
Add Adjusted Taxable Gifts Made After 1976 (Value on Date of Gift)	+ 12,000	
Estate Tax Computation Base	762,000	
Tentative Tax From Table Below	252,980	
Less Gift Tax Actually Paid After 1976	− 0	
Actual Tax on Taxable Estate	252,980	
Less Unified Credit (1987)†	−192,800	−192,800
Federal Estate Tax Due	$ 60,180	

*If your taxable estate is less than $600,000 (assuming the full unified credit is available in 1987 and beyond), no federal tax is due. For 1986 the federal credit is $155,800, which allows a taxable estate of $500,000 to pass tax-free.

†There may be other credits, such as a credit for foreign death taxes and death taxes paid to a state, that may be applicable to your estate.

Gift and Estate Tax Rate Schedule

If The Amount Is		Tentative Tax Is		
Over	But Not Over	Tax +	%	On Excess Over
$ 0	$ 10,000	$ 0	18%	$ 0
10,000	20,000	1,800	20	10,000
20,000	40,000	3,800	22	20,000
40,000	60,000	8,200	24	40,000
60,000	80,000	13,000	26	60,000
80,000	100,000	18,200	28	80,000
100,000	150,000	23,800	30	100,000
150,000	250,000	38,800	32	150,000
250,000	500,000	70,800	34	250,000
500,000	750,000	155,800	37	500,000
750,000	1,000,000	248,300	39	750,000
1,000,000	1,250,000	345,800	41	1,000,000
1,250,000	1,500,000	448,300	43	1,250,000
1,500,000	2,000,000	555,800	45	1,500,000
2,000,000	2,500,000	780,800	49	2,000,000
2,500,000	3,000,000	1,205,800	53*	2,500,000
3,000,000		1,290,800	55*	3,000,000

*Beginning in 1988, the 53% and 55% brackets disappear and taxable amounts over $2,500,000 will be taxed at 50%.

Reprinted from Internal Revenue Code (CCH) § 2,001 (July 15, 1985).

ESTATE PLANNING 101

Estate planning, like every field of law, has its own specialized vocabulary. Before you can review your will or read the rest of this chapter, you need to be sure that you understand the basic vocabulary and concepts. If you're an estate planning sophisticate, you can skip this section. If not, you will be a sophisticate by the end of it.

What Is Probate?

Probate is an administrative process to prove that a will is valid, and that the person who created and signed it—the **testator**—was mentally competent and acting without undue influence at the time the will was made. It is the probate court's duty to administer the estate so that all the instructions in the will are executed faithfully.

Any number of horror movies depicting a dear, sweet elderly aunt subjected to coercion by her greedy, ruffian nephew have driven home the importance of this process of "proving" a will. In its absence, there would be many more ruffian heirs.

A will is simply a set of instructions written or dictated by the testator, telling how and to whom assets are to be distributed, as well as other considerations such as the transfer of responsibilities for minor children. All assets in the will must be placed in the hands of the probate court. Most states have exemptions for small estates.

A trust is also a written agreement that deals with the transfer of assets and responsibilities of the creator of the trust, the **settlor** or **trustor**. The main difference between a will and a trust is that the assets may avoid probate in a trust. Living trusts avoid probate. Testamentary trusts must be presented for probate because they are found within the will itself. For assets in a trust to avoid probate, the trust must be a living or **Inter Vivos trust** and not attached to the will.

Table 8-2 lists the cast of characters in the estate process. When there is a trust, similar persons perform similar functions but are called by different names.

TABLE 8-2 Who's Who in the Estate Process

In a Will	In a Trust	Without a Will	Duties
Testator	Settlor/Trustor	Decedent	Owner of Assets
Executor	Trustee	Administrator	In Charge of Assets
Attorney	Attorney	Attorney	Provides Legal Assistance
Legatee	Beneficiary	Heir	Receives Assets

Executors, **trustees** and **administrators** may be individuals or corporations. **Legatees** and **beneficiaries** may also be corporate entities—charities, for example.

We have shown you some of the value of the probate process, yet the book *How to Avoid Probate* has had a great following. Why would you want to avoid probate? As with most legal processes, probate has virtues and vices. Many people feel that the disadvantages of probate outweigh the advantages. Let's take a look:

Advantages of Probate

1. When an estate has been probated and its assets distributed, no creditor can make claim against the assets.
2. If heirs believe a property has been overvalued in probate, thus increasing the potential estate tax, the lawyer or executor can bring in an independent appraiser who appears before the judge. The judge may approve the new appraiser or take a middle-ground position between the independent appraiser and court-appointed one.
3. An estate is a separate taxable entity and may provide opportunities to reduce taxes by shifting income to an heir or keeping it in the estate a bit longer if the estate's tax bracket is lower than the heir's.
4. It costs more for an attorney to draft the living trust than to draft a will.

Disadvantages of Probate

1. Probate is costly. The fees are set by law, but they are for ordinary services. If the attorney does extraordinary work, the fees may be greater. To give you a sense of how these run, in California the fees are four percent of the first $15,000, three percent of the next $85,000, two percent of the next $900,000 and one percent of values above $1 million. The executor may charge the same fees. Therefore, if the executor does not waive his or her fees, double the amounts above. The fees are based on gross, not net, values. If there are highly-leveraged properties in the estate, the fees really work to the heir's disadvantage. A $1 million building with a $900,000 mortgage will count as $1 million in assessing the fees, not $100,000. When Richard and Trish Walter created their living trust, probate fees would have been either $17,150 for ordinary services of the attorney and $34,300 if the executor did not waive his or her fee.
2. Probate is time consuming. Estate settlement often takes between one and two years. Furthermore, assets in probate often suffer from lack of management and overly conservative management during the settlement process. It often takes a month or more to receive court permission to sell an asset. Due to time delays, an executor might

not be able to respond to a sudden decline in the stock market, for example. Executors tend to be very conservative during probate because of their liability if they are judged to be less than prudent.
3. Probate is a public process. Probate gives unknown creditors an opportunity to make claims against the estate. For this process to work, the will must be a matter of public record. Some people market lists of estates going through probate and heirs may be bombarded with phone calls and letters.

Now that you have a basic understanding, let's turn to your own will and analyze its provision.

If You Have a Will—Understanding the Important Provisions

Worksheet 28 asks you to review your current will or estate plan. Legal language is strange to those not trained in it, but it is not as impenetrable as you might think. Read over your will and note the key factors on the worksheet. Who are your executors, guardians, trustees and their successors? Is property distributed to your heirs outright or in trust? If it is in trust, who gets the income and who receives the principal? How and when is the principal distributed? In a typical unified credit trust, for example, the surviving spouse is the income beneficiary and the children are the ultimate beneficiaries. With a trust created to manage the assets of minor children, the children are usually the income beneficiaries and the ultimate beneficiaries. Principal is often distributed in full when they are 21, or in portions at various ages.

If you have a living trust, you—or you and your spouse—are probably the trustees.

Now that you know the basics about your own will, we will describe some estate planning techniques and considerations. You can judge what you have against them and feel satisfied that your plan is on target, or decide how to change it.

TRUSTS—KEEPING YOUR WEALTH INTACT

Revocable Living (*Inter Vivos*) Trusts

The Probate Avoidance Trust

The main benefit of this **revocable living trust** is that it allows assets to bypass probate. It does not, however, avoid the Federal Estate Tax or a State Inheritance Tax, if there is one in the state in question. The second benefit is that it allows the settlor (owner) to also be the trustee. In other words, the settlor has control of the assets. The settlor may invest, borrow, sell, etc., without anyone else's consent.

WORKSHEET 28   **REVIEWING YOUR CURRENT ESTATE PLAN**

	HUSBAND	WIFE
Executor	Wife	Husband
Successor executor	brother Jim	brother Ed
Property Distributed Outright:		
Item or dollar amount and recipient:	5,000, State U	5,000, State U
Item or dollar amount and recipient:		
Item or dollar amount and recipient:		
Item or dollar amount and recipient:		
Item or dollar amount and recipient:		
Item or dollar amount and recipient:		
Item or dollar amount and recipient:		
Property Distributed in trust: Trustees:	Wife	Husband
Successor trustees:	brother Jim	brother Ed
Name(s) of beneficiary(ies)	Sally John	Sally John
Ultimate beneficiary(ies)	Sally John	Sally John
Distribution of principal (timing and amount)	100% at 21	100% at 21
Do you have a living trust? Trustee(s)	no	no

Other provisions _____

More than one person can be a trustee. For example, a husband and wife may have a joint revocable living trust as co-trustees, with two signatures being required to perform legal acts involving trust assets. The two-signature provision is optional, of course.

When the settlors die, the successor trustee pays the death transfer taxes and distributes the assets to the beneficiaries, thus dissolving the trust.

The experience of Ellie Wilson's heirs illustrates the benefit of a living trust. Ellie had a revocable living trust. She put all her major assets into it except one. When she died, her son, who was successor trustee, was able to distribute all assets from the trust in one day to his brothers and sister. The one asset that was not in trust took five years to go through probate.

Sometimes, a client may want the trust to continue after death. In that case, a **"pour-over" arrangement** allows assets that were left out of the trust to be placed in trust for the beneficiary. In that way, a parent can provide for special cases, such as ensuring that a disabled child is taken care of for the rest of the child's life, or just making sure assets are protected until a child is mature enough to handle them. A "pour-over" provision is also used when the trust does not continue, because it provides for the distribution of all assets under the trust instructions.

For the trust to function, assets must be titled to the trust. The "one asset" left out of Ellie's trust was left out because she failed to retitle it. It should have been changed from Ellie B. Wilson to Ellie B. Wilson, Trustee, The Ellie B. Wilson Trust of February 4, 1987.

The Marital Deduction Trusts

These revocable living trusts are probate-avoidance trusts that can take one of three forms: The survivor's trust, the exemption trust or the "Q-tip" trust. In each case, the key event is the death of the first spouse.

The Survivor's Trust. An example is the best way to describe this complicated type of marital deduction trust, so let's look at the case of Sam and Mary. They establish a joint revocable living trust we'll call the "family trust." When Sam dies (or whoever dies first), his assets pour over into a marital trust. There are now two trusts: Trust A, which is the survivor's trust, and Trust B, where Sam's assets reside. Some call the second trust itself a "marital trust," while others call it the "B" trust of an "A/B" trust. Call it anything you like, but what it does is prevent Sam's assets from combining with Mary's assets, which would create one huge pile that the state inheritance tax and federal estate tax people could devastate at Mary's death.

The purpose is to keep the estate divided so that the values of both halves of the estate are kept under the Federal Estate Tax Exemption. The trade-offs for Trust "B" are the following:

- Mary receives the income from capital.
- In addition, she can receive five percent of the capital per year, or $5,000, whichever is greater.
- She can have additional capital if it is required for her health, support or education.
- She may act as a co-trustee of Sam's trust.
- All income from the "B" trust is taxable to her and is added to her income from her "A" trust.
- Upon her death, all assets in Sam's "B" trust pass to the beneficiaries, free from inheritance and federal estate tax and free of probate.

Of course Mary, the survivor in this example, has total control of her survivor's Trust "A" and may do with it whatever she wishes.

Thousands of dollars can be saved with the marital trust. Because only the survivor's estate will be taxed on her death, one effective strategy is to place growth investments (inflation hedges) in the "B" trust. No matter how large it grows over Mary's lifetime, it will not be subject to tax.

If Mary needs more capital, it would be better for her to penetrate her own "A" trust, deliberately reducing it to below the federal exemption. This would allow her to pass it on to her beneficiaries without death transfer taxes. As a general rule, you should keep high-income, no-growth investments in the "A" trust and growth investments in the "B" trust.

Now, what happens if Sam and Mary's estate is large enough to exceed the two federal exemptions (more than $1.2 million)? Whatever assets pass from spouse to spouse, do so today without federal death transfer tax. But anything above the current exemption for state and Federal transfer tax will be subject to taxation in the "B" trust because the capital in the "B" trust is left to its ultimate beneficiaries, not to Mary. Whatever the predeceased spouse passes to someone other than the surviving spouse, even if it passes into a trust for survivor's benefit, passes free of estate tax only if it is $600,000 or less. Amounts over that are subject to tax of a minimum of 37 percent! That's why the exemption trust was created.

The Exemption Trust. The exemption trust works just like the marital (A/B) trust, with one exception: It has a built-in statement saying that only those assets that are exempt from federal estate taxes can pour into the "B" trust. The balance of the combined estate passes directly to the spouse and is exempt from federal estate taxes.

As the federal exemption rose each year, peaking in 1987 at $600,000, the exemption trust automatically plugged in the current exemption amount. That is why the language in your estate plan may read like a formula rather than simply stating that $600,000 be placed in trust. Only when the surviving spouse dies is her estate taxed. Whatever is above the federal exemption is finally taxed in the survivor's estate, but that survivor may have had use of the tax money for many years before losing it to the state and federal governments. To increase the tax savings, the survivor could begin giving part of her estate away to the beneficiaries, providing it would not injure her financial independence. This is in addition to the suggestion given above about placing growth assets in the non-taxable trust.

Q-tip Trust. To discuss the Q-tip trust, let's stay with Sam and Mary, but this time we picture both of them in a second marriage. Sam has three children from his first marriage and Mary has two from her previous marriage. Sam and Mary love each other but they love their separate children, too. If they put everything into joint tenancy, when one of them dies, the survivor gets the whole estate. When the survivor dies, guess whose children will be left with nothing? Right, the one who died first.

Usually, people like Sam and Mary enter into the second marriage with separate property. Let's say Sam has $400,000 and Mary has $100,000. While Sam is living, Mary is amply taken care of through his investment income, his pension, and Social Security, which he generously uses for their combined living expenses. As time passes, Sam begins wondering how Mary is going to get along financially when he's gone if at his death his estate goes to his children. His pension and Social Security will stop, so she won't have those to count on. Sam is too old to make term or ordinary life insurance practical to use. Besides, he's already had a couple of heart attacks.

Sam seeks advice of an estate attorney who recommends a Qualified Terminal Interest Trust, popularly called a Q-tip. It starts with a single revocable living trust, that will bypass probate (as joint tenancy would have done). So instead of his assets going to Mary and then to her children, his estate pours into this Q-tip trust, that provides for Mary's benefit during her widowhood. At her death, Sam still has control of the assets in that trust. In a manner of speaking, he reaches out from the grave and passes his assets on to his children. It's a valuable instrument that can assure that Sam's children are his ultimate heirs without compromising Mary's financial security.

If their estate is large, Sam and Mary may use an **"ABC" trust.** Trust A holds Mary's share as the survivor, Sam's share goes into two trusts: Trust B (the Q-tip), and Trust C, an exemption trust. Trust C is never taxed and Trust A and B are not taxed until Mary dies.

The Totten Trust. The Totten Trust is another estate planning technique used extensively at banks and savings institutions. Often called a "poor man's will" because no formal trust instrument need be prepared, simply signing a savings signature card establishes the trust. Thus, if Sam Jones opens a savings account registered "Sam Jones, Trustee for Susan Jones," he establishes a Totten Trust.

This situation has other advantages besides easy establishment. **The Totten Trust** avoids probate, allows tighter control of property, and makes changing beneficiaries a simple matter. It does not require the agreement of a trustee as does a living trust which creates a contract between trustor and trustee.

The Totten Trust is easy to create, easy to abrogate, and is opened free of charge by most banks. In addition, the trust is not of public record so it remains a private matter. Savings institutions keep the account secret.

The Totten Trust is also easy for the beneficiary to execute. When the owner of the trust dies, the beneficiary presents the banker with a certified copy of the death certificate and the asset is transferred immediately to the beneficiary. On the minus side, although the Totten Trust avoids probate, it does not save taxes.

Generally, a formal living trust tailor-made by an attorney is appropriate for larger estates. When an estate consists primarily of savings accounts and little else, the Totten Trust is a useful estate planning instrument. While other living trusts often extend over the lifetimes of several people, the Totten Trust ends on the owner's demise. However, this trust, as well as other living trusts, may be revoked at any time during the settlor's or trustor's lifetime. This gives the trustor great flexibility.

Irrevocable Trusts

Assets placed in irrevocable trusts cannot be retrieved by the settlor. The assets are irrevocably given away—not to individuals but to the trust for the benefit of people and institutions, such as hospitals and churches. Also, the settlor cannot receive any income (except in a charitable trust or private annuity), nor can the settlor have any control over the assets. The settlor cannot, for example, force the trustee to do anything other than what is permitted by the trust instrument. The trustee may listen to the settlor's suggestions but is under no obligation to follow the settlor's requests. In other words, absolutely every attribute of ownership must be taken from the settlor. The trustee, on the other hand, must religiously abide by the trust instructions.

Now the good news: Not only does an irrevocable trust avoid probate, but it is also exempt from both state inheritance and federal estate tax. However, if the beneficiaries are individuals, there will be gift taxes to pay.

The following is an example of the type of estate that would benefit from an irrevocable trust:

Mary, a wealthy widow and mother of three children who spend as if the money will never end, wants to reduce the size of her estate by preventing its future growth. If she gives it to the children, Tom will buy a new Maserati, Bill will buy a sailboat he can't afford to maintain, and Sue will put a down payment on a $600,000 house she and her husband want. Mary loves her children and dislikes paying taxes. What can she do?

Mary can put some of her assets into an irrevocable trust, thus stopping future growth in her own estate of that capital (and growth of the tax bite along with it), and give the children annuity income for the next ten years or so. Or, she can let the income accumulate in the trust for a period of time. Later, she might distribute one-third of the trust assets to each child, then distribute the balance in another five years. Mary can allot it any way she wishes, but once she signs the trust, she can't change the plan.

In making the gift into the trust, she will not have to pay a gift tax on any amount over $10,000 she gives to each child because she may use part of her lifetime exemption at this time and avoid the gift tax. As you know, the lifetime exemption is enough to avoid taxes on an estate of $600,000 in 1987.

The Charitable Trust With Remainder Interest

Sometimes you can "give it away" and be better off. This technique, the **charitable remainder trust** works best for people who have appreciated assets *and* charitable intent.

A charitable trust with a remainder interest made sense for Marge. Marge, an elderly widow with a handicapped daughter, needed income. She had two stocks in her portfolio that paid low dividends and were currently valued at $240,000. Marge's cost for the stock was only $14,000 so, if she sold it, the capital gains tax would be over $60,000! The trust works like this: A person may give to charity without creating a gift tax. A gift of this kind also allows a deduction from one's income of up to 30 percent of the person's adjusted gross income. Any additional amount of the gift not allowed for deduction can be carried forward to the next taxable year for a total of six years. Now, one need not restrict this gift to a charity directly; it can be given to a trust specifically and exclusively for a charity. The deduction is based on the present value of what will eventually go to the charity. In addition to giving cash to a charity, one can also give stocks, even stocks with high capital gains.

The donor asks an officer or an administrator employed by the charity to act as trustee, which the charity has no reason to refuse. The trustee is asked to sell those growth stocks as soon as the trustee gets them in the trust and then reinvest the money into a corporate bond mutual fund. Most trustees will consider this, but it cannot be bound in writing that they do so. They do it because it makes sense.

Marge's attorney drew up a charitable trust and put the two growth stocks into it. Marge and her daughter will receive a specified dollar amount of income from the trust for as long as they live. Now, if the trustee would sell those stocks yielding 1.8 percent of $4,320 to buy a corporate bond fund yielding 8 percent or $19,200, this one change would increase her income by 444 percent on the asset values involved. The whole thing can be done without a capital gains tax because the stock was sold within the charitable trust and all qualified charities and charitable trusts are income-tax-exempt.

Because the widow's handicapped daughter could be expected to live another 30 plus years, the charitable deduction was minimal. But if you take the difference in Marge's and her daughter's income per year and stretch that out for 37½ years (the life expectancy of a 44-year-old female), the difference before taxes is $558,000—nearly 2.3 times more than the capital she gave away!

One of the key aspects of this trust, in terms of capital gains tax savings, is for the trustee to sell the growth assets when the trustee gets them. Now, the trustee doesn't legally need to sell the assets. Indeed, if the trustee was bound in writing, it would affect the validity of the trust. However, if the change is prudent and conservative, it's hard to imagine the trustee not making it. In any event, the income beneficiary (and settlor, in this case) can require the trustee to pay her a minimum annual income such as six percent of the value of the capital.

Many other fascinating, productive trusts and legal devices are available for estates today. But, before you see an attorney, learn as much as you can.

OTHER ESTATE PLANNING ISSUES

Distributing Assets to Children

The Life Insurance Council reports that 90 percent of all people who receive inheritances have nothing left at the end of five years. If you have children, we recommend that you protect them from this scenario. The Walters' approach made a great deal of sense. The children were income beneficiaries until they were 25 years old. Then they would receive one-third of their inheritance. They would have five years to either manage it well or learn how easily it could slip through their fingers. At the end of five years, they would receive a second distribution of principal, and a final distribution would be made ten years after the original one.

If you feel your children will be financially mature at an earlier age, you might want to make different distribution arrangements. If you are concerned about their maturity, but have difficulty with the concept of keeping assets in trust to age 30 or beyond, a compromise might suit you. You can keep the assets in trust but give the trustee discretion to make principal payments for specified purposes such as the purchase of a home or the starting of a business.

Specific Bequests and Gifts

If you know your sister would love a piece of jewelry that you inherited from your mother, or you want to make a gift to your favorite college or charity then, by all means, make a specific bequest in your will.

Bequests to charities remove the amount donated from your taxable estate. Bequests to minors should be given to a trustee for their benefit if they would, for example, require the minor to enter into a contract. Minors may not legally do this.

We offer one caution to you. If you are married and wish to make a specific bequest, be sure that it will not compromise your spouse's financial security. Jack Addison's will contained a specific bequest of $25,000 to his cousin. Unfortunately, in the time between drafting his generous bequest and his death, he stopped working and interest rates dropped drastically. Jack's wife, Lana, saw $2,000 of annual income disappear due to this bequest. Although she was still financially comfortable, in the frightening interlude between Jack's death and the time she finally realized that she would do well financially, the bequest added to her grief. It might have been better if the bequest to Jack's cousin took place at the second spouse's death.

Bequests are gifts that occur after the testator's death. You can make lifetime gifts, and they often make a great deal of sense. Gifts have both income tax and estate tax consequences that we will describe shortly, but first we want to correct a common misconception. Many people think that if you make a gift, you receive a tax deduction. This is true only if you give a gift to a qualified charity. The way a gift affects your taxes is that it may remove a stream of income from your tax return. Let's say that Richard and Trish make a gift of a $10,000 stock investment to one of their adult children. The stock pays a $500 annual dividend and the Walters paid a total of 36 percent combined Federal and state taxes. The Walters have given up the income and its accompanying $180 tax liability. If their daughter is in the lower 20 percent combined state and federal bracket, she will pay only $100 in tax. This shifting of income (see Chapter 10 for more on income shifting) resulted in greater after-tax income from the investment.

The gift also served to reduce estate taxes because the Walters removed the $10,000 (plus whatever appreciation they might have achieved on it) from their taxable estate. When we last looked at Richard and Trish's situation, their estate exceeded $1 million. They would be in a 41 percent marginal estate bracket. The $10,000 they gave to their daughter today would have shrunk to $5,900 if they left it in their estate!

If you want to make gifts, just be sure that they will not compromise your financial security. We've talked to many people who ask if they should place their home or other assets in joint tenancy with a son or daughter to avoid probate. When you do this, you have made a gift of property that may have tax consequences, and you may have traded estate tax savings for capital gains taxes without seeing which tax would be less.

Death, the Only Way to Avoid Capital Gains Taxes

Now that we have brought up the subject of capital gains versus estate taxes, we should describe that situation more fully. Actually, death is not the only way to avoid paying capital gains taxes—you can give appreciated assets to charity as we described earlier. It is true, however, that at death the government forgives all capital gains taxes. Assets receive what is called a **stepped up basis** at the date of death, or the alternate valuation date six months after death. Because **capital gains** are computed on the difference between the basis and the current market value, and a new basis is set at the current market value, capital gains are effectively erased.

In contrast, gifts carry the donor's basis and are not stepped up in basis when the donor dies. Let's go back to the example of putting a child's name on the deed of the home of his or her surviving parent. This strategy would avoid probate, but the child's half of the property would not receive a step-up in basis at the parent's death. Only the parent's half would have its capital gain erased. If the parent's estate had been under $600,000 and the child had waited until the parent died, there would be no estate tax. If the property was sold soon after, there would be no capital gains tax. If, on the other hand, the parent made a gift of a one-half interest, there would be no estate tax, but there would be a greater capital gains tax when the child sold the home.

Seek the advice of a lawyer before doing transactions like this. In the above example, the parent and child created a tax by making the gift.

Ownership of Property

Estate planning includes decisions regarding the way that property interests are held. Property is usually divided into **real property**—land and buildings—and **personal property.** There are a number of ways that property can be owned.

Individual ownership means that the owner of a piece of property holds it in his or her own name and has complete discretion over it.

Joint ownership exists when two or more individuals have ownership rights or interests in the property. There are several types of joint interests:

Joint Tenancy, with right of survivorship, is often called a "will substitute" because the property automatically passes to the surviving joint owner or owners in the event of the death of one owner. Joint tenancy ownership is not limited to husbands and wives. Because of its nature, joint tenancy titling cannot be overridden by a will. Be sure that the way you have assets titled does not interfere with what you wish to accomplish in your will. If you want your sister to receive your interest in a piece of property that you own jointly with another, then the titling must be other than joint tenancy.

Tenancy by Entirety applies to property held jointly by a husband and wife. In some states, this type of titling gives the husband control and the right to all of the income.

Tenancy in Common does not carry a right of survivorship. The presumption in the two forms of joint ownership noted above is that the owners have equal interest (50 percent each for husband and wife); tenants in common may have unequal interests.

Not all property owned by married couples is jointly owned, nor does the surviving spouse always have rights to property owned by the deceased spouse. Except in community property states, only property that is titled as joint tenancy property or in tenancy by entirety is jointly held.

In **community property states**—Arizona, California, Idaho, Louisiana, Nevada, New Mexico, Texas and Washington—the forms of ownership are the same as those used above. There are, however, laws that govern the ownership of property by married persons. In community states, you might title a property in individual name, but it would still be viewed as community property.

Laws vary from state to state but, generally, **separate property** is property owned by either spouse at the time of marriage. Inheritances or personal injury settlements during the marriage are separate property, as are any assets bought with separate property funds or (in some states) the income from separate property.

The income of both spouses is a community asset and assets acquired with earned income are **community assets.** At death, each spouse can dispose of his or her half of community property by will.

Community property taken from one of the eight states listed above into a non-community property, or common law state, remains community property.

Community property has an important tax advantage. When an owner of community property dies, both halves of the asset receive a stepped-up basis. In contrast, only the decedent's half of joint tenancy property receives a step-up in basis. Thus, if property was held as community property, there may be a smaller capital gains tax to be paid in the event that the surviving spouse sells the asset.

As you can see, property ownership laws can have a great impact on your estate plan and on your estate tax. Become familiar with the laws of your state and understand their implications. Don't simply check a box under ownership the next time you acquire an asset. Know what each box means and check the one that fits your objectives and circumstances.

Durable Power of Attorney

The Durable Power of Attorney is a powerful legal tool, yet many people are unaware of it. The durable power of attorney can eliminate the need for embarassing court proceedings if you become incapacitated and cannot manage your own financial affairs or make important decisions. When you execute this power, you (the principal) give someone specified authority to act on your behalf.

In some states this power expires when you become incapacitated, but in other states it remains effective until it is revoked or the principal dies. When the durable power functions in the latter way, it allows you and your loved ones to avoid the expense and the court oversight required in conservatorship proceedings.

The durable power may be drafted to suit your own needs and you can even decide when it will take effect. Most people have it take effect upon signing or in the event of incapacity because, in many cases, it would be impossible to predict when it might be needed. Individuals with Alzheimer's disease or terminal cancer often are forewarned before incapacity strikes, but others are not.

The person you select as your **attorney-in-fact** should be someone you trust implicity, for he or she will have substantial power over your financial assets and even your physical person. You can have the power drafted to exclude certain powers. If, for example, you do not want your home sold during your lifetime, you can specifically state that the attorney-in-fact does not have the authority to sell it.

Discuss this power of attorney with your attorney. If he or she advises you to have one drafted, select your attorney-in-fact with great care.

If this alternative is not available to you and a Living Trust is appropriate, you can name a standby trustee for your living trust who would perform some of the same functions that an attorney-in-fact would perform.

SUMMARY

You now have a working vocabulary of estate planning and a foundation of knowledge regarding a number of estate planning techniques. Put what you have learned to work by calling your attorney to update your plan or by identifying someone to create a plan for you. If you have read this chapter and find that what you already have is exactly what you need, we congratulate you. You are in the tiny well-prepared minority—soon to be joined by the rest of our readers.

LIFE INSURANCE—DO YOU NEED IT?

There are really only two reasons for owning life insurance: to protect dependents in the event of a wage-earner's premature death and to pay estate taxes when there is insufficient liquidity. The first reason is a fairly obvious one—if your spouse would be left in greatly reduced circumstances if you died or you have children whose educational goals would go unrealized, life insurance is a necessity. But, under these circumstances, it is a necessity only if you die before you have enough time to build an estate of your own. When your net worth has grown sufficiently, you can afford to "self insure" for these risks. In the meantime, this is a risk you should transfer by purchasing life insurance.

The second reason for purchasing life insurance is best illustrated by the school teacher whose husband left her 100 percent ownership of a large apple ranch. The ranch has been in the family for 50 years and is no longer in the midst of a rural area. It has been overtaken by development in surrounding areas and the land has appreciated substantially. It is worth approximately $1 million. The rest of Mrs. Lee's estate is worth approximately $250,000 and includes a few investments and her personal property. She lives primarily on her husband's Social Security and her teacher's pension. If Mrs. Lee were to die today, the tax on her estate would be $448,300. Where would it come from? Her children are not rich. They could sell the ranch, but selling it in time to pay the estate taxes might mean they would be forced to sell at a bad time, or that they would be at a great disadvantage in negotiating a sale. Individuals purchase life insurance in cases like this to keep their heirs from being forced to sell or having to **"distress sell"** an asset.

You can see from our comments above that if no one is dependent on you to earn a living and you have no estate liquidity problem, you probably don't need insurance. If someone is dependent upon you, turn to Worksheet 29 to estimate your need for life insurance. The approach shown here is simple and complete instructions are given on the worksheet.

Now That You Know How Much You Need, What Do You Need?

Insurance comes in many types—term, ordinary or whole life, universal, limited pay and endowment. And there are variations of each type. Term insurance, for example, comes as level term, decreasing term, mortgage insurance, annual renewable term and the like.

Every kind of life insurance, except various forms of term insurance, combine an investment feature with insurance. Term is pure death protection. Although other forms of insurance have their applications, we recommend **term insurance** a vast majority of the time. In our opinion, combining investment with insurance makes sense only in specific cases. The rest of the time, we recommend that you do your own investing. An insurance company, like a bank, is a financial intermediary. You lend it money, it invests the money, earns enough to cover its operating costs and provide a profit to its shareholders (unless it is a mutual company) and then provides a return to its policy holders. Investing directly can be much more rewarding. In general, you should separate your pure death protection from your investing by purchasing term insurance.

We recommend that you avoid **credit life insurance** and **accidental death and dismemberment insurance** (AD&D). Both of these forms of insurance can be costly. Your need for **credit life insurance** can be met by including in your insurance needs analysis sufficient money to pay off existing debts.

AD&D coverage can appear inexpensive because it is subject to so many conditions that it probably rarely pays a death benefit—a reassuring thought when you are flying! Furthermore, life insurance coverage should be based on the needs of dependents or estate tax payments, not on the cause of death.

Irrevocable Life Insurance Trusts

When we discussed Mrs. Lee and her apple ranch above, we failed to mention that purchasing life insurance to pay estate taxes may exacerbate the

Estate Planning Strategies: Taking Care of Your Heirs

WORKSHEET 29   FIGURING OUT HOW MUCH LIFE INSURANCE

The purpose of life insurance is to guarantee your family a comfortable life if you die young. Consequently you should err on the high side when calculating your coverage. That does not mean sacrificing all present niceties for the possibility of turning your relatives into Rockefellers. It does mean carrying enough protection to preserve your family's current standard of living. You can arrive at a suitable amount of coverage by using this worksheet. If both spouses have paying jobs, make a copy of the worksheet and do the figures for each breadwinner.

This exercise aims to nail down how much insurance you need while your children are growing up. It does not include the much larger sums required to finance a surviving spouse's later life or retirement. The presumption these days is that he or she could take care of that. But families with lifelong dependents—a handicapped child, for example—should ask a financial planner for help in their calculations.

Most of the lines on the worksheet explain themselves. Here's some coaching for those that don't:

Line 1. In two-paycheck households, start by lumping together both after-tax incomes. Payroll deductions for retirement funds and health insurance count as take-home pay; life insurance deductions do not.

Line 2. People usually spend a third of their income on themselves. You may want to figure more or less than that.

Line 6. In totaling your present assets, don't forget Individual Retirement Accounts, company savings plans and survivor's benefits from your pension fund.

Lines 7 and 8. Consider here whether your spouse, if she or he is now working, would wish to stay home with the children for a year or two if you die. Then subtract that year or two from the number on line 4. If your spouse would choose not to work for several years, don't count on any take-home pay. Enter 0 on line 7.

Line 10. Social Security survivor benefits can become a major source of income. Table A, at right, indicates the annual amounts currently paid to a non-
(continued)

1. Current total family take-home pay (annual) $ 36,000
2. One-third of your own take-home pay $ 7,000
3. Annual family expenses without you $ 29,000
   (line 1 minus line 2)
4. Number of years until your youngest child   x   10
   finishes high school
5. Total family expenses (line 3 times line 4) $ 290,000
6. Savings and investments $ 50,000
7. Spouse's annual take-home pay $ 12,000
8. Number of years of that income   x   10
9. Total spouse contribution $ 120,000
   (line 7 times line 8)
10. Total Social Security benefits $ 69,432
11. Total assets and income $ 239,432
    (add lines 6, 9 and 10)
12. Total income deficit $ 50,568
    (line 5 minus line 11)
13. Average annual income deficit $ 5,057
    (line 12 divided by line 4)
14. Lump sum that, if invested, would provide $ 49,000
    the amount on line 13 for the number
    of years on line 4
    (factor from Table B times $1,000)
15. College costs per child $ 24,000
16. Number of college-bound children   x   1
17. Total college costs $ 24,000
    (line 15 times line 16)
18. Funeral and estate costs $ 15,000
19. Lump sum for a mortgage or $ 75,000
    emergency fund (optional)
20. Total lump sum needed at death $ 163,000
    (add lines 14, 17, 18 and 19)
21. Present life insurance coverage $ 48,000
22. Total insurance needed $ 115,000
    (line 20 minus line 2)
    (if negative, you have more than you need)

Copyright 1987. Money Magazine. Reprinted with permission.

WORKSHEET 29 (Continued)

working spouse and children and the maximum available per family. Benefits decline swiftly for a working spouse earing more than $6,000 a year. Children continue collecting until they graduate from high school or turn 19, whichever comes first. A spouse's benefits expire after the youngest child reaches age 16. Estimate your total benefits by counting the years of maximum and lesser benefits at your income level in the table. Multiply the benefits by the number of years you would collect them and add the results. (For further help, call your local Social Security office or write to the Social Security Administration, Office of Public Inquiries, Baltimore, Md. 21235.)

Line 14. The average annual income deficit resulting from your death (line 13) overstates what your family would need unless you adjust the amount for investment income. Much of the lump sum you are calculating could earn interest or dividends for several years before the whole amount is spent. The number shown in Table B, at left, most nearly corresponding to your annual deficit and the years your family would need income (line 4) is a factor that, when multiplied by $1,000, approximates the lump sum needed. It is based on the conservative assumption that after taxes and inflation the fund would earn a 2% return.

Line 15. Enter an amount here if you want your insurance to finance the college education of your child or children. Four years at a private college, including room and board, now costs an average of $40,100, and public colleges average $22,416. For children at least five years away from college, those amounts should be adjusted now for inflation. Assuming 5% annual increases, raise them to $52,000 and $28,600—and in five years review them against actual costs.

Line 18. Funeral and estate costs, including the settlement of debts, generally amount to one year's take-home pay.

Line 19. If you wish, you can provide money that your family could use to pay off the mortgage or keep for emergencies.

Line 21. Take into account any coverage you already have from your employer as well as your own policies.

FIGURING OUT HOW MUCH LIFE INSURANCE

Table A: Social Security benefits. Here are estimates of annual survivor payments for your spouse and children.

WORKER'S PRESENT AGE		WORKER'S 1986 INCOME		
		$20,000	$30,000	OVER $40,000
25	Benefit per survivor	$6,312	$7,764	$9,060
	Maximum family benefit	14,940	18,132	21,132
35	Benefit per survivor	6,228	7,716	8,724
	Maximum family benefit	14,795	18,000	20,352
45	Benefit per survivor	6,216	7,488	7,944
	Maximum family benefit	14,772	17,484	18,528
55	Benefit per survivor	6,216	7,224	7,572
	Maximum family benefit	14,760	16,872	17,544
65	Benefit per survivor	5,868	6,804	7,092
	Maximum family benefit	13,908	15,888	16,560

Source: Social Security Administration

Table B: Lump-sum factors. Here are the amounts needed to replace income (multiply by $1,000).

DOLLAR AMOUNT (FROM LINE 13)	NUMBER OF YEARS (FROM LINE 4)								
	5	7	9	11	13	15	16	17	18
$5,000	24	33	41	49	57	65	72	79	85
10,000	48	65	82	98	114	129	143	157	170
15,000	71	98	123	147	170	193	214	235	255
20,000	95	130	164	196	227	257	286	313	340
25,000	118	163	205	245	284	321	357	391	425
30,000	142	195	245	294	340	385	428	469	510
35,000	166	227	286	343	397	449	500	548	594
40,000	189	260	327	391	454	513	571	626	679
45,000	213	292	368	440	510	578	642	704	764
50,000	236	325	408	489	567	642	713	782	849
55,000	260	357	449	538	624	706	785	860	934
60,000	283	390	490	587	680	770	856	938	1,019
65,000	307	422	531	636	737	834	927	1,016	1,104
70,000	331	454	571	685	794	898	999	1,095	1,188
75,000	354	487	612	734	850	962	1,070	1,173	1,273

Copyright 1987. MONEY Magazine. Reprinted with permission.

problem Mrs. Lee is trying to solve. After all, any life insurance she purchases will also be subject to estate tax, and she is already in a 41 percent marginal bracket. She would have to purchase nearly twice the amount of insurance as the estate tax owed so that, after the taxes were paid on the insurance proceeds, there would still be enough to pay the rest of the estate tax bill.

One solution to this problem is for Mrs. Lee's children to own the policies on her life and to pay the premiums. Mrs. Lee could make gifts each year of enough to pay the premiums.

Another alternative would be a life insurance trust that could have been established before Mr. Lee died. If the trust owns the policies and pays the premiums, then the proceeds of the life insurance would not have been part of Mr. Lee's estate. If the children were the beneficiaries of the trust, Mrs. Lee could have been the income beneficiary of the trust and he would remain out of her taxable estate too. The trust could assure that the insurance proceeds were not taxed in either of the senior Lee's estates. This objective would be accomplished only if the policies were placed in the trust more than three years before Mr. Lee's death, and if the mechanisms for paying the premiums were properly structured.

Life insurance trusts can be very effective for young people who have great insurance needs, but they should be carefully drafted by a lawyer to be sure that they will fulfill all the legal requirements to protect them from estate taxes.

LIFE INSURANCE OPTIONS

If you need insurance, a variety of options are available. The primary division of life insurance is between term and whole-life insurance. Within these two categories there are varying types of policies, and new types of "whole or cash value" insurance contracts are evolving. The main difference between term and whole-life is that **term insurance** is pure protection for temporary needs, while **whole-life insurance** is considered permanent insurance and combines pure protection with a savings plan.

In general, we recommend building your own protection via a well-managed investment portfolio instead of paying an insurance company for protection. This is not practical during those early years when you are building your net worth. Self-insuring must wait until you are financially independent.

Life insurance is most needed at the beginning of your adult life when there are dependents to support and little cash flow. Your insurance needs tend to be the highest when your ability to pay premiums is at its most limited. As time passes, your net worth will increase and your dependents will become financially independent; but, until you have accumulated sufficient financial wealth, insurance is necessary. In these situations, term insurance is usually recommended over whole-life, because it is less expensive. Term insurance is the affordable alternative but, in your younger years, price is not the only argument in favor of term insurance. If you are considering whole life, ask yourself if you want to invest through an insurance company? You would probably earn greater returns by investing directly.

Several types of policies can help you in your decision whether to "buy term and invest the difference" or use "whole or permanent" to build up long-term cash values.

Term Insurance

Annual Renewable Term

The premium for annual renewable term insurance starts out at a low rate, then increases each year if the level of protection remains level. You are allowed to renew the policy every year until age 75 or 100, depending on the provisions of the specific policy. This is by far the most recommended version of term insurance.

Decreasing Term

The premium remains level, but the amount of insurance declines over time with decreasing term insurance. There is almost no advantage to decreasing term, because it is hard to predict exactly how much protection will be needed in the future. The most common use of decreasing term, mortgage insurance, is for paying off your home mortgage. This protection tends to be too expensive in your younger years. In addition, you may not want to pay off a home mortgage. Given the tax deductibility of mortgage interest and the non-deductibility of most other interest expenses, a low-interest rate mortgage may also be one of the least desirable debts to pay off early.

Level Term

This version of term insurance is by far the least desirable due to front-loading the premium. The premium and protection remain level throughout the stated time period, as the cost of pure insurance rises each year. This means that in the early years you pay more than your share. You are, in essence, allowing the insurance company the use of your money in the beginning, and losing the potential of future growth of this capital if you were to invest it.

Deposit Term

Deposit term was invented to reduce the high cost of early cancellations of insurance policies. Cancellation of policies is a serious economic problem for insurance companies due to the high initial cost of issuing policies. Initial costs include sales commissions, underwriting, administration and medical examinations that are not ordinarily recovered in the first few years. As an incentive for insureds to remain with the company, policyholders deposit a lump-sum at the beginning of the term with the intention of remaining with the policy for a stated term. If they stay with the policy, they are returned their deposit at the end of the specified period along with interest. The insurance company keeps the lump-sum if they cancel. This type of policy results in a loss of the use of the money on deposit. The insured might have earned a higher rate of return had he invested on his own.

Whole Life or Cash Value Policies

In traditional whole-life policies the face amount and premiums remain at the same level for the lifespan of the policyholder. Because the premium is averaged over a client's lifetime, the premium is higher than would otherwise be necessary in the early years, just when a person is least likely to afford the cost. This premium is also higher than term insurance due to the savings feature. Some portion of the premium goes to accumulating a cash surrender value. Although whole-life is often sold on the grounds of a forced tax-deferred savings plan, the dollars allocated to this savings feature could be earning higher interest in your own investment portfolio. In addition, the beneficiaries of the policy never receive the accumulated cash value. Instead, they only receive the face value. If you cannot motivate yourself to save, whole-life insurance may work for you. It turns your savings program into a bill that must be paid each month, quarter or year. Below are variations on the traditional whole-life policy.

Universal Life

This new product offers additional flexibility to permanent insurance. The death benefit is determined when initially purchased, and thereafter the policyholder may change the death benefit to suit his or her needs. Part of the premium pays for insurance, while another portion goes into a savings fund, after deducting certain fees and charges. In reality, it may take several years before any interest is earned on this savings fund due to the additional costs involved. Again, we recommend that you do your own investing rather than working through a financial intermediary.

Variable Life

In several ways, variable life is similar to buying term insurance and investing the difference. You control the allocation of your investments into an equity, money market or bond portfolio. The other portion of your premiums pay for the monthly mortality charge. This may become an increasingly popular product as insurance companies link up with mutual fund managers who have excellent track records.

Endowment

This type of insurance policy pays the face amount of the policy, if you are still living on a designated date, or to a beneficiary if you die before that date. The premiums on this policy are high because you are funding for a specified period. Popular uses of endowment policies are for retirement programs or college education. In general, we advise our clients to avoid this type of policy, because it is expensive and your after-tax premium dollars compound at a slow rate.

Conclusion

You may need pure protection in the early years of your life and term insurance is a relatively inexpensive way to provide it. It allows you time to build up a sufficient living estate. Having done so, you will no longer need insurance. Because it is hard to predict how much life insurance you will need in the future, buying permanent insurance for unnecessary protection could waste your money. In addition, the cash value of these policies may grow at a slower rate than you could achieve in your own portfolio due to the additional costs involved and general pooling of insurance funds.

There may be exceptions to this general rule. The "inside build-up" of cash value in life insurance policies is not subject to tax. If you are considering a life insurance policy, compare the after-tax rate of return with other investments.

Life insurance is useful and often necessary at certain stages in life. Under some circumstances it can work as a good financial planning tool but, for most of us, it is better to build strong portfolios so that we can eventually "self-insure" and eliminate the expense of life insurance. Instead of finding the best life insurance, focus on the performance of your investments to provide for your future needs.

CHAPTER NINE

FINANCIAL INDEPENDENCE

GETTING RIGHT ON THE MONEY

Johnny Paycheck captured our imaginations with his song, "Take This Job and Shove It." Whether you love your work or not, most of us dream about the kind of economic freedom that would allow us to express the same sentiment—perhaps, however, less colloquially. We would like to express it with the knowledge that our lifestyle would remain at least at its present level. Unfortunately, dreams of freedom don't come true for the majority of our fellow citizens. The median income of men over 65 is $10,450 per year. For women in the same age group, the median is $6,020. Remember that the median is the 50th precentile. This statistic means that one-half of our male senior citizens live on less than $10,450 and more than half of their female counterparts live on less than $6,020. Over three million seniors live below the poverty line. Those income and poverty statistics include Social Security benefits. What would they do without it?

For anyone under forty we recommend not counting on Social Security. For those between 40 and 50, we recommend counting on less than one-half. The Social Security system was not structured to provide a living for those over 65, it was structured to avoid abject poverty. Yet many senior citizens rely on Social Security as their major source of income.

How did this tragedy happen? Americans have the lowest savings rate of any industrialized nation. The savings rate changes over time, but it hovers around four percent. That means Americans save only four percent of what they earn. Other industrialized nations, Germany and Japan among them, show savings rates in the 10 percent to 14 percent range.

This is a sobering picture if you think about it for a moment. Most of us will work for about 45 years of our lives—less if we extend our educations or retire early. At age 65, the average life expectancy is just over 14 years for men and 17 years for women. That means we may need to set aside enough during those 45 working years to support us for another 14–17 years.

If you are like most people, you struggle to pay the bills each month. By the time you have paid for the rent or the mortgage, for food, clothing, taxes, utilities, and automobile expenses, there may be very little left over from your paycheck. We're going to suggest that you add yet another creditor to your list: yourself. Not only that, but we suggest that you pay yourself first. We can assure you that you will never get ahead unless you invest for your future well being.

Now that we have depressed you, let's look at what you can do. The first thing to do is start now. You need to save only $85 per month to be a millionaire if you start at age 25. (Refer back to the chart on page 11.) If you wait twenty years, it will take over $1,000 per month. Time and the miracle of compounding are your greatest allies. Here are a few tips to help you reach financial independence:

1. Set a savings goal and meet it based on your overall goals. This chapter will show you how. If you wait until your next salary increase to save, that isn't good enough. If, after reading all of this, you still think that saving is something for tomorrow, you do not have the attitude you need to be financially successful.
2. Develop a technique for managing your cash flow that makes it easy for you to reinvest all of the income and capital gains from your investments and easy for you to save. (The system described below may be just what you need.)
3. Get more out of your investments. Look at your current investments (if you've worked your way through Chapter 5, you have already done this). Make sure you are getting the highest returns consistent with being prudent.
4. Find every legal way to reduce your taxes. Keep a few more dollars each year from wending their way to Washington, D.C. or your state capital. There are still ways to reduce your taxes; and qualified retirement plans offer the greatest opportunity.

If you do these things, your chance of becoming financially independent is great. We've already focused on the legions who don't make it. Now let's look at those who do. You will see that the formula for success is simple. The successful few differ from the unsuccessful many in these ways:

- They are more likely to have written down what they want to accomplish. You have already done that.
- They save systematically. Either you do that already, or you started today.
- They reinvest all income and growth on the money they have saved. It's the only way that your investments will compound.
- They reduce their taxes to the extent that it is prudent to do so.
- They monitor and track their portfolios and reposition them when better opportunities are available or when existing investments are not performing.

MANAGING YOUR CASH FLOW: THE THREE-BIN SYSTEM

If you had your choice, would you rather be like a well-run corporation or like the Social Security system, which is teetering on the edge of bankruptcy? It's not a fair question, is it? The Social Security system was rescued from the brink of bankruptcy and most people believe it will be back to the brink again. How could you want to be like it?

When we talk about being like a well-run, profitable corporation, we mean managing your cash flow like one. If we haven't whetted your appetite yet, then let us tell you about the best feature of the system you are about to learn: if you use it, you don't have to have a budget. It takes a little figuring to set the system up, but when you do, it runs very simply.

We've devised a method that we'll call the **three-bin system.** It works for a wide variety of people, from young people who are trying to save, to retired people who want to keep from dipping into their capital living, instead, on the income from it. It is called the three-bin system because it involves distributing your cash flow into three different accounts (Figure 9–1).

If you are in the capital accumulation years, which extend from your first summer job until you retire, the challenge is to make sure some of what you earn belongs to you and finds its way into your **"capital account."** Once there, it should grow and compound untouched until you need it to realize one of your important goals—homeownership, a sabbatical for child rearing, retirement and the like.

If you are in the capital-using years of retirement, you want to manage your cash flow so that you avoid dipping into your capital too early or too deeply.

If you remember the write-ups on how the Social Security system got into such trouble, it was because Social Security was being funded on a cash-flow basis. That means that all the money flowing in was considered to be spendable. Social Security ignored the fact that it should be setting aside money today for those who were promised benefits in the future. Now, the Social

Security recipients of the future are paying full freight for people receiving benefits today with little hope of reaping similar benefits for themselves in the future. We all know what has happened to the system and the continuing concerns. The baby boom generation will probably pay into Social Security and receive nothing close to what its parent's generation received. The generation behind the baby boom may pay for Social Security and receive no benefits themselves.

Unfortunately, many of us run our households on a cash flow basis too, ignoring liabilities that are accruing—property taxes, income taxes, insurance payments, our desire for a great vacation. Unlike Social Security, we can't tax others to increase our revenue, so the problems created by cash-flow management make themselves readily and painfully apparent. What accrual accounting does is recognize that some liabilities are adding up every day, although the bills for them have not shown up. It makes sure that you set aside a little every day so that the money is there to pay the bill when it arrives. No pain, no strain.

Once you establish your system, when those large and infrequent bills show up, you'll already have set aside the money to pay them. Any three bins will do, but we suggest a checking account for running your household and dispersing funds, a bank market rate account for the second bin—your household accrual account—and a money market mutual fund (taxable or not, depending upon your bracket) for capital accumulation. The first two bins are for running your household. The second of these, the accrual account, is used to set aside money on a regular monthly basis to pay for non-monthly expenses such as vacations or insurance premiums. The third is a "holding tank" for monies either awaiting investment or set aside for the fulfillment of major financial goals.

When you get this system working properly, there will be very few surprises in running your household. When those larger, infrequent bills show up, the money will have been set aside to pay them. It takes a year for the accrual system to work its magic since annual accrued liabilities are funded on a monthly basis. There won't be a perfect match the first year between the rate of accrual and the need for cash. If you have some seed money to start this account, it will help. If not, be patient. You will have to use checking account monies to make up the deficit. It will work.

Let's say that you have analyzed your expenses and your taxes and that you are sure your tax liability will be covered by withholding. Table 9–1 illustrates your monthly take-home pay, remaining expenses and your savings goal.

Using the three-bin system with this spending plan, you would put $200 per month into your money market fund for later investing. You would add any cash flow received from other investments to this amount so that you would always reinvest your income, dividends, and capital gains, taking advantage of the opportunity for compound growth. Each month you would add $230 to your accrual account and you would draw money from that account when your auto or homeowner's insurance came due, to pay property taxes and when

Table 9-1 Monthly Income, Expenses and Savings

	Annual Take Home Pay		$24,000
LESS:	Savings Goal		(2,400)
	Fixed Monthly Expenses		(12,000)
	Variable Monthly Expenses		(6,840)
	Accrued Expenses (annualized)		
	Property Taxes	1,000	
	Auto Insurance	500	
	Homeowners Insurance	260	
	Vacation	1,000	
	Accrual Funding Total		(2,760)
			-0-

Monthly Funding for Accrued Expenses $2,760 / 12 = $230

Figure 9-1 The Three-Bin System

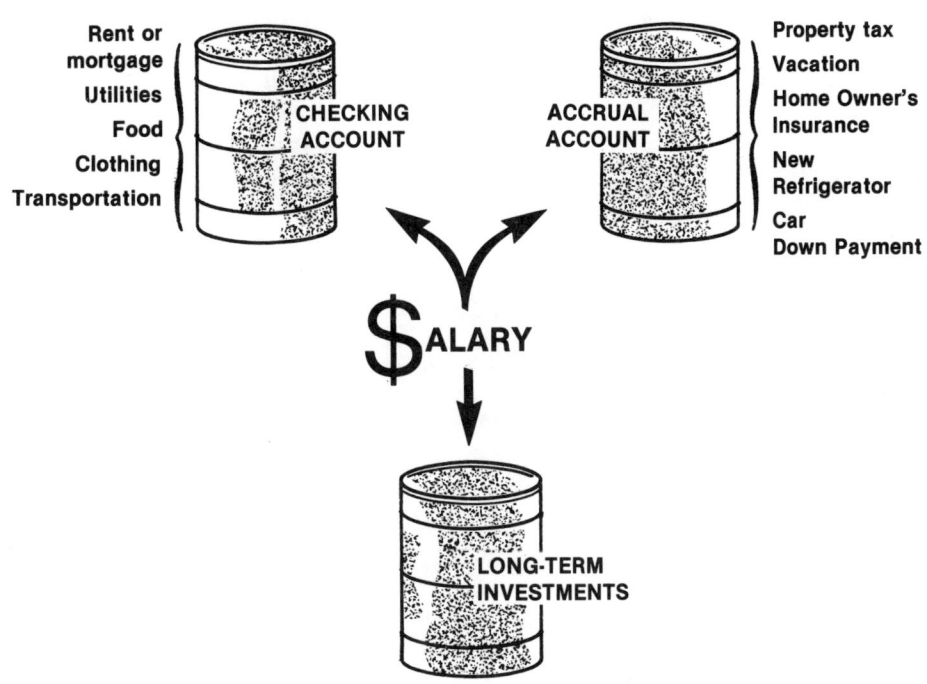

it is time for your vacation. Notice that with this method, you won't have to put your vacation, or anything else, on credit cards. Remember that during the first year there won't be a perfect match between the balance in your accrual account and your accrued expenses unless you seed the accrual account with some start-up money. You can see exactly how this will work by charting your accrual balance against the timing of expenses. Look at Table 9-2 to see how the accrual account works and you can see exactly how monies will come in evenly every month and flow out unevenly as the bills arrive to be paid.

Go through this same process for your own household. Add up your infrequent bills, and divide the total by twelve. Then do a chart of how money comes in and flows out. Show the balance as negative whenever money needed from the accrual account is more than what has been deposited. You could make the system work perfectly the first year if you could seed the account in the first year with an amount of money equal to the largest negative balance the accrual will have. In our example, the largest negative is $270 and you can see that, if you use that amount of seed money, the accrual account will never have a negative balance.

Table 9-2 How The Accrual Account Works

Month	Paid In	Spent		Balance	Balance Using $270 Seed Money
January	$ 230	Auto Insurance	$500	(270)	0
February	230			(40)	230
March	230			190	460
April	230	Property Tax	500	(80)	190
May	230			150	420
June	230			380	650
July	230			610	880
August	230	Vacation	1,000	(160)	110
September	230	Homeowners' Insurance	260	(190)	80
October	230			40	310
November	230			270	540
December	$ 230	Property Tax	$500	0	270

One of the best cash flow management techniques you can use is to avoid credit card debt. With the change in the tax laws, the cost of credit usage just rose drastically—and it was no bargain before! Jane and Michael Brent kicked their substantial credit card habit when they realized that if they invested the amount they were currently spending on credit card interest—their balance averaged just over $15,000 and interest was $3,000 last year—

in a good growth mutual fund, they would have $50,000 at the end of eight years. Believe us, your local bank really has done nothing to deserve that large a piece of your net worth. Pay cash and keep the interest for yourself.

Table 9–3 gives us a quick look at the rising cost of credit. If you had been in a 50 percent marginal bracket in 1986 and had an average balance of $15,000, the after-tax cost of credit would stack up like this as we move into the new law:

Table 9–3 The Cost of Credit Cards

Year	1986	1987	1988
Amount Charged	$15,000	$15,000	$15,000
Interest Rate (19%)			
Interest Cost	2,850	2,850	2,850
Amount Deductible	100%	65%	40%
Tax bracket	50%	38.5%	28%
Tax Savings	1,425	712	315
Your Cost of Credit	$ 1,425	$ 2,138	$ 2,535

The out-of-pocket cost of credit has risen from $1,425 to $2,535 in the illustration above. That is a 78 percent increase! Although we hope your credit card balances are nowhere near as high, the percentage increase will be the same. Don't use credit cards. Their use is one of the greatest barriers to increasing your net worth.

ACCUMULATING CAPITAL TO MEET GOALS OTHER THAN FINANCIAL INDEPENDENCE

People who have trouble motivating themselves to save often find that deciding what they want to save *for* solves the problem. If you have no financial goals, why would you choose to save rather than spend? When you make a spending decision under those circumstances, you have to choose between something and nothing. When you have a goal to save for, you choose between something and something. When you completed Worksheets 1 and 2, you defined your major financial goals and attached a price tag to each and a date when you would need the money to achieve that goal.

When you complete this chapter, you will know what it will take to accumulate the desired amount of capital by the time that you need it. If, for example, you need $10,000 five years from now and can invest it in something that will grow at eight percent, you could set aside $6,712 this year or $136 every month during the next five years. Thanks to compounding, accumulating capital is a bit easier than you might think—if you start soon enough. If, however, you wish to make an expenditure in the future, it is likely to cost more than it will today due to inflation. Remember that all your "price tags" are in today's dollars. Let's assume you want to accumulate a down payment for a house and you need $20,000 today to buy the kind of house you have in mind. Your goal is to buy the house in five years and you estimate that inflation in real estate values will be about five percent during that period. Read across the top of Table 9-4 until you find five percent and down the table until you find five years. At the point where that column and row intersect, you'll find the number 1.28. Multiply that by $20,000 for an estimate of what you will need in five years—$25,525.

Table 9-4 Future Cost Factors for Pricing Your Financial Goals

Years Until Goal is Reached	Inflation Rate Between Now and Realization of Your Goal		
	5%	8%	12%
1	1.05	1.08	1.12
2	1.10	1.17	1.25
3	1.16	1.26	1.40
4	1.22	1.36	1.57
5	1.28	1.47	1.76
6	1.34	1.59	1.97
7	1.41	1.71	2.21
8	1.48	1.85	2.48
9	1.55	1.99	2.77
10	1.63	2.16	3.11
15	2.08	3.17	5.47
20	2.65	4.66	9.64
25	3.39	6.85	17.00
30	4.32	10.06	29.96
35	5.52	14.79	52.80
40	7.04	21.72	93.05
45	8.99	31.92	163.99
50	11.47	46.90	289.00

Table 9-5 shows what you need to do to save annually to accumulate $1,000 over various periods of time. To accumulate $1,000 in five years you need to save $170 per year, if you can earn an eight percent after-tax rate of return. Your goal is to save $25,525. Divide that number by $1,000 and multiply to find the number of $1,000 "chunks" you'll need to accumulate. Multiply that by the annual saving required to accumulate $1,000. The calculation looks like this:

1. Take the amount you want to have accumulated in five years: $25,525.
2. Divide by $1,000; 25,525/1000 = 25.525
3. Multiply the result by the table value: $170 × 25.525 = $4,339. This is the amount you will need to save each year to meet your goal of buying a home.

If you follow this plan, when five years rolls around, you will have accumulated the down payment.

Table 9-5 Amount to Invest Annually If You Wish to Accumulate $1,000

Years Until Funds Are Needed	Rate of Return (After-Tax)		
	5%	8%	12%
1	$952.38	$952.93	$892.85
2	464.57	445.16	421.16
3	302.10	285.22	264.59
4	220.96	205.48	186.82
5	172.36	157.83	140.55
6	140.02	126.22	110.02
7	116.97	103.77	88.50
8	99.74	87.05	72.59
9	86.37	74.15	60.43
10	75.72	63.92	50.88
15	44.14	34.10	23.95
20	28.80	20.24	12.39
25	19.95	12.67	6.69
30	14.33	8.17	3.70
35	10.54	5.37	2.07
40	$ 7.88	$ 3.58	$ 1.17

Go through this procedure to see what you need to save to meet all your intermediate term goals. Calculating what you need to save to be financially independent will be covered in the next section.

ACCUMULATING CAPITAL FOR FINANCIAL INDEPENDENCE

Worksheet 30 gives a step-by-step method for arriving at the annual savings necessary for you to be financially independent. It takes into account your pension plan and Social Security. As noted earlier, if you were born at the leading edge of the baby boom, 1946 or later, we recommend you not count on any Social Security benefits being available. If you were born between 1936

WORKSHEET 30   **HOW CLOSE ARE YOU NOW?**

1. Gross annual income you will need after you leave work in today's dollars $ 48,000

2. The sum needed to provide that income
   Divide line 1 by .057 if you will retire at 50, .063 at 55, .069 at 60, or (.076 at 65) $ 631,578

3. One-time transition costs, like moving expenses or capital to start a business $ 50,000

4. Total amount needed *Line 2 plus line 3* $ 681,578

5. Pensions   a. Yearly benefit $ 7,200
   b. Total pension *Multiply amount on 5a by 11.1 if your pension will begin at age 50, 10.7 at 55, 10.1 at 60 or (9.3 at 65). Then multiply that number by a factor from column A* $ 66,960

6. Social Security   a. Yearly benefit $ —0—
   b. Total benefit *Multiply amount on line 6a by 13.7. Then multiply that number by a factor from column A.* $

7. Postretirement jobs
   a. Estimated annual earnings from new jobs, part-time work or other sources, not including your investments $ —0—
   b. Total earnings during retirement *Multiply amount on line 7a by 17.7 if you plan to leave work at 50, 16.3 at 55, 14.6 at 60 and 12.7 at 65. Then multiply that number by a factor from column A.* $ —0—

8. Money needed from savings *Line 4 minus lines 5b, 6b and 7b* $ 614,618

9. Amount you have saved already $ 150,000

10. What your savings will grow to by the time you stop working
    Line 9 times a factor from column B $ 328,500

11. Total additional savings you will need *Line 8 minus line 10* $ 286,118

12. Amount you will need to save each year $ 9,728
    Line 11 times a factor from column C

Number of years between now and when you will begin receiving additional income	Column A
1	.962
2	.925
3	.889
4	.855
5	.822
6	.790
7	.760
8	.731
9	.703
10	.676
15	.555
20	.456
25	.375

Number of years between now and when you will stop working	Column B	Column C
1	1.04	1.000
2	1.08	.490
3	1.12	.320
4	1.17	.235
5	1.22	.185
6	1.27	.151
7	1.32	.127
8	1.37	.109
9	1.42	.095
10	1.48	.083
15	1.80	.050
20	(2.19)	(.034)
25	2.67	.024

Copyright 1986. MONEY Magazine. Reprinted with permission.

and 1946, assume that you will be eligible for about half of what people with earnings histories similar to yours receive today. For information regarding your Social Security benefits, write to the Social Security Administration. Table 9–6 illustrates the amount you can expect to receive from Social Security.

Table 9–6 Estimated Social Security Benefits for Retired Workers*

Year of Birth	Current Annual Earnings			
	25,000–30,000	30,000–35,000	35,000–40,000	Social Security Maximum
1922	$7,716	8,676	9,468	10,104
1923-27	8,100	9,060	9,744	10,368
1928-32	8,676	9,564	10,104	10,728
1933-37	9,384	9,924	10,548	11,268
1938-42	9,744	10,368	11,004	11,724
1943-47†	10,104	10,824	11,544	12,168

*Actual benefits are based upon a complex formula which takes each years' earnings into account. For more detailed information, write to Social Security Administration.

†For planning purposes, we recommend that any one born at the leading edge of the "baby boom" or later not count on Social Security benefits being available.

When you analyze your retirement capital needs, you will want to go through the calculations twice: once using the desired income and age at which you want to be financially independent and once using the age you expect to retire and the minimum, or "no frills" lifestyle. By using these two combinations, you will have analyzed the most aggressive goal first and looked at what you will have to set aside today to fund it. Your second analysis involves working longer and spending less, a more modest goal that will take fewer assets from today's lifestyle.

When you know what savings goal you are aiming for, we recommend you set up a monthly savings program. It might consist of adding to portfolio positions you established in Chapter 5, or adding new elements to your portfolio. Finding an interesting place to put the money you save will motivate you to save.

WHAT IF YOUR GOALS CONFLICT?

If you add up all your savings goals and you can't possibly save that much, what can you do?

You can reevaluate your goals and set priorities. Perhaps it is worth it to reduce current spending to the extent necessary to meet all the other goals. If not, you can decide which of your longer-term goals are most important and shorten the list of things you are trying to accomplish.

Some of the goals may lend themselves to being postponed. A delay of a year or two on some of your shorter-term goals may make a big difference in how much you need to save.

Maybe your investments will perform better than you expect. That would be a fortunate turn of events. If you recalculate your financial independence savings need on Worksheet 30, you may find that you are making progress faster than you expected and will be able to allocate some savings to other purposes. We caution you, however, about trying to make up for insufficient savings by expecting your portfolio to turn out miracles. That strategy forces you to put your capital at increasingly greater risk to increase the rate of return.

There may be some untapped earning potential in your family. The children could set aside some of their earnings from part-time work to pay for their college educations. Grandparents may want to make gifts for that purpose. If you have a non-working spouse, you could look at the value of that against other important goals.

You can set a savings goal today with the idea of stepping it up in the future. Consider capping your living expenses at their current level and allocating all increases in income to savings. Even a "50 percent to lifestyle/50 percent to savings" commitment for further salary increases will lead to a substantial increase in savings over the longer run.

SPECIAL FUNDING OPPORTUNITIES FOR FINANCIAL INDEPENDENCE/RETIREMENT

Using tax-qualified retirement plans gives the greatest boost to retirement funding. IRAs—for taxpayers still eligible to make tax-deductible contributions—are a good example. Let's assume that you are in a 31 percent combined marginal bracket and your IRA contribution is fully deductible in your state.

As you can see in Table 9–7, a tax deductible plan allows you to invest pre-tax dollars and those dollars compound tax free. Notice that the IRA has a $52 advantage after one year and a $1,229 advantage after ten years. With every passing year the difference between the IRA and saving with after-tax dollars will be greater.

All tax-qualified plans have this characteristic of having contributions that are deductible from taxable income. Some are deducted when you file your tax return, others are deducted from your W-2 statement of earnings, others involve employer contributions and are not considered part of your salary (although they are definitely part of your compensation).

Individual Retirement Accounts

Unfortunately, the rules regarding IRAs were tightened by the Tax Reform Act of 1986 and many people who were able to deduct their IRAs from their

Table 9-7 The Benefits of IRAs

	IRA	No IRA
What you earned	$2,000	$2,000
What went to taxes	(0)	(620)
What was left	$2,000	1,380
How much did it earn at 12%	240	165
How much did you keep	240	114
Total Value After One Year	$2,240	$1,494
If you wanted to withdraw your funds after one year:		
Taxes on Withdrawal	694	0
Amount you would keep	$1,546	$1,494
If you wanted to withdraw your funds after ten years:		
Amount you would keep	$4,286	$3,057

income in computing their taxes now will be unable to do so. If one of the following describes you, you are eligible to deduct the full $2,000 contributions.

- You're single and do not actively participate in a retirement plan.
- You're married and neither you nor your spouse participates in a retirement plan.
- You are single, participate in a retirement plan but your adjusted gross income is less than $25,000.
- You are married, either you or your spouse participates in a retirement plan and your joint adjusted gross income is less than $40,000.

If either of the following describes you, you are in the "phase out range" and your adjusted gross income determines how much you may contribute:

- You are single, participate in a retirement plan and your adjusted gross income is between $25,000 and $35,000.
- You are married, either you or your spouse participates in a retirement plan and your adjusted gross income is between $40,000 and $50,000.

If you cannot deduct IRA contributions, should you make one anyway? Yes—if you have some time to take advantage of the tax-free compounding. Assume that you earned 12 percent on your IRA funds and that you are in a 31 percent combined marginal bracket. After ten years of contributions, you would have $27,123. The same contribution outside of an IRA would net you only $21,936 after withdrawing your funds and paying the taxes.

Retirement Plans for the Self-Employed and for Corporations

Whether you are self-employed or the owner of a corporation, you can save on a tax-deferred basis by establishing a retirement plan for your company. Before you decide to do so, you should sit down with a pension plan consultant to analyze the available structures and how they would work for you. IRS rules regarding pension plans are complex and unforgiving. Failing to meet the legal requirements may result in the disqualification of your plan.

You could established a defined contribution plan in which the contribution you make is known, but the eventual benefit you receive at retirement depends on investment performance in the interim. There are two kinds of defined contribution plans, profit sharing and money purchase plans. If you choose the first type of plan, you will be limited to a 15 percent contribution—that is, 15 percent of compensation—and it will be voluntary. If you choose a money purchase plan, you may contribute up to 25 percent and whatever contribution level you select will be mandatory.

The law allows you to contribute up to 25 percent or $30,000, whichever is less, to a defined contribution plan. Most people combine a 15 percent profit sharing plan with a 10 percent money purchase plan. The two add up to a total of 25 percent, so that they allow you to contribute the maximum permitted by law. By combining them in this way, you also have considerable flexibility. You have a mandatory 10 percent contribution and a voluntary contribution of up to 15 percent. If you have a bad year, you can limit your contribution to the mandatory 10 percent figure.

When you own your own business, one important factor in establishing a retirement plan is the amount you will have to contribute on behalf of employees. When you meet with your pension consultant, discuss this matter at length. A pension plan is a plus when it comes to retaining good employees, so you will have to do a careful analysis of the costs and benefits.

Defined Benefit Plans

Defined benefit plan contributions are based on the amount of money you need to contribute to receive a particular benefit at retirement. These kinds of plans are usually based on a formula for years of service and age. The amount contributed on your behalf is based on complex actuarial calculations. Now that you know that the limitation on defined contribution plans is $30,000, an example of a defined benefit plan might help. Bill Sherbourne, 65, retired from the Federal government and set up his own business as a mediator. He earned $100,000 his second year in business. Because of his age, a defined benefit plan was definitely superior to a defined contribution plan. Bill was able to shelter $55,000 of income due to his pension contribution. This would be a great advantage to him, especially if he ultimately chooses to retire in two to three years.

Tax Sheltered Annuities or 403(b) Plans

These retirement plans are available to employees of non-profit organizations and you may contribute up to $9,500 per year. Your school district, hospital or university, has pre-approved investment choices from which you may select.

The method of contribution is by "salary reduction." You elect to divert a certain percentage of your salary to the plan and your W-2 form shows your earnings net of the contribution.

You may invest in fixed income or variable annuities. Your choice should be based on your overall portfolio objectives. Keep in mind, however, that income-oriented investments have just kept up with inflation over the past 50 years while growth investments—the type you find in variable annuities—have exceeded inflation by several points.

Deferred Compensation Plans or 401(k) Plans

These are also called **Cash or Deferred Arrangements** (CODAs). Like the tax-sheltered annuity described above, you elect to contribute a particular amount and it may be placed in investment alternatives that have been evaluated by your employer. Contributions to these are limited to $7,000 per year.

Non-Qualified Deferred Compensation Plans

These are generally available to executives or other senior employees of corporations. The employee elects to defer compensation and the employer promises to pay it over a specified period of years at retirement, separation or some other specific date. This plan allows you to defer compensation beyond the limitation for qualified plans. You can take advantage of these plans for even greater tax reduction and tax deferred compounding. You should be aware, however, that the plan may treat you as a general creditor of the corporation. As such, you may never get your money back if it goes bankrupt. Be conservative in the amount you defer. Keep in mind the number of years of deferral—the longer the time, the greater the risk—and the total percentage of your net worth that you place in this plan.

Company Savings or Thrift Plans

Many companies that had thrift or savings plans have changed to 401(k) plans so that employees can deduct their contributions. If your company has not, the plan may still be an excellent savings vehicle. The funds invested compound tax deferred *and* your company may match your savings dollar-for-dollar or fifty cents on the dollar—providing an immediate return on your investment. Whether you are an employer or an employee, research the retirement plans available to you and establish and/or participate in them. Tax-deferred savings is the best way to accelerate the growth of your net worth.

CHAPTER TEN

FINANCING A COLLEGE EDUCATION

THE RISING COST OF A COLLEGE EDUCATION

A college education can add $250,000 to $500,000 to a lifetime of earnings. It is obviously well worth the price, but college is an expensive proposition and the costs are rising faster than inflation. As you read in Chapter 3, it now costs $17,000 for a year at many top private universities. That includes room, board and tuition only. Add pocket money and transportation from home to school, and the price tag seems astronomical.

How can you hope to put your children through college? The best advice is to start planning early. For most families, it is not practical to redirect $17,000 of current income for four years, or even the $6,000 it takes to attend state colleges and universities. With 18 years to plan, the task becomes considerably easier. Use time to give you a head start in providing for your children's college. Even if you have only a few years, there are strategies you can use to accumulate funds at a faster rate—with a little help from Uncle Sam.

What Will It Cost?

College funding is like the rest of the goal-setting process. We think about the goal in terms of what it costs today. Then we must adjust it for inflation or other factors that will increase costs in the future. In assessing the amount needed, follow the same procedure you followed in Chapter 9. Let's assume that you have decided to send Junior to a state college with a cost of $6,000 per year for tuition, books, room and board. When you add travel to and from school in September and June, plus two more round trips for the Christmas holidays and spring recess, the price tag climbs to $28,000 for four years. If Junior wants a car or other luxuries, you reason, he can acquire them with summer earnings.

Take the $28,000 in today's dollars and adjust it to future dollars using the table below. We have assumed that college costs will rise at approximately eight percent—a rate higher than current inflation, but lower than this year's rise in college costs. Find the entry on Table 10-1 for the number of years until your child graduates from high school and multiply that value times $28,000. The figure you calculate will be a slight overestimate of college costs because it assumes that all the money needed will be available when the child starts college. Actually you have a few more years before the whole fund is needed.

Table 10-1 Future Cost Factors For A College Education (Assuming 8% Inflation)

Years Until High School Graduation	Multiply Today's Cost By This Factor to Figure Future Cost
1	1.08
2	1.17
3	1.26
4	1.36
5	1.47
6	1.59
7	1.71
8	1.85
9	1.99
10	2.16
11	2.33
12	2.52
13	2.72
14	2.94
15	3.17
16	3.43
17	3.70
18	3.99

Table 10-2 Amount To Invest Annually Per $1,000 of College Expenses

Years Until High School Graduation	Rate of Return (After-Tax)			
	5%	8%	12%	15%
1	$952.38	$925.93	$892.85	$869.57
2	464.57	445.16	421.16	404.45
3	302.10	285.22	264.59	250.46
4	220.96	205.48	186.82	174.14
5	172.36	157.83	140.55	128.98
6	140.02	126.22	110.02	99.34
7	116.97	103.77	88.50	78.57
8	99.74	87.05	72.59	63.35
9	86.37	74.15	60.43	57.80
10	75.72	63.92	50.88	42.83
11	67.03	55.63	43.22	35.71
12	59.83	48.79	37.00	29.98
13	53.77	43.08	31.85	25.31
14	48.59	38.24	27.56	21.47
15	44.14	34.10	23.95	18.28
16	40.26	30.53	20.88	15.61
17	36.87	27.44	18.27	13.36
18	33.85	24.72	16.02	11.47

Table 10-2 shows the annual savings required to accumulate $1,000. Divide the value you arrived at above by $1,000 and multiply the result by the table value. That is the amount you will need to save each month.

Saving that amount was easier before the Tax Reform Act of 1986, but there are still some strategies left, as you will read in the next section.

FUNDING STRATEGIES

Before the Tax Reform Act of 1986, there were many more tax-advantaged ways to fund a college education. Some opportunities have been foreclosed due to the "kiddie tax." Those that remain have a reduced value due to lower marginal brackets. There are, however, still some valuable strategies available that we can review.

Income Shifting

The central feature of most college funding strategies has been income shifting. Income shifting is a tax reduction strategy that lends itself to college funding. It involves shifting income—and the tax consequences of that income—from higher-bracket family members to lower-bracket family members. What it achieves is an overall reduction in tax so that the family is able to keep more of what is earned. What better occasion to shift income from parent to child than saving for college. Income will flow from parent to child anyway. Why not do it in a way that reduces taxes?

We are all aware, however, that we can't just turn a paycheck over to Junior and subtract it from our taxable income. That is called **"assignment of income"** and it has been thoroughly litigated with the IRS emerging victorious.

The courts insist that you can't give away only the "fruit" and expect to shift the income to the lower-bracket taxpayer, you must give away the tree—the asset—as well.

Let's look at an example. Sam Lenhardt will be 14 this year. His parents are concerned about putting Sam through college and assume it will take at least $20,000. They have a $10,000 certificate of deposit. They decide to make a gift to Sam that he invests in an income and growth stock mutual fund. The fund has been paying approximately four percent in dividends and realizing ten percent in capital gains. What have Sam's parents accomplished? If they kept the $10,000 and made the same investment, their $1,400 annual yield would shrink to $910 after they pay a combined 35 percent state and Federal tax. Sam, on the other hand, can earn up to $3,000 without tax liability, so he will be able to keep all $1,400. Over the next four years, if the Lenhardts had kept the money, it would have grown to $14,167. By shifting the income to Sam and taking advantage of his lower bracket, the fund will grow to $16,889. They have added more than $2,700 to Sam's college fund without spending a penny.

Another possibility would be for the Lenhardts to take an appreciated asset that they felt had matured and should be liquidated. If they liquidated it in their tax bracket, the after-tax proceeds would be smaller than if Sam did the same. The Lenhardts have $10,000 in a small-growth company that has appreciated from their original $7,500 investment. They feel that the growth curve for the company has slowed due to competition and it is time to lock in their gains by selling the stock. If they sell it, after state and federal tax on the gain, there will be $9,200 left. Had they made a gift of it to Sam, he could have sold it and realized the full $10,000.

That, as they say, is the good news about income shifting. The strategy was more effective when the gap between parental federal brackets (50 percent) and children's brackets (zero) was greater than today's 28 percent spread. The bad news is that if you shift more than $1,000 to a child younger than Sam (under 14 for this tax year), it will be brought back to be taxed in your marginal bracket.

For income shifting to operate as we have described, you must take into account the "fruit" and "tree" analogy that developed as this part of the tax law was being fought in the courts. The Lenhardt's strategies will work only if they give away the asset. It is not enough to give up the stream of income ("fruit"). Using this strategy means that when your child reaches the age of majority, the money is his or hers. All you have is parental influence to make sure the money goes to Princeton rather than Porsche. Parental influence can, however, be formidable.

Employing Your Children

If you own your own business, you have an income shifting opportunity unaffected by the kiddie tax. You can put your children to work in your business. To satisfy the IRS, the children must actually work for the company and you must pay them reasonable wages for the work they do. Assume that your daughter worked in your office as a word processor and earned $5,000. She could put $2,000 in an IRA. If she started at 13, five years later she would have accumulated $12,705. If she saved the rest, she would have more than twice as much for her college fund. The economics of it work this way: if you wanted to give your daughter one dollar to go to college, your firm would have to earn $1.54, and pay it to you. You would report it on your income and pay 35 percent combined state and federal tax, leaving one dollar after-tax for your daughter. By employing her, your firm has to earn only one dollar to give your daughter one dollar for college.

What If You Already Have a Clifford Trust or UGMA Account?

Historically, one of the best college funding mechanisms was a Clifford Trust—also called a **reversionary trust.** You could place assets in the trust, pay all of the income out to the beneficiaries and, at the end of ten years and one day, the asset would revert to you. (You never gave away the "tree," but that was okay as long as you parted with it for ten years and a day.) Since TRA 1986, the income from Clifford Trusts is taxed at the parent's bracket if the child is under 14.

If you established a custodial account under the Uniform Gift to Minors Act and it throws off more than $1,000 of income to a child under 14, you have the same problem as the parents who established a Clifford Trust. Consider investing the funds in a tax-exempt or tax-deferred vehicle to avoid tax—municipal bonds, Series EE bonds, growth securities, annuities, raw land. We'll cover the specifics of these in the next section.

2503(c) Trust

This is a minor's trust that is exempt from the requirement that a trust must distribute income to qualify for the $10,000 gift exclusion. Because the 2503(c) trust lets you retain income, it may allow for effective college funding, especially for parents who established Clifford trusts and UGMA accounts with high-income generating investments that cannot be changed. The trust is a tax-paying entity with it own tax bracket. Trust tax brackets are such that the first $5,000 of income generated by a trust and retained (if it is paid out, it is taxable to the beneficiary) is taxed at 15 percent. The minor's trust will enable you to shift income from a 28 percent bracket to a 15 percent bracket, and there also may be state tax savings.

This trust has another interesting feature. The beneficiary of the trust has a six-month period to ask for the funds in the trust. This period occurs when the beneficiary is 21. If no request is made, the trustee may keep the funds in trust until the beneficiary is age 25. Although there is a legal requirement that beneficiaries be notified of their right to funds in the trust, parent-trustees of irresponsible 21-year-olds have been known to wait until their children are sound asleep, walk into their rooms and in the barest of whispers say, "Junior, if you want your trust fund you'll have to request it from me in the next six months."

INVESTMENT VEHICLES FOR COLLEGE FUNDING

Series EE Bonds

Not spectacular in their yields, Series EE Bonds are very safe—barring a collapse of the government. They yield about six percent if held to maturity and no tax need be paid until they are cashed. When your child is over 14, you can cash the bonds without worrying about the kiddie tax. Depending on the child's total income in the year they are cashed, the bonds may be cashed-in tax free or in your child's 15 percent tax bracket.

Zero-Coupon Bonds

The chief virtue of "zeroes" is that you know exactly what they will be worth at the end of the term. Unfortunately, they are an investment that pays no interest along the way. They are bought at discount, the maturity value includes an interest component and the interest you did not receive is subject to tax. (Unless you invest in zero-coupon municipal bond.) We prefer to see taxable "zeroes" used only in retirement plans when the tax treatment becomes a non-issue.

Life Insurance

Because the tax-free buildup of insurance value was one of the few investments to emerge unscathed from TRA 1986, insurance policies are more interesting than ever. An insurance contract could assure your child of a college fund in two ways. If you die, the death benefit would be available. If not, you can take a loan against the cash value. The investment accumulates tax-deferred, and if you borrow the cash value, you are not taxed on the accumulated earnings. If you keep the policy in force, you will never pay income taxes on it. As we said in the insurance section in Chapter 8, choose insurance as an investment vehicle only if the after-tax return is competitive with other investments.

Life Insurance Annuities

These also have the advantage of tax-deferred income and/or growth. You can invest in some high-performance mutual funds of all types through the annuity contract and defer all tax. Variable annuities have a guarantee that, in the event of your death, your heirs will never get less from the annuity than you put into it. Unlike a life insurance policy, when you take funds from an annuity, you will have to pay the tax that has been deferring. In addition, you may be subject to a tax penalty if you take assets before the age of 59½. Don't let this last factor dissuade you. Take a careful look at your situation and at the available annuities. The value of tax-free compounding may outweigh the eventual tax penalty.

Other investments, such as growth mutual funds, do not offer tax deferral but may be an excellent way to accumulate funds. If you started a college fund at your child's birth and added $50 per month to a fund that averaged a 12 percent yield, you would accumulate $38,000 by the time the child was 18. The value of that would be reduced by inflation, but it would give you a great start.

Other Sources of Assistance

Pre-paid Tuition. Duquesne University began a prepayment program for college tuition. A payment today of $13,000 covers tuition in ten years, when it is estimated that the tuition will cost $54,000. There are problems with this idea and they concern us deeply. What if your child does not want to go to college, or does not want to go to the college you prepaid? Worse yet, what if he or she was not qualified for admission? The rate or return required to increase $13,000 to $54,000 in ten years is 15.3 percent. It's an interesting coincidence that that is the exact yield of the 50th ranked mutual fund over the last ten years. Keep the money, keep your flexibility and make wise investment decisions. If your child decides not to go to college, you'll have $54,000 to accomplish other goals.

Scholarships. Scholarships are available to outstanding students as recognition of their accomplishments. Talk to the high school counselor or the financial aid office of the college your child plans to attend. There are many good reference books on this subject, including *The College Cost Book* published by the College Board.

Student Loans. Several Federal government financial aid programs offer loans that must be paid back with interest, grants that do not have to be repaid and work-study programs that provide on-campus paid jobs.

Part-Time Employment. Your child can work part-time and still do well in college. Students who work in college often organize their time better and, as many parents have told us, they seem to appreciate their educations more. College work is very demanding, however, and we would recommend that your son or daughter limit working to fifteen or twenty hours a week during the school year.

The best student jobs may be those on campus. In work-study programs based on financial need or student assistant programs, students can work in the library, the cafeteria or the financial aid office. Wherever students are working, everyone recognizes that his or her first job is to be a student. Schedules are shuffled to accommodate finals week and other adjustments are made because of the importance of an education. And campus jobs are very time-efficient; there is almost no time spent commuting to work.

SUMMARY

College funding, like every other aspect of planning, is easiest when you have the longest possible time to accomplish it. If your children are getting older and you haven't begun, the tax-advantaged strategies can help you get there a bit faster. Part-time work during summer vacations from high school and part-time work during college can let Junior help with the cost of his education. Compromising on schools—community college for two years and university for two more—is a viable strategy for reducing costs.

THE WORKBOOK: CREATE YOUR PERSONAL FINANCIAL PLAN

Instructions for filling in worksheets:

The following worksheets are designed to be used by people in a wide variety of financial and family circumstances. Not all of them may apply to your financial situation.

Some of the forms ask you to specify under whose name the investment is registered. In those cases, the following codes may be helpful:

H: Head of household (or primary wage-earner); Individual Ownership of property or financial instrument.
S: Spouse (or second wage earner); Individual Ownership of property or financial instrument.
JT: Joint tenancy
TC: Tenancy-in-common (Note percent of ownership and names of other tenants.)
CP: Community property.

In some cases, columns are labeled with letters. These letters are used in formulas necessary for simple calculations that help you evaluate your investments. For example:

A Number of stocks you bought	B Original Price Per Share	C Current Price Per Share	D Dollars Earned $((C-B)\times A)$
100	$5.00	$6.00	$100

Finally, remember to enclose losses and any other negative sums in parentheses so that you won't forget to subtract them when you are calculating totals.

WORSHEET 1   **DREAMS AND OBLIGATIONS**

1) What are your short-term (next five years) dreams and goals? Write them in the order of importance. Then estimate the amount of money you will need to realize these dreams and when you will need that money.

	DREAM/GOAL	DOLLARS NEEDED	TIMING
1			
2			
3			
4			
5			

2) Now, do the same for your more long-term goals. Start with goals you would like to reach in five to ten years and finish with any goals you have for the distant future (other than financial independence).

	DREAM/GOAL	DOLLARS NEEDED	TIMING
1			
2			
3			
4			
5			

WORKSHEET 1 (Continued)   **DREAMS AND OBLIGATIONS**

1) What are your short-term obligations? Include those obligations that will become due in five years or less.

	OBLIGATION	AMOUNT OF OBLIGATION	TERMS OF PAYMENT	DATE WHEN OBLIGATION WILL BE FULLY PAID
1				
2				
3				
4				
5				
6				
7				
8				
9				
10				
11				
12				
13				
14				
15				
16				
17				
18				
19				
20				

2) What are your long-term obligations? Include those obligations (your mortgage may be one example) that will take more than five years to pay for.

	OBLIGATION	AMOUNT OF OBLIGATION	TERMS OF PAYMENT	DATE WHEN OBLIGATION WILL BE FULLY PAID
1				
2				
3				
4				
5				
6				
7				
8				

WORSHEET 2   **FINANCIAL INDEPENDENCE AND RETIREMENT**

1) At what age do you wish to be financially independent? _____

2) At what age do you expect to retire? _____

3) What is the annual income you will need at retirement in today's dollars?

         Minimum $ _____   Desired $ _____

4) Do you anticipate any extraordinary major expenditures? _____

PURPOSE OF EXPENDITURE	AMOUNT	APPROXIMATE DATE
1		
2		
3		
4		

5) What kind of lifestyle would you select for yourself at retirement or if (and when) you are financially independent and are no longer required to work for an income?

_____

_____

_____

_____

_____

_____

_____

WORSHEET 3 **ESTATE DISPOSITION QUESTIONS**

1. Do you or your spouse expect to inherit a substantial amount of property? Indicate estimated amounts and sources.

2. Do your children have substantial estates in their own right and income from salary or investments, etc.?

3. Do you and your spouse have wills? When were they last revised?

4. If a revocable living trust is appropriate for you, who would you select as Trustees and successor Trustees?

5. Do you plan to leave substantial gifts to charity at your or your spouse's death? Indicate any intended charities and approximate amounts.

6. Would you be willing to make outright gifts to your children and grandchildren or other relatives at this time if there were estate and income tax advantages to be gained?

7. Have you used any Estate Transfer Credit in making gifts? If so, how much has been used up?

8. Are you contributing to the support of any parent, relative or in-law? Indicate any such person, relationship and annual amount. Might any of the above depend on you for financial support in the future?

WORKSHEET 3 (Part Two) — ESTATE CONSIDERATIONS

Please answer the following questions for the adults in your household—whether or not they are employed outside the home. Note any relevant comments in the space provided.

	IF HUSBAND DIES	IF WIFE DIES
1. What would your family's minimum after-tax monthly income requirement be in today's dollars?		
2. To what degree is the surviving spouse capable of handling financial affairs?		
3. Would the surviving spouse obtain or continue employment?		
4. What would the estimated pre-tax monthly income of the spouse be?		
5. Would the surviving spouse continue to live in your present home?		
6. Should the home mortgage be paid off?		

7. Estate Planning Objectives (Select one from each category):

   ☐ Maximize Assets Available to Spouse ☐ Simplicity and Flexibility
   ☐ Maximize Assets Available to Children ☐ Maximize Estate Tax Savings

8. Are there any assets you would not consider liquidating upon a death to provide for your family's monthly income needs?

   _____

Comments: _____

_____

_____

_____

WORKSHEET 4   **EDUCATIONAL GOALS**

CHILD'S NAME					
1 YEARS UNTIL COLLEGE					
2 COST PER YEAR					
3 NUMBER OF YEARS					
4 TOTAL COST					
5 PERCENT YOU WILL PAY					
6 FUNDS NEEDED					

WORKSHEET 5   **GENERAL STATISTICS**

PERSONS

1	HEAD OF HOUSEHOLD		DATE OF BIRTH		AGE	
2	SPOUSE		DATE OF BIRTH		AGE	
3	CHILDREN: NAMES & AGES					

ESTIMATED INCOMES 19 _____

	DESCRIPTION	HEAD OF HOUSEHOLD		SPOUSE		COMBINED	
		MONTHLY	ANNUAL	MONTHLY	ANNUAL	MONTHLY	ANNUAL
4	SALARY						
5	PROFESSIONAL INCOME						
6	ALIMONY						
7	INCOME FROM ANNUITIES						
8	PENSION						
9	PENSION						
10	SOCIAL SECURITY						
11	OTHER						
12	INVESTMENTS						
13	TOTAL						

CASH FLOW FOR LAST YEAR

14	INCOME FROM ALL SOURCES	
15	LESS: FEDERAL TAXES	( )
16	STATE TAXES	( )
17	FICA*	( )
18	LOCAL TAXES	( )
19	AFTER-TAX CASH FLOW	
20	LESS: LIVING EXPENSES	( )
21	DISCRETIONARY INCOME	

*1986 FICA: 7.15% of earnings to a maximum of $42,000 in earnings. Maximum Tax = $3,003.
For self-employed: 12.3% to a maximum tax of $5,166.
1987 FICA: 7.15% of earnings up to $43,800. Maximum tax is $3,131.70.
For self-employed: 12.3%, maximum tax is $5,387.40.

WORKSHEET 6   **ESTIMATED LIVING EXPENSES FOR 19 _____**

COMMITTED EXPENSES		MONTHLY	OR	ANNUAL

Residence:
   Rent or
   Mortgage Payment
      Interest rate
      Original balance
      Origination date
      Term of loan
      Current balance
   Property tax
   Household garden help
   Water/trash
   TV Cable
   Other housing costs

Automobile:
   Payments
      Interest rate
      Original balance
      Origination date
      Term of loan
      Current balance
   Gas/oil
   Maintenance/repairs
   Parking
   Other transportation/commuting costs

Insurance:
   Homeowners/renters insurance
   Life
   Medical
   Disability
   Personal liability
   Auto insurance
   Other

Household/Personal Expenses:
   Utilities/fuel
   Telephone
   Groceries/liquor
   Clothes/dry cleaning
   Personal care
   Medical/dental care
   Prescription drugs

Miscellaneous:
   Alimony
   Support of relatives
   Education

         TOTAL

WORSHEET 6 (Continued)   **ESTIMATED LIVING EXPENSES FOR 19 _____**

DISCRETIONARY EXPENSES	MONTHLY	OR	ANNUAL

Residence:
    Home improvements
    Furniture/linens/etc.

Entertainment:
    Dining out
    Recreation
    Vacations
    Babysitters
    Memberships/clubs
    Hobbies

Miscellaneous:
    Charitable contributions
    Gifts/holiday gifts
    Work-related expenses
    Lunches
    Books/periodicals
    Legal/accounting/financial services
    Other Tax Deductible:

    Other non-deductible:

       TOTALS

Total living expenses:
    (Committed and Discretionary)

Are you planning any major purchases
or expecting any unusual fluctuations
in these amounts?

WORKSHEET 7   RISK MANAGEMENT: CASUALTY AND LIABILITY

AUTO INSURANCE	AUTO 1	AUTO 2	AUTO 3	Note any changes needed in any of the preceding policies or provisions (See Chapter 7)
Make and model				
Bodily injury liability				
Property damage liability				
Medical payments				
Underinsured motorists				
Collision (yes/no)				
Collision deductible				
Comprehensive (yes/no)				
Comprehensive deductible				
Company				
Premium and frequency				

WORKSHEET 7 (continued)   **RISK MANAGEMENT: CASUALTY AND LIABILITY**

Homeowner's Insurance	Primary Residence	Second Home	Rental Property	Other	Note Needed Changes
Location					
Market value					
Dwelling					
Appurtenant structures					
Unscheduled property					
Living expenses					
Personal liability					
Medical payments (per person and per occurence)					
Deductible					
Scheduled property					
Inflation guard					
Replacement value					
Burglar/smoke alarm					
Earthquake/flood					
Company					
Premium and frequency					

Umbrella Coverage (yes/no) _____ Coverage Amount _____

Required Underlying Coverage: Automobile _____ Homeowners _____

Premium and Frequency: _____ Company _____

WORKSHEET 8   **RISK MANAGEMENT: MEDICAL AND DISABILITY**

I. DISABILITY INCUME INSURANCE

	POLICY 1	POLICY 2	POLICY 3	POLICY 4
Insurance company and policy number				
Who is insured on this policy?				
Amount of monthly benefit				
Length of time before benefits begin				
Length of benefits A. For illness:				
B. For accident:				
Premiums and frequency				
Definition of disability (own occupation, any occupation, or split definition)				
Other notes about policy				

WORKSHEET 8 (Continued)   RISK MANAGEMENT: MEDICAL AND DISABILITY

2. MEDICAL INSURANCE (If your medical care is provided through an HMO, note that information here.)

	POLICY 1	POLICY 2	POLICY 3	POLICY 4
Insurance company and policy number				
Who is insured on this policy?				
Premiums and frequency				
Deductible				
Coinsurance (percent you must pay)				
Stop loss (maximum amount you are liable for each year)				
Major medical limit				
Other notes about policy				

3. DENTAL INSURANCE

	POLICY 1	POLICY 2
Insurance company and policy number		
Who is insured?		
Premiums and frequency		
Deductible		
Coinsurance percent		
Annual limit		
Other provisions or notes		

WORKSHEET 9

LIFE INSURANCE

	A	B	C	D	E	F	G	H	I	J	K	L
	INSURANCE COMPANY	**POLICY NUMBER**	**INSURED**	**OWNER**	**BENEFICIARY**	**TYPE OF POLICY**[1]	**FACE VALUE**	**ANNUAL PREMIUMS**	**CASH VALUE BEFORE LOANS**[2]	**POLICY LOANS**	**NET CASH VALUE (I-J)**	**NET INSURANCE PROTECTION (G-J)**
1												
2												
3												
4												
5												
6												
7												
8												
9												
10												
										TOTAL		

[1] Term, Whole or Ordinary, Universal, Single Premium Whole Life or Other
[2] Tables provided in your policy will show estimated cash value. This will not include accumulated dividends.

WORKSHEET 10   **DISABILITY INCOME NEEDS**

	IF HUSBAND WERE DISABLED	**IF WIFE WERE DISABLED**
What would be your family's after-tax minimum monthly income requirements?		
Would your spouse obtain or continue employment?		
Estimated pre-tax monthly income of spouse		
Anticipated retirement date		
Would your family's educational objectives change?		
Comments		

DISABILITY NEEDS ANALYSIS

		IF HUSBAND WERE DISABLED	**IF WIFE WERE DISABLED**
Family Income Need			
Less:	Spouse's income		
	Disability benefits		
	Social security disability		
	Portfolio income (6% of working assets)		
	Adjustment for taxes		
Disability Insurance Needed			

WORKSHEET 11　　　　　CASH AND EQUIVALENTS

A REGISTRATION	B DATE DEPOSITED	C DESCRIPTION	D MATURITY DATE	E CURRENT VALUE	F YIELD (PERCENT)	G INCOME (E × F)	H REMARKS
1							
2							
3							
4							
5							
6							
7							
8							
9							
10							
11							
12							
13							
14							
15							
16							
17							
18							
19							
20							
TOTAL							

WORKSHEET 12 — FIXED INCOME SECURITIES (Bills, Notes, Bonds and Preferred Stock)

	A	B	C	D	E	F	G	H	I	J	K	L
	REGISTRATION	PURCHASE DATE	NUMBER OF BONDS	DESCRIPTION	COUPON OR DIVIDEND	MATURITY DATE	COST PER UNIT	PRESENT PRICE PER UNIT	MARKET VALUE (C × H)	CURRENT YIELD	ANNUAL INCOME	CAPITAL GAIN OR LOSS (I − C × G)
1												
2												
3												
4												
5												
6												
7												
8												
9												
10												
11												
12												
13												
14												
15												
16												
17												
18												
19												
20												
TOTAL												

WORKSHEET 13

NOTES RECEIVABLES (Mortgages/Loans)

REGISTRATION	DESCRIPTION	ORIGINAL AMOUNT	YEAR OF ORIGINATION	INTEREST RATE	ANNUAL PAYMENTS RECEIVED	MATURITY DATE	BALLOON PAYMENT	BALANCE
1								
2								
3								
4								
5								
6								
7								
8								
9								
10								
11								
12								
13								
14								
15								
16								
17								
18								
19								
20								
TOTAL								

WORKSHEET 14

COMMON STOCK

REGISTRATION	PURCHASE DATE	NUMBER OF SHARES	DESCRIPTION	TOTAL COST	$ PRESENT					DIVIDEND YIELD (PERCENT)	CAPITAL GAIN OR LOSS
					PRICE PER SHARE	MARKET VALUE	PER SHARE INCOME	ANNUAL INCOME		
1										
2										
3										
4										
5										
6										
7										
8										
9										
10										
11										
12										
13										
14										
15										
16										
17										
18										
19										
20										
TOTAL										

WORKSHEET 15

MUTUAL FUNDS

REGISTRATION	NAME OF FUND	PRESENT NUMBER OF SHARES	CURRENT DOLLARS PER SHARE	CURRENT VALUE	DIVIDEND PER SHARE	ANNUAL INCOME	CURRENT YIELD	LATEST CAPITAL GAINS DISTRIBUTION		ORIGINAL PURCHASE DATE	ORIGINAL COST
								DOLLAR PER SHARE	DOLLAR AMOUNT		
1											
2											
3											
4											
5											
6											
7											
8											
9											
10											
11											
12											
13											
14											
15											
16											
17											
18											
19											
20											
TOTAL											

WORKSHEET 16

REAL PROPERTY

A REGISTRATION	B DESCRIPTION	C ESTIMATED MARKET VALUE	D BALANCE ON MORTGAGE	E ESTIMATED NET EQUITY (C-D)	F ORIGINAL COST	G YEARS HELD	H CAPITAL GAIN OR LOSS
1							
2							
3							
4							
5							
SUBTOTAL							
TOTAL							

WORKSHEET 17   **RENTAL UNIT ANALYSIS: Income and Cash Flow**

Name of property: _____

Current year: _____

TAXABLE INCOME

Gross Rents   _____

    Subtract Cash Expenses: Property taxes   (_____)

                                       Insurance   (_____)

                                       Miscellaneous expenses   (_____)

                                       Interest on mortgage   (_____)

                                       Depreciation   (_____)

Taxable Gain or Loss   _____

CASH FLOW BEFORE AND AFTER TAX

Gross Rents   _____

    Subtract: Cash Expenses
                                       (property taxes, insurance
                                       and miscellaneous expenses) (_____)

                                       Mortgage payments   (_____)

Pre-Tax Cash Flow   _____

    Add Back: Taxes Saved on Loss
      (loss multiplied by your marginal tax bracket)   _____

OR

    Subtract: Taxes Paid on Gain   (_____)
      (gain multiplied by your marginal tax bracket)

After-Tax Cash Flow   _____

WORKSHEET 18 RENTAL UNIT ANALYSIS: Estimated Return on Investment

Name of property: _____

TAXABLE GAIN OR LOSS

Market Value _____

    Subtract: Real Estate Commission (6%)   (_____)

                     Purchase price   (_____)

                     Improvements   (_____)

    Add: Accumulated depreciation   + _____

Unrealized Gain (Loss) _____

CASH TO YOU UPON SALE

Market Value _____

    Subtract: 6% Commission   (_____)

                     Mortgage balance   (_____)

    Subtotal: Pre-tax equity   _____

    Subtract: Deferred capital gains tax   (_____)
                     (unrealized gain or loss multiplied
                     by marginal tax bracket)

After-Tax Equity _____

After-Tax Yield on After-Tax Equity _____
(after-tax cash flow from Worksheet 17
divided by after-tax equity)

Appreciation _____
(subtract purchase price from current market value)

Purchase Date _____

Average Annual Appreciation _____
(appreciation divided by years you have held property.
See Appendix B to calculate compound rate of appreciation.)

WORKSHEET 19

ENERGY

REGISTRATION	DESCRIPTION	PURCHASE DATE	PERCENT OWNED OR NUMBER OF UNITS	COST PER UNIT	ESTIMATED VALUE	ANNUAL INCOME	YIELD	PRESENT ESTIMATED GAIN OR LOSS
1								
2								
3								
4								
5								
6								
7								
8								
9								
10								
11								
12								
13								
14								
15								
16								
17								
18								
19								
20								
TOTAL								

WORKSHEET 20 — EXOTICS: Gold funds, Precious Metals, Precious Stones, Art, Stamps, Etc.

| REGISTRATION | PURCHASE DATE | DESCRIPTION | QUANTITY | TOTAL COST | ESTIMATED PRESENT DOLLARS ||| YIELD | ESTIMATED CAPITAL GAIN OR LOSS |
					PER SHARE OR UNIT VALUE	TOTAL VALUE	ANNUAL INCOME		
1									
2									
3									
4									
5									
6									
7									
8									
9									
10									
11									
12									
13									
14									
15									
16									
17									
18									
19									
20									
TOTAL									

WORKSHEET 21   **BUSINESS**

Owner's name _____

How is the business registered?   Sole proprietor _____

                                  Partnership   _____

                                  Corporation   _____

Percent of business owned _____ %

Approximate value of business (100%) _____

Value of your share of the business _____

How did you arrive at the total value of your business?

_____

_____

_____

_____

_____

_____

_____

_____

_____

WORKSHEET 22

OTHER INVESTMENTS

REGISTRATION	PURCHASE DATE	DESCRIPTION	NO. OF UNITS	TOTAL COST	$ ESTIMATED PRESENT			YIELD	PRESENT ESTIMATED GAIN (LOSS)
					PER UNIT VALUE	TOTAL VALUE	ANNUAL INCOME		
1									
2									
3									
4									
5									
6									
7									
8									
9									
10									
11									
12									
13									
14									
15									
16									
17									
18									
19									
20									
TOTAL									

WORKSHEET 23   **SUMMARY OF ASSETS AND INCOME**

RESERVE ASSETS

	DESCRIPTION	NET VALUE
1	LIFE INSURANCE PROTECTION	
2	HOME EQUITY (Current Market Value Less Mortgage Balance(s))	
3	BUSINESS, PENSION AND PROFIT-SHARING BENEFITS	
4	TOTAL RESERVE ASSETS	

	WORKING ASSETS	NET VALUE	DOLLAR INCOME	PERCENT YIELD	PERCENT OF WORKING ASSETS	ESTIMATED APPRECIATION
5	SAVINGS TYPE ACCOUNTS					
6	BILLS, BONDS, NOTES AND PREFERREDS					
7	NOTES AND RECEIVABLES					
8	COMMON STOCK					
9	MUTUAL FUNDS					
10	REAL ESTATE					
11	ENERGY					
12	EXOTICS					
13	OTHER					
14	TOTAL WORKING ASSETS					
15	TOTAL ESTATE VALUE					

			REMARKS:
16	MONTHLY INCOME		
17	MONTHLY COST OF LIVING		
18	SURPLUS OR (DEFICIT)		

WORKSHEET 24   **CAPITAL ANALYSIS: Present Portfolio**

Note: Perform this analysis for only those investments that can be repositioned.

Present Portfolio

	DESCRIPTION	AMOUNT	PERCENT OF WORKING ASSETS	INCOME	YIELD	AMOUNT TAXABLE	TAXES	EXPECTED APPRECIATION	NET AFTER TAXES
1	SAVINGS-TYPE ACCOUNTS								
2	BILLS, NOTES, BONDS AND PREFERRED STOCK								
3	COMMON STOCK								
4	MUTUAL FUNDS								
5	REAL ESTATE								
6	ENERGY								
7	EXOTICS								
8	OTHER								
9	**TOTAL**								

WORKSHEET 25   CAPITAL ANALYSIS: Proposed Portfolio

Proposed Portfolio

	DESCRIPTION	AMOUNT	PERCENT OF WORKING ASSETS	INCOME	YIELD	AMOUNT TAXABLE	TAXES	NET AFTER TAXES	EXPECTED APPRECIATION
1	SAVINGS-TYPE ACCOUNTS								
2	BILLS, NOTES, BONDS AND PREFERRED STOCK								
3	COMMON STOCK								
4	MUTUAL FUNDS								
5	REAL ESTATE								
6	ENERGY								
7	EXOTICS								
8	OTHER								
9	**TOTAL**								

Comparing Portfolio Performance Before and After Adjustment

	DESCRIPTION	INCOME	YIELD	NET AFTER TAXES	EXPECTED APPRECIATION
1	BEFORE ADJUSTMENTS				
2	AFTER ADJUSTMENTS				
3	DOLLAR DIFFERENCE				
4	PERCENTAGE DIFFERENCE				

WORKSHEET 26 — COMPARING NET INCOME, BALANCING AND LIQUIDITY FACTORS

Note: The difference between this form and the preceding one is that you now can look at your portfolio as an entirety.

ESTIMATED INVESTMENT INCOME AND TAXES

DESCRIPTION	INVESTMENT INCOME	TAXES	NET INCOME AFTER TAXES
CURRENT PORTFOLIO	$	$	$
PROPOSED PORTFOLIO	$	$	$

YIELD

DOLLAR DIFFERENCE	$	$	$
PERCENTAGE DIFFERENCE		%	%

APPRECIATION

DOLLAR DIFFERENCE	$
PERCENTAGE DIFFERENCE	%

BALANCING FACTOR

CURRENT PORTFOLIO			PROPOSED PORTFOLIO		
DEFLATION HEDGES	$	%	%	$	DEFLATION HEDGES
INFLATION HEDGES	$	%	%	$	INFLATION HEDGES
TOTAL	$	%	%	$	TOTAL

LIQUIDITY FACTOR

CURRENT PORTFOLIO			PROPOSED PORTFOLIO		
LIQUID	$	%	%	$	LIQUID
NONLIQUID	$	%	%	$	NONLIQUID
TOTAL	$	%	%	$	TOTAL

Remarks on Total Portfolio:

_____

_____

_____

WORKSHEET 27 — ESTIMATING THE SIZE OF YOUR ESTATE

DESCRIPTION	HUSBAND	PERCENT OF TOTAL ESTATE	WIFE	PERCENT OF TOTAL ESTATE	COMBINED TOTAL	COMBINED PERCENT OF TOTAL ESTATE
LIFE INSURANCE PROTECTION[1]						
RESIDENCE (NET EQUITY)[2]						
BUSINESS, PENSION, AND PROFIT-SHARING PLAN[3]						
SAVINGS-TYPE ACCOUNTS						
BILLS, NOTES, BONDS, AND PREFERRED STOCKS						
MORTGAGES AND LOANS						
COMMON STOCK						
MUTUAL FUNDS						
REAL ESTATE						
ENERGY						
EXOTICS						
OTHER						
TOTAL						

[1] Life insurance will be part of the estate of the "owner" of the policy.

[2] If property is jointly owned, the presumption will be that 50% of the value is owned by each spouse.

[3] Although assets may be titled separately, in the eyes of the law, they may be jointly owned. Unless you are sure that the property is jointly owned or sure that a particular percentage is owned by each spouse, assume 50% is attributable to each estate.

WORKSHEET 28   **REVIEWING YOUR CURRENT ESTATE PLAN**

	HUSBAND	WIFE
Executor	_____	_____
Successor executor	_____	_____
Property Distributed Outright:		
Item or dollar amount and recipient:	_____	_____
Item or dollar amount and recipient:	_____	_____
Item or dollar amount and recipient:	_____	_____
Item or dollar amount and recipient:	_____	_____
Item or dollar amount and recipient:	_____	_____
Item or dollar amount and recipient:	_____	_____
Item or dollar amount and recipient:	_____	_____
Property Distributed in trust:		
Trustees:	_____	_____
	_____	_____
Successor trustees:	_____	_____
	_____	_____
Name(s) of beneficiary(ies)	_____	_____
	_____	_____
	_____	_____
	_____	_____
	_____	_____
Ultimate beneficiary(ies)	_____	_____
	_____	_____
Distribution of principal (timing and amount)	_____	_____
Do you have a living trust? Trustee(s)	_____	_____

Other provisions _____
_____

WORKSHEET 29 — FIGURING OUT HOW MUCH LIFE INSURANCE

The purpose of life insurance is to guarantee your family a comfortable life if you die young. Consequently you should err on the high side when calculating your coverage. That does not mean sacrificing all present niceties for the possibility of turning your relatives into Rockefellers. It does mean carrying enough protection to preserve your family's current standard of living. You can arrive at a suitable amount of coverage by using this worksheet. If both spouses have paying jobs, make a copy of the worksheet and do the figures for each breadwinner.

This exercise aims to nail down how much insurance you need while your children are growing up. It does not include the much larger sums required to finance a surviving spouse's later life or retirement. The presumption these days is that he or she could take care of that. But families with lifelong dependents—a handicapped child, for example—should ask a financial planner for help in their calculations.

Most of the lines on the worksheet explain themselves. Here's some coaching for those that don't:

Line 1. In two-paycheck households, start by lumping together both after-tax incomes. Payroll deductions for retirement funds and health insurance count as take-home pay; life insurance deductions do not.

Line 2. People usually spend a third of their income on themselves. You may want to figure more or less than that.

Line 6. In totaling your present assets, don't forget Individual Retirement Accounts, company savings plans and survivor's benefits from your pension fund.

Lines 7 and 8. Consider here whether your spouse, if she or he is now working, would wish to stay home with the children for a year or two if you die. Then subtract that year or two from the number on line 4. If your spouse would choose not to work for several years, don't count on any take-home pay. Enter 0 on line 7.

Line 10. Social Security survivor benefits can become a major source of income. Table A, at right, indicates the annual amounts currently paid to a non-
(continued)

1. Current total family take-home pay — $ _____
2. One-third of your own take-home pay — $ _____
3. Annual family expenses without you (line 1 minus line 2) — $ _____
4. Number of years until your youngest child finishes high school — X _____
5. Total family expenses (line 3 times line 4) — $ _____
6. Savings and investments — $ _____
7. Spouse's annual take-home pay — $ _____
8. Number of years of that income — X _____
9. Total spouse contribution (line 7 times line 8) — $ _____
10. Total Social Security benefits — $ _____
11. Total assets and income (add lines 6, 9 and 10) — $ _____
12. Total income deficit (line 5 minus line 11) — $ _____
13. Average annual income deficit (line 12 divided by line 4) — $ _____
14. Lump sum that, if invested, would provide the amount on line 13 for the number of years on line 4 (factor from Table B times $1,000) — $ _____
15. College costs per child — $ _____
16. Number of college-bound children — X _____
17. Total college costs (line 15 times line 16) — $ _____
18. Funeral and estate costs — $ _____
19. Lump sum for a mortgage or emergency fund (optional) — $ _____
20. Total lump sum needed at death (add lines 14, 17, 18 and 19) — $ _____
21. Present life insurance coverage — $ _____
22. Total insurance needed (line 20 minus line 2) (if negative, you have more than you need) — $ _____

Copyright 1987. Money Magazine. Reprinted with permission.

WORKSHEET 29 (Continued)

working spouse and children and the maximum available per family. Benefits decline swiftly for a working spouse earing more than $6,000 a year. Children continue collecting until they graduate from high school or turn 19, whichever comes first. A spouse's benefits expire after the youngest child reaches age 16. Estimate your total benefits by counting the years of maximum and lesser benefits at your income level in the table. Multiply the benefits by the number of years you would collect them and add the results. (For further help, call your local Social Security office or write to the Social Security Administration, Office of Public Inquiries, Baltimore, Md. 21235.)

Line 14. The average annual income deficit resulting from your death (line 13) overstates what your family would need unless you adjust the amount for investment income. Much of the lump sum you are calculating could earn interest or dividends for several years before the whole amount is spent. The number shown in Table B, at left, most nearly corresponding to your annual deficit and the years your family would need income (line 4) is a factor that, when multiplied by $1,000, approximates the lump sum needed. It is based on the conservative assumption that after taxes and inflation the fund would earn a 2% return.

Line 15. Enter an amount here if you want your insurance to finance the college education of your child or children. Four years at a private college, including room and board, now costs an average of $40,100, and public colleges average $22,416. For children at least five years away from college, those amounts should be adjusted now for inflation. Assuming 5% annual increases, raise them to $52,000 and $28,600—and in five years review them against actual costs.

Line 18. Funeral and estate costs, including the settlement of debts, generally amount to one year's take-home pay.

Line 19. If you wish, you can provide money that your family could use to pay off the mortgage or keep for emergencies.

Line 21. Take into account any coverage you already have from your employer as well as your own policies.

FIGURING OUT HOW MUCH LIFE INSURANCE

Table A: Social Security benefits. Here are estimates of annual survivor payments for your spouse and children.

WORKER'S PRESENT AGE		WORKER'S 1986 INCOME		
		$20,000	$30,000	OVER $40,000
25	Benefit per survivor	$6,312	$7,764	$9,060
	Maximum family benefit	14,940	18,132	21,132
35	Benefit per survivor	6,228	7,716	8,724
	Maximum family benefit	14,795	18,000	20,352
45	Benefit per survivor	6,216	7,488	7,944
	Maximum family benefit	14,772	17,484	18,528
55	Benefit per survivor	6,216	7,224	7,572
	Maximum family benefit	14,760	16,872	17,544
65	Benefit per survivor	5,868	6,804	7,092
	Maximum family benefit	13,908	15,888	16,560

Source: Social Security Administration

Table B: Lump-sum factors. Here are the amounts needed to replace income (multiply by $1,000).

DOLLAR AMOUNT (FROM LINE 13)	NUMBER OF YEARS (FROM LINE 4)								
	5	7	9	11	13	15	16	17	18
$5,000	24	33	41	49	57	65	72	79	85
10,000	48	65	82	98	114	129	143	157	170
15,000	71	98	123	147	170	193	214	235	255
20,000	95	130	164	196	227	257	286	313	340
25,000	118	163	205	245	284	321	357	391	425
30,000	142	195	245	294	340	385	428	469	510
35,000	166	227	286	343	397	449	500	548	594
40,000	189	260	327	391	454	513	571	626	679
45,000	213	292	368	440	510	578	642	704	764
50,000	236	325	408	489	567	642	713	782	849
55,000	260	357	449	538	624	706	785	860	934
60,000	283	390	490	587	680	770	856	938	1,019
65,000	307	422	531	636	737	834	927	1,016	1,104
70,000	331	454	571	685	794	898	999	1,095	1,188
75,000	354	487	612	734	850	962	1,070	1,173	1,273

Copyright 1987. MONEY Magazine. Reprinted with permission.

WORKSHEET 30   **HOW CLOSE ARE YOU NOW?**

1. Gross annual income you will need after you leave work in today's dollars $ _____

2. The sum needed to provide that income
   Divide line 1 by .057 if you will retire at 50, .063 at 55, .069 at 60, or .076 at 65 $ _____

3. One-time transition costs, like moving expenses or capital to start a business $ _____

4. Total amount needed *Line 2 plus line 3* $ _____

5. Pensions   a. Yearly benefit $ _____
   b. Total pension *Multiply amount on 5a by 11.1 if your pension will begin at age 50, 10.7 at 55, 10.1 at 60 or 9.3 at 65. Then multiply that number by a factor from column A* $ _____

6. Social Security   a. Yearly benefit $ _____
   b. Total benefit *Multiply amount on line 6a by 13.7. Then multiply that number by a factor from column A.* $ _____

7. Postretirement jobs
   a. Estimated annual earnings from new jobs, part-time work or other sources, not including your investments $ _____
   b. Total earnings during retirement
   Multiply amount on line 7a by 17.7 if you plan to leave work at 50, 16.3 at 55, 14.6 at 60 and 12.7 at 65. Then multiply that number by a factor from column A. $ _____

8. Money needed from savings *Line 4 minus lines 5b, 6b and 7b* $ _____

9. Amount you have saved already $ _____

10. What your savings will grow to by the time you stop working
    Line 9 times a factor from column B $ _____

11. Total additional savings you will need *Line 8 minus line 10* $ _____

12. Amount you will need to save each year $ _____
    Line 11 times a factor from column C

Number of years between now and when you will begin receiving additional income	Column A
1	.962
2	.925
3	.889
4	.855
5	.822
6	.790
7	.760
8	.731
9	.703
10	.676
15	.555
20	.456
25	.375

Number of years between now and when you will stop working	Column B	Column C
1	1.04	1.000
2	1.08	.490
3	1.12	.320
4	1.17	.235
5	1.22	.185
6	1.27	.151
7	1.32	.127
8	1.37	.109
9	1.42	.095
10	1.48	.083
15	1.80	.050
20	2.19	.034
25	2.67	.024

Copyright 1986. MONEY Magazine. Reprinted with permission.

WORKSHEET 31 — **RUNNING BALANCE SHEET AND CASH-FLOW STATEMENT**

DATES REVIEWED:	DATE:		DATE		DATE:		DATE:	

WORKING ASSETS

DESCRIPTION	$	%	$	%	$	%	$	%
SAVINGS-TYPE ACCOUNTS								
BILLS, NOTES, BONDS AND PREFERRED STOCKS								
MORTGAGES AND NOTES								
COMMON STOCK								
REAL ESTATE								
EXOTICS								
OTHER								
SUB-TOTAL								
TOTAL WORKING ASSETS								

RESERVE ASSETS

INSURANCE PROTECTION								
HOME EQUITY								
BUSINESS NET WORTH								
TOTAL RESERVE ASSETS								
TOTAL ESTATE VALUE								

INCOME AND LIVING EXPENSES

INVESTMENTS								
SALARY								
PENSIONS								
SOCIAL SECURITY								
TOTAL INCOME								
TOTAL LIVING EXPENSES								

WORKSHEET 32

SUMMARY OF SALES FOR CALENDAR YEAR

REGISTRA-TION	PURCHASED					SOLD				CAPITAL GAIN (LOSS)		$ INCOME
	DATE	NUMBER OF SHARES, UNITS OR % OF OWNERSHIP	DESCRIPTION	TOTAL COST	DEPRECIA-TION, PROFIT EXEMPTION & OTHER ADJUSTMENTS	TOTAL ADJUSTED COST	DATE	NUMBER OF SHARES, UNITS OR % OF OWNERSHIP	$ PER SHARE, UNIT, % OWNER-SHIP	$ PROCEEDS	SHORT-TERM	LONG-TERM	CURRENT NET TO SALE DATE
1													
2													
3													
4													
5													
6													
7													
8													
9													
10													
11													
12													
13													
14													
15													
16													
17													
18													
19													

APPENDIX A: WHERE TO GO FOR ADDITIONAL HELP

The most important thing you can do for your financial plan is to get started on it. At this point, you have already completed the critical first steps of the process: You have defined your goals, developed an overview of your present financial situation and considered various financial strategies that will help you meet your goals. If you've completed the worksheets, you've also analyzed different investment options and have made decisions about changes you would like to make in your financial portfolio.

Now all you have to do is make a phone call to your broker, write a few checks and watch your money start to roll in.

Or is it?

Before you start spending the money you expect to earn, ask yourself a few questions. Are you sure you've made the right decisions? Are you ready to implement your plan? Do you need professional help? Or do you need more information before you finalize your investment decisions?

RECOMMENDED RESOURCES AND READING

It's not difficult to find out information about financial issues and strategies. If you're going to be doing your own financial planning, start with the *Wall Street Journal* and *Money* magazine. We also recommend *Financial Planning Under the New Rules,* by Lindsay K. Wyatt and Elizabeth S. Styers (Longman, 1987). These books describe how various investment vehicles work, taking into account recent tax legislation.

Mutual funds and investment and brokerage services are advertised in the major consumer magazines. Remember that if you are doing your own planning, a discount broker can save you money. Send for the prospectus of any fund you are considering and read it carefully. You might find it helpful to consult one of a growing number of financial newsletters that evaluate stocks and mutual funds. Remember that in every case, past performance of an investment vehicle is no guarantee of future returns. The following is a partial list of resources:

Money Guide to Mutual Funds–Annual rankings of 658 funds
Money magazine and *Forbes Magazine*–Ongoing information on all investment vehicles and strategies
Available on newstands.

Value Line Investment Survey–Newsletter Service that evaluates 1,700 stocks on an ongoing basis
Value Line, Inc., 711 Third Avenue, New York, N.Y. 10017

Fortune Investment Information Directory–Directory of places to go for further information on stocks, bonds, municipal bonds, options, mutual funds
The Drushkin Publishing Group, Inc., Sluice Dock, Guilford, Conn. 06437

Dow Jones News/Retrieval–One line resource for investors. Stock performance, earnings, economic forecasts, reports from major brokerage houses
JJN/R Membership Kit, PO Box 300, Princeton, N.J. 08543

Mutual Fund Values–Morningstar Inc., 53 West Jackson, Chicago, Ill. 60604

Growth Fund Guide–Growth Fund Research Inc., Growth Fund Research Building, Box 6600, Rapid City, S.D. 57709

United Mutual Fund Selector–Information, analysis, performance comparisons on over 800 funds
212 Newberry Street, Boston, Mass. 02116

The Outlook, Standard and Poor's Corporation–Newsletter that analyzes stock market trends and makes recommendations
25 Broadway, New York, N.Y. 10004

Weisenberger Investment Companies Service–*The Mutual Fund Current Performance and Dividend Record, The Mutual Fund Investment Report*
Warren, Gorham, and Lamont, 210 South Street, Boston, Mass. 02111

The Mutual Fund Forecaster–Institute for Economic Research, 3471 N. Federal Highway, Fort Lauderdale, Fla. 33306

Donoghue's Mutual Fund Almanac–Box 540, Holliston, Mass. 01746

WHO NEEDS PROFESSIONAL HELP?

Financial planners tend to give different answers when asked to describe their clientele. Some planners only work with the very wealthy. It's not uncommon for a planner to limit a clientele to those with a net worth of $250,000 or more and an income of at least $100,000.

Other planners enjoy working with a middle class clientele or with young professionals. Working with people who are not yet rich gives them a chance to feel that they've really helped someone through their profession; at the same time, upwardly mobile young clients can be expected to amass a greater net worth and turn into good—perhaps even wealthy—long-term clients.

Still other planners believe that anyone and everyone can benefit from the use of a personal financial planner.

The only attitude that all planners seem to share is that there are no rigid cutoff criteria. Your financial situation is a personal issue, and whether or not you can benefit from professional help depends as much on your attitude as on your income. The following guidelines may help.

- Do-it-yourself planning makes sense for single people with incomes of less than $50,000 and married couples with incomes of less than $100,000 who are financially stable.
- Regardless of your income, you may want to consider financial planning if you fall into one of the following categories:
    1. You just don't have time to manage your financial situation.
    2. You have children and you would like to plan for their college education.
    3. You are expecting a windfall—perhaps an inheritance.
    4. Your income fluctuates wildly. Perhaps you're in a volatile field such as the arts: actors, for example, can have extremely lucrative years followed by long, dry spells.
    5. Your tax circumstances are unusual or complicated—say you sold an asset or had an unusual jump in income.
    6. You are a small business owner or an entrepreneur.

Doing your own planning is also a wonderful idea for people who expect to consult a financial planner in the future. By getting started on your own, you will be ready to use the services of a planner as effectively as possible. And, by understanding the process, you will have a better idea of what questions to ask and what to expect.

Financial planners tend to look on do-it-yourself planning as accountants look on do-it-yourself tax returns. When you are young and your tax situation is straightforward, it makes sense to file your own tax return. As your income increases and your net worth grows, it becomes more and more likely that you will benefit from hiring a professional. As your taxes become more complicated, there are more things to consider, the cost of making mistakes is greater, and the likelihood of an audit becomes greater, too. One April 14th you sit down and decide that you'd probably save time and money—not to mention headaches—if you hired a pro.

An old legal maxim tells us: "A lawyer who represents himself has a fool for a client." No matter how knowledgeable you are about financial issues, you will lack objectivity in constructing your own financial plan. If your situation is complicated, you may find that a visit to a planner can untangle some webs.

What Should You Know Before You Start Looking for a Financial Planner?

Financial planning is a service and you, as the prospective client, have the right to expect that it will meet your needs. Be prepared to spend some time looking for the right financial planner for you. You wouldn't pick a doctor's name out of the phone book; nor should you blindly call a financial planner and hope for the best.

Start by asking your friends, associates and family. Who has used a financial planner? What did they think about the person and his or her work?

Professional associations (see pages 246 & 247) provide another source of references. Your lawyer or accountant may also be able to make a recommendation. Finally, look in the business section of your local newspaper. Are any financial planners consistently interviewed? Or do any planners write articles? What do you think of what they have to say?

We've found that some simple tactical planning can yield impressive results. When you have a few names of planners, start calling them. Tell each planner how you got his or her name. Ask "Who, aside from yourself, would you recommend as the best planner in this area?" When the same name keeps turning up time after time, you've got a potential planner.

Finally, seminars provide you with an excellent opportunity to size up a prospective planner. Planners frequently give seminars in order to attract new clients. The topics range from a general overview of financial planning to specific tax-related issues. Seminars are often advertised in your local paper, or they may be sponsored by community groups or schools. Choose a topic that interests you and sign up. The seminar will give you the chance to evaluate the planner. Is this someone you could talk to honestly about your goals and your financial situation? Is he or she someone you could trust? First impressions can speak volumes about a person, and by attending a seminar, you can gain valuable information and evaluate a prospective advisor. However, many excellent planners work only by word-of-mouth, not seminars, so you may miss some qualified planners if you use this method exclusively.

Financial planning is a relatively new field, and financial planners come from a variety of backgrounds with different educational credentials and professional experiences. It is important to realize that at this point in the profession's evolution, there are no restrictions on who may or may not call himself a financial planner. Your ten-year-old daughter can hand out business cards calling herself a financial planner, and so can any one of a number of salespeople who may be more concerned with their commission than with your overall financial well-being.

If you are looking for a financial planner, you will want someone who has appropriate academic credentials, who has experience in the field, who is a member of one or more of the financial planning's professional associations, who is involved in continuing education classes and who subscribes to a code of ethics. You will want someone who is technically proficient and who <u>puts your needs and goals first</u>. It is <u>your</u> financial plan—and <u>your</u> financial independence—that is at stake.

Part of the reason that financial planning is so popular right now is that it's such a good idea. If you've made your way through the worksheets in this book, you probably feel—perhaps for the first time—that you are in control of your financial situation; that your money is starting to work for you. With annual updates and a plan that changes as you do, your situation can only get better. That's what planning is about, and that's one reason that there is an increasing interest in the field.

Unfortunately, there are a number of people who have jumped on the financial planning bandwagon who don't really belong on it. You may have already been approached by a "financial planner" only to find out that his or her idea of a financial plan is for you to buy whatever he or she is selling. National consumer magazines are full of advertisements for companies that offer "total financial planning." Some planners criticize that many of these services actually have nothing to do with true financial planning. Clients may receive a document that looks like a financial plan, but critics charge that these plans are often commonsense, superficial boilerplates that exist as a glitzy sales tool for the products available through the vendor and its affiliates or subsidiaries. The result: the client gets several financial products that may or may not be related to his financial goals. So-called "free" financial plans that lure the client in the door may be worth exactly what they cost. *Caveat emptor.*

As financial planners point out, financial planning is not the process of selling you financial products; it is the process of defining goals and devising strategies that can help to meet them. But to confuse the issue further, that doesn't mean that you should steer away from financial planners who sell financial products. How a planner gets paid—whether by commission or fee, or some combination, should be of less concern to you than how using the services of that planner will affect your financial balance sheet.

How Do Financial Planners Get Paid?

Fee-Only Planners. Fee-only planners make recommendations. Their job is analysis, not implementation. They may advise you to buy shares of a mutual fund, but, whether the fund is "load" or "no-load," they do no selling and receive no commission. Fee-only planners tend to think of themselves as "pure" planners, and they claim that because they are free from the pressure of earning money through commissions, they can be more objective and can make recommendations that are based solely on their clients well-being. There is one catch: The stereotype is that fee-only planners usually work with the very rich. All of their income is generated by fees, which can sometimes be very high. A few planners charge as little as $300, but more often the fees are much higher. A wealthy client with a complicated financial portfolio could pay upwards of $25,000 for the plan—and that doesn't count the cost of implementing it. If you do use a fee-only planner, you should be aware that having a plan is only one part of the process. It does you no good unless you implement it by buying the financial products recommended and making use of the strategies and procedures in your plan.

Fee-Plus-Commission Planners. An increasing number of financial planners split their practices into two segments. The advisory part of the process functions like the fee-only planner's business. The planner constructs the financial plan, taking into account the client's goals and concerns. He makes recommendations on both financial products that could help clients achieve their goals and on strategies and procedures that, while necessary to a financial plan, would not necessarily generate further income (i.e., commission) for the planner. The second segment is the implementation, where the client may choose to buy the recommended products. The planner then may receive a commission on certain investment vehicles. While critics, among them fee-only planners, charge that fee-plus-commission planners cannot be objective if they stand to gain from the sale of some financial products, many planners have chosen the fee-plus commission structure because they feel that it enables them to broaden their client base and compensates them for the time it takes to select, monitor and track the investments that make up a complete financial plan. Like a doctor who earns a fee by recommending surgery, or an attorney who earns a fee by recommending that you draw up a will, fee-plus-commission planners may earn income from their recommendations. Their long-term success requires that they act in the best interest of their client.

Commission-Only Planners. Commission-Only Planners also construct financial plans, but they receive commissions on products they sell. While objectivity is an issue often raised by critics, financial planners who work on a commission-only basis often construct affordable, helpful plans for their clients. Repeat business is one of the most important ways financial planners have of ensuring their own success, and good financial planners—regardless of their commission structures—know that they can only retain satisfied clients. Also, commission-only planners often are more affordable for clients with small current net worths. The plans may be less in-depth, but if you don't have $25,000 to invest, you certainly don't need a plan that costs that much.

What Qualifications Should Your Financial Planner Have?

While financial planners are not required to have any particular certifications to set up shop, there is not dearth of organizations, designations and credentials in the field. In fact, a financial planners business card can sometimes look like alphabet soup. To confuse the matter further, many designations that were earned in other areas are beneficial to the financial planner. Ask any planner you are considering using which designations he or she holds. If you don't know what the initials mean ask what they stand for and what the planner had to achieve to earn them. Listed below are some of the better known designations in the field.

CFP or Certified Financial Planner –A designation given by the College for Financial Planning. The CFP course generally takes two years to complete, and comprises six classes in financial planning.

ChFC or Chartered Financial Consultant**–**This designation is offered by the American College of Insurance in Bryn Mawr, Pennsylvania. The program of study includes 10 comprehensive courses covering different financial planning topics.

Both the ChFC and the CFP designations are generally regarded as evidence that the planner has a broad-based background in the various areas of financial planning, and has met recognized academic standards in the field.

CLU or Chartered Life Underwriter**–**This is an insurance designation given by the American College of Insurance. The program includes courses in risk management, insurance, taxes and investments.

RHU or Registered Health Underwriter**–**Health insurance designation.

CPA or Certified Public Accountant**–**Many CPAs have branched into the financial planning arena because their skills in taxation matters are transferable, and their clienteles are good financial planning prospects. CPAs who are financial planners work on a fee-only basis because the CPA regulations forbids commissions on the sale of products. In any event, most planners work with accountants—and you should, too—on issues of taxation.

JD or Juris Doctor**–**Attorneys, like accountants, often find that they have both transferable knowledge and a ready clientele for financial planning services. In addition, lawyers can be involved in many issues of financial planning, including wills, probate issues, trusts, estate planning, charitable giving, as well as tax laws.

Registered Investment Adviser**–**You should be aware that SEC regulations forbids providing investment recommendations for a fee unless the planner is registered with the Securities and Exchange Commission. However, "registered investment adviser" is neither a designation nor a degree; it indicates merely that the financial planner has been duly registered.

Registered Representative, N.A.S.D.**–**Registered Representatives have passed examinations given by the National Association of Securities Dealers and are licensed to sell securities.

MBA, MSFS or Master of Business Administration and Master of Science in Financial Services**–**These graduate business degrees are university degrees, not industry designations. Some colleges are offering programs in financial services and financial planning. While these degrees have no bearing on the planner's experience, they do indicate a strong base of academic knowledge.

Where Can I Find Out More About Financial Planning?

Several financial planning organizations have sprung up to meet the growing number of financial planners. Some have rigid entrance requirements; others have none. Many offer continuing education programs, including seminars, regional and national conventions, and courses. Ask your planner about her continuing education activities. The financial environment is changing on a daily basis. If your planner took her last tax course two years ago, chances are she's way out-of-date.

The following organizations can provide you with further information about financial planners in your area:

- IAFP or International Association for Financial Planning
  Two Concourse Parkway
  Suite 800
  Atlanta, Georgia
  (800) 241-2148
  Membership Requirements: Active in Financial Services
  Sponsors annual national convention, regional conventions and educational seminars.

- IAFP Registry of Financial Planning Practitioners
  Stringent requirements, including CFP designation, submission of an approval financial plan, continuing education courses, three years of experience, client references and passing a comprehensive exam. The IAFP will provide a list of planners in your area who have met these standards.

- ICFP or Institute of Certified Financial Planners
  Two Denver Highlands
  10065 East Harvard Avenue
  Suite 320
  Denver, Colorado
  (303) 751-7600
  Membership Requirements: Must have the CFP designation

- International Association of Registered Financial Planners
  4127 West Cyprus Street
  Tampa, Florida
  (813) 875-7352
  Membership Requirements: College degree, three years experience or an industry-recognized designation. Members must also meet requirements in life and health insurance, and must qualify for at least one securities license. Members are granted RFP designation upon admittance. Sponsors annual national meeting and regional meetings.

- National Association of Personal Financial Advisors
  PO Box 7833
  Chicago, Illinois
  (312) 577-4450
  Membership Requirements: One year of fee-only planning experience and maintenance of a fee-only financial planning practice.
  Sponsors annual national meeting and regional meetings.

- ASCLU or American Society of Chartered Life Underwriters
  270 Bryn Mawr Avenue
  Bryn Mawr, Pennsylvania
  (215) 896-4300
  Membership Requirements: Members must hold the CLU or ChFC designation.
  Sponsors annual national meeting, regional meetings for 240 chapters.

- AICPA or American Institute for Certified Public Accountants
  1211 Avenue of the Americas
  New York, New York
  (212) 575-6200
  Personal Financial Planning Division
  Membership Requirements: CPA designation and entry examination.
  Sponsors national meeting.

Choosing the Right Planner

You've gotten references from your personal and professional networks, and you've asked the planner about his credentials, experience and background. How do you know you've made the right choice?

This question comes down to a personal issue. Do you like the planner? Is this someone you feel you can trust?

When you have your first meeting with a planner, you should be prepared with a list of your goals and a complete accounting of your financial situation. Bring this workbook with you, if you've gone through it; it will simplify the data gathering process.

The planner may be interviewing you for your financial data—that's part of the job, and that's a criterion that may be used in deciding whether to take you on as a client. But remember that the preliminary meeting is a chance for you to evaluate the planner, too. Does he or she seem truly interested in your personal goals? Or does he or she appear to be primarily interested in selling you something? Is the planner positive about you and the possibility of working with you? Treat the session like a job interview: you're both exploring the possibility of a long-term relationship, and it has to work for both of you in order to be worthwhile.

APPENDIX B: CALCULATIONS AND FORMULAS

ESTIMATED REAL ESTATE VALUES FORM

SAMPLE CALCULATION:

1. CURRENT VALUE OF REAL ESTATE $100,000
2. PURCHASE PRICE OF REAL ESTATE   50,000
3. NUMBER OF YEARS SINCE PURCHASE   5

STEPS:

A. Divide current value by purchase price. $100,000/50,000 = 2

B. Find the row in Future Value Factors Table for the number of years you have held the property;

C. Scan the row until you come to the number closest to the result of your calculation in Step A, "2". Look up the column to read the percent at the top, 15%. This property has had nearly a 15% compound annual rate of return.

PRESENT VALUE TABLES

YEARS	1%	2%	3%	4%	5%	6%	7%
1	1.0100	1.0200	1.0300	1.0400	1.0500	1.0600	1.0700
2	1.0201	1.0404	1.0609	1.0816	1.1025	1.1236	1.1449
3	1.0303	1.0612	1.0927	1.1249	1.1576	1.1910	1.2250
4	1.0406	1.0824	1.1255	1.1699	1.2155	1.2625	1.3108
5	1.0510	1.1041	1.1593	1.2167	1.2763	1.3382	1.4026
6	1.0615	1.1262	1.1941	1.2653	1.3401	1.4185	1.5007
7	1.0721	1.1487	1.2299	1.3159	1.4071	1.5036	1.6058
8	1.0829	1.1717	1.2668	1.3686	1.4775	1.5938	1.7182
9	1.0937	1.1951	1.3048	1.4233	1.5513	1.6895	1.8385
10	1.1046	1.2190	1.3439	1.4802	1.6289	1.7908	1.9672
11	1.1157	1.2434	1.3842	1.5395	1.7103	1.8983	2.1049
12	1.1268	1.2682	1.4258	1.6010	1.7959	2.0122	2.2522
13	1.1381	1.2936	1.4685	1.6651	1.8856	2.1329	2.4098
14	1.1495	1.3195	1.5126	1.7317	1.9799	2.2609	2.5785
15	1.1610	1.3459	1.5580	1.8009	2.0789	2.3966	2.7590
16	1.1726	1.3728	1.6047	1.8730	2.1829	2.5404	2.9522
17	1.1843	1.4002	1.6528	1.9479	2.2920	2.6928	3.1588
18	1.1961	1.4282	1.7024	2.0258	2.4066	2.8543	3.3799
19	1.2081	1.4568	1.7535	2.1068	2.5270	3.0256	3.6165
20	1.2202	1.4859	1.8061	2.1911	2.6533	3.2071	3.8697
21	1.2324	1.5157	1.8603	2.2788	2.7860	3.3996	4.1406
22	1.2447	1.5460	1.9161	2.3699	2.9253	3.6035	4.4304
23	1.2572	1.5769	1.9736	2.4647	3.0715	3.8197	4.7405
24	1.2697	1.6084	2.0328	2.5633	3.2251	4.0489	5.0724
25	1.2824	1.6406	2.0938	2.6658	3.3864	4.2919	5.4274
26	1.2953	1.6734	2.1566	2.7725	3.5557	4.5494	5.8074
27	1.3082	1.7069	2.2213	2.8834	3.7335	4.8223	6.2139
28	1.3213	1.7410	2.2879	2.9987	3.9201	5.1117	6.6488
29	1.3345	1.7758	2.3566	3.1187	4.1161	5.4184	7.1143
30	1.3478	1.8114	2.4273	3.2434	4.3219	5.7435	7.6123
31	1.3613	1.8476	2.5001	3.3731	4.5380	6.0881	8.1451
32	1.3749	1.8845	2.5751	3.5081	4.7649	6.4534	8.7153
33	1.3887	1.9222	2.6523	3.6484	5.0032	6.8406	9.3253
34	1.4026	1.9607	2.7319	3.7943	5.2533	7.2510	9.9781
35	1.4166	1.9999	2.8139	3.9461	5.5160	7.6861	10.6766
36	1.4308	2.0399	2.8983	4.1039	5.7918	8.1473	11.4239
37	1.4451	2.0807	2.9852	4.2681	6.0814	8.6361	12.2236
38	1.4595	2.1223	3.0748	4.4388	6.3855	9.1543	13.0793
39	1.4741	2.1647	3.1670	4.6164	6.7048	9.7035	13.9948
40	1.4889	2.2080	3.2620	4.8010	7.0400	10.2857	14.9745
41	1.5038	2.2522	3.3599	4.9931	7.3920	10.9029	16.0227
42	1.5188	2.2972	3.4607	5.1928	7.7616	11.5570	17.1443
43	1.5340	2.3432	3.5645	5.4005	8.1497	12.2505	18.3444
44	1.5493	2.3901	3.6715	5.6165	8.5572	12.9855	19.6285
45	1.5648	2.4379	3.7816	5.8412	8.9850	13.7646	21.0025
46	1.5805	2.4866	3.8950	6.0748	9.4343	14.5905	22.4726
47	1.5963	2.5363	4.0119	6.3178	9.9060	15.4659	24.0457
48	1.6122	2.5871	4.1323	6.5705	10.4013	16.3939	25.7289
49	1.6283	2.6388	4.2562	6.8333	10.9213	17.3775	27.5299
50	1.6446	2.6916	4.3839	7.1067	11.4674	18.4302	29.4570

PRESENT VALUE TABLES

YEARS	8%	9%	10%	11%	12%	13%	14%
1	1.0800	1.0900	1.1000	1.1100	1.1200	1.1300	1.1400
2	1.1664	1.1881	1.2100	1.2321	1.2544	1.2769	1.2996
3	1.2597	1.2950	1.3310	1.3676	1.4049	1.4429	1.4815
4	1.3605	1.4116	1.4641	1.5181	1.5735	1.6305	1.6890
5	1.4693	1.5386	1.6105	1.6851	1.7623	1.8424	1.9254
6	1.5869	1.6771	1.7716	1.8704	1.9738	2.0820	2.1950
7	1.7138	1.8280	1.9487	2.0762	2.2107	2.3526	2.5023
8	1.8509	1.9926	2.1436	2.3045	2.4760	2.6584	2.8526
9	1.9990	2.1719	2.3579	2.5580	2.7731	3.0040	3.2519
10	2.1589	2.3674	2.5937	2.8394	3.1058	3.3946	3.7072
11	2.3316	2.5804	2.8531	3.1518	3.4786	3.8359	4.2263
12	2.5182	2.8127	3.1384	3.4985	3.8960	4.3345	4.8179
13	2.7196	3.0658	3.4523	3.8833	4.3635	4.8981	5.4924
14	2.9372	3.3417	3.7975	4.3104	4.8871	5.5348	6.2613
15	3.1722	3.6425	4.1772	4.7846	5.4736	6.2543	7.1379
16	3.4259	3.9703	4.5950	5.3109	6.1304	7.0673	8.1372
17	3.7000	4.3276	5.0545	5.8951	6.8660	7.9861	9.2765
18	3.9960	4.7171	5.5599	6.5436	7.6900	9.0243	10.5752
19	4.3157	5.1417	6.1159	7.2633	8.6128	10.1974	12.0557
20	4.6610	5.6044	6.7275	8.0623	9.6463	11.5231	13.7435
21	5.0338	6.1088	7.4003	8.9492	10.8038	13.0211	15.6676
22	5.4365	6.6586	8.1403	9.9336	12.1003	14.7138	17.8610
23	5.8715	7.2579	8.9543	11.0263	13.5523	16.6266	20.3616
24	6.3412	7.9111	9.8497	12.2392	15.1786	18.7881	23.2122
25	6.8485	8.6231	10.8347	13.5855	17.0001	21.2305	26.4619
26	7.3964	9.3992	11.9182	15.0799	19.0401	23.9905	30.1666
27	7.9881	10.2451	13.1100	16.7387	21.3249	27.1093	34.3899
28	8.6271	11.1671	14.4210	18.5799	23.8839	30.6335	39.2045
29	9.3173	12.1722	15.8631	20.6237	26.7499	34.6158	44.6931
30	10.0627	13.2677	17.4494	22.8923	29.9599	39.1159	50.9502
31	10.8677	14.4618	19.1943	25.4104	33.5551	44.2010	58.0832
32	11.7371	15.7633	21.1138	28.2056	37.5817	49.9471	66.2148
33	12.6761	17.1820	23.2252	31.3082	42.0915	56.4402	75.4849
34	13.6901	18.7284	25.5477	34.7521	47.1425	63.7774	86.0528
35	14.7853	20.4140	28.1024	38.5749	52.7996	72.0685	98.1002
36	15.9682	22.2512	30.9128	42.8181	59.1356	81.4374	111.8342
37	17.2456	24.2538	34.0039	47.5281	66.2318	92.0243	127.4910
38	18.6253	26.4367	37.4043	52.7562	74.1797	103.9874	145.3397
39	20.1153	28.8160	41.1448	58.5593	83.0812	117.5059	165.6873
40	21.7245	31.4094	45.2593	65.0009	93.0510	132.7816	188.8835
41	23.4625	34.2363	49.7852	72.1510	104.2171	150.0432	215.3272
42	25.3395	37.3175	54.7637	80.0876	116.7231	169.5488	245.4730
43	27.3666	40.6761	60.2401	88.8972	130.7299	191.5901	279.8392
44	29.5560	44.3370	66.2641	98.6759	146.4175	216.4968	319.0167
45	31.9204	48.3273	72.8905	109.5302	163.9876	244.6414	363.6791
46	34.4741	52.6767	80.1795	121.5786	183.6661	276.4448	414.5941
47	37.2320	57.4176	88.1975	134.9522	205.7061	312.3826	472.6373
48	40.2106	62.5852	97.0172	149.7970	230.3908	352.9923	538.8065
49	43.4274	68.2179	106.7190	166.2746	258.0377	398.8814	614.2395
50	46.9016	74.3575	117.3909	184.5648	289.0022	450.7359	700.2330

PRESENT VALUE TABLES

YEARS	15%	16%	17%	18%	19%	20%
1	1.1500	1.1600	1.1700	1.1800	1.1900	1.2000
2	1.3225	1.3456	1.3689	1.3924	1.4161	1.4400
3	1.5209	1.5609	1.6016	1.6430	1.6852	1.7280
4	1.7490	1.8106	1.8739	1.9388	2.0053	2.0736
5	2.0114	2.1003	2.1924	2.2878	2.3864	2.4883
6	2.3131	2.4364	2.5652	2.6996	2.8398	2.9860
7	2.6600	2.8262	3.0012	3.1855	3.3793	3.5832
8	3.0590	3.2784	3.5115	3.7589	4.0214	4.2998
9	3.5179	3.8030	4.1084	4.4355	4.7854	5.1598
10	4.0456	4.4114	4.8068	5.2338	5.6947	6.1917
11	4.6524	5.1173	5.6240	6.1759	6.7767	7.4301
12	5.3503	5.9360	6.5801	7.2876	8.0642	8.9161
13	6.1528	6.8858	7.6987	8.5994	9.5964	10.6993
14	7.0757	7.9875	9.0075	10.1472	11.4198	12.8392
15	8.1371	9.2655	10.5387	11.9737	13.5895	15.4070
16	9.3576	10.7480	12.3303	14.1290	16.1715	18.4884
17	10.7613	12.4677	14.4264	16.6722	19.2441	22.1861
18	12.3755	14.4625	16.8790	19.6733	22.9005	26.6233
19	14.2318	16.7765	19.7484	23.2144	27.2516	31.9480
20	16.3665	19.4608	23.1056	27.3930	32.4294	38.3376
21	18.8215	22.5745	27.0336	32.3238	38.5910	46.0051
22	21.6447	26.1864	31.6293	38.1421	45.9233	55.2061
23	24.8915	30.3762	37.0062	45.0076	54.6487	66.2474
24	28.6252	35.2364	43.2973	53.1090	65.0320	79.4968
25	32.9190	40.8742	50.6578	62.6686	77.3881	95.3962
26	37.8568	47.4141	59.2697	73.9490	92.0918	114.4755
27	43.5353	55.0004	69.3455	87.2598	109.5893	137.3706
28	50.0656	63.8004	81.1342	102.9666	130.4112	164.8447
29	57.5755	74.0085	94.9271	121.5005	155.1893	197.8136
30	66.2118	85.8499	111.0647	143.3706	184.6753	237.3763
31	76.1435	99.5859	129.9456	169.1774	219.7636	284.8516
32	87.5651	115.5196	152.0364	199.6293	261.5187	341.8219
33	100.6998	134.0027	177.8826	235.5625	311.2073	410.1863
34	115.8048	155.4432	208.1226	277.9638	370.3366	492.2235
35	133.1755	180.3141	243.5035	327.9973	440.7006	590.6682
36	153.1519	209.1643	284.8990	387.0368	524.4337	708.8019
37	176.1246	242.6306	333.3319	456.7034	624.0761	850.5623
38	202.5433	281.4515	389.9983	538.9100	742.6506	1020.6747
39	232.9248	326.4838	456.2980	635.9139	883.7542	1224.8097
40	267.8635	378.7212	533.8687	750.3783	1051.6675	1469.7716
41	308.0431	439.3165	624.6264	885.4464	1251.4843	1763.7259
42	354.2495	509.6072	730.8129	1044.8268	1489.2664	2116.4711
43	407.3870	591.1443	855.0511	1232.8956	1772.2270	2539.7653
44	468.4950	685.7274	1000.4098	1454.8168	2108.9501	3047.7184
45	538.7693	795.4438	1170.4794	1716.6839	2509.6506	3657.2620
46	619.5847	922.7148	1369.4609	2025.6870	2986.4842	4388.7144
47	712.5224	1070.3492	1602.2693	2390.3106	3553.9162	5266.4573
48	819.4007	1241.6051	1874.6550	2820.5665	4229.1603	6319.7488
49	942.3108	1440.2619	2193.3464	3328.2685	5032.7008	7583.6986
50	1083.6574	1670.7038	2566.2153	3927.3569	5988.9139	9100.4383

COMPUTING YOUR INCOME TAX

Current Portfolio, Tax Projection (19 _____)

INCOME	CASH FLOW	FEDERAL TAX EFFECT	STATE TAX EFFECT
Non-Investment Income			
Salary			
Professional Income			
Pension			
Social Security			
Royalties, Oil and Mineral			
Income Annuity			
Other Non-Investment Income			
Total Non-Investment Income			
Investment Income			
Interest — Treasury Bills			
Interest — Banks, Savings and Loans			
Interest — Treasury Bonds and Notes			
Interest — Municipal Bonds			
Interest — Other Tax-Free Bonds			
Interest — Corporate Bonds			
Mortgage Income			
Deferred Annuity			
Single Premium Life Insurance			
Dividends on Stock			
Real Estate Income			
Energy Income (Oil, Gas)			
Dividends on Gold Shares			
Other Investment Income			
Total Investment Income			
Total Income			
Adjustments to Income			
IRA			
KEOGH			
Other			
Adjusted Gross Income			
Itemized Deductions (Exclude St. Tx.)			
State Taxable Income			
State Tax			
Total Deductions			
Federal Exemptions			
Total Deductions and Exemptions			
Federal Taxable Income			
Federal Tax			

COMPUTING YOUR INCOME TAX

Proposed Portfolio, Tax Projection (19 _____)

INCOME	CASH FLOW	FEDERAL TAX EFFECT	STATE TAX EFFECT
Non-Investment Income			
Salary			
Professional Income			
Pension			
Social Security			
Royalties, Oil and Mineral			
Income Annuity			
Other Non-Investment Income			
Total Non-Investment Income			
Investment Income			
Interest — Treasury Bills			
Interest — Banks, Savings and Loans			
Interest — Treasury Bonds and Notes			
Interest — Municipal Bonds			
Interest — Other Tax-Free Bonds			
Interest — Corporate Bonds			
Mortgage Income			
Deferred Annuity			
Single Premium Life Insurance			
Dividends on Stock			
Real Estate Income			
Energy Income (Oil, Gas)			
Dividends on Gold Shares			
Other Investment Income			
Total Investment Income			
Total Income			
Adjustments to Income			
IRA			
KEOGH			
Other			
Adjusted Gross Income			
Itemized Deductions (Exclude St. Tx.)			
State Taxable Income			
State Tax			
Total Deductions			
Federal Exemptions			
Total Deductions and Exemptions			
Federal Taxable Income			
Federal Tax			

GLOSSARY

Abrogate
A legal term meaning do away with or abolish by authoritative action.

Adjusted Cost Basis
The original cost of property plus improvements, less the total depreciation taken against the property during the years the investor owns it.

Adjusted Working Assets
All assets in a client's estate as they look *after* the financial planner has made his recommendations.

Annuity
Insurance contracts that pay a named person a pre-specified income. The term "annuity" also applies to any instrument that pays a fixed payment over a period of time.

Bond
A debt obligation, usually of a corporation or a government, federal, state or local. A bond is evidence of debt on which the issuing company usually promises to pay bondholders a specified amount of interest for a specified length of time and to repay the loan in full on the expiration date. Bonds issued by state and local governments are called "Municipals."

Bond Fund
A mutual fund with a portfolio that consists primarily of bonds. The emphasis of the fund is on income rather than growth.

Broker/Dealer
An individual or firm that buys and sells securities, either as a principal for its own account or as an agent for others. In the securities industry, a principal is called a "dealer" and an agent is called a "broker."

Capital Gains and Losses
Profit or loss from the sale of a capital asset. A capital gain, under current federal income tax laws, may be a short-term (six-month or less) capital gain or a long-term (more than six months) capital gain. A short-term capital gain

is taxed at the full income tax rate; a long-term capital gain is subject to a lower tax.

Certificate of Deposit
A money market instrument issued by banks. The time CD is characterized by its set date of maturity and interest rate, and its wide acceptance as a highly negotiable short-term investment vehicle.

Charting Service
A service that plots market trends on a graph, using its own market indicators. The objective is to predict the future movement of a stock or of the market as a whole.

Commission
A commission (as distinguished from a "concession") is generally considered to be a charge added to the gross price of securities purchased or deducted from the gross price of securities sold. While a commission may occur in a retail transaction between a broker/dealer and a customer or in a "wholesale" transaction between broker/dealers, a concession is more likely to occur between a broker/dealer and the issuer of a security.

Community Property
Property acquired by a married couple during their marriage, not including gifts or inheritances. However, gifts and inheritances of a spouse may be converted to community property by that spouse.

Concession
An amount included in the gross price of a transaction, which is retained by or payable to the broker or dealer executing the transaction.

Debt Service
The term used to describe the amount of payment necessary to cover principal and interest, usually on a loan against real estate.

Direct Participation Programs
Securities that provide for flow-through tax consequences regardless of the structure of the legal entity chosen for their distribution. They include, but are not limited to, oil and gas programs, real estate programs, and the like. (Article III, Sec. 34 of Rules of Fair Practice of NASD.)

Dividend
The payment designated by the board of directors of a corporation to be distributed pro-rata among the shares outstanding. On preferred shares, it is generally a fixed amount. On common shares, the dividend varies with the fortunes of the company and the amount of cash on hand, and it may be omitted

if business is poor or the directors decide to withold earnings to invest in plant and equipment. Sometimes a company will pay a dividend out of past earnings even if it is not currently operating at a profit.

Equity
In real estate, equity is the difference between the present balance owed on a piece of property and its present market value.

Estate Planning
Work performed by an estate attorney to ensure that a person's entire assets are working for the benefit of that person and the person's heirs or beneficiaries. It includes the setting up of wills or trusts.

Exotics
Items such as paintings, stamps, diamonds, antiques and precious metals that are bought for investment purposes, but which are not standard investment vehicles.

Face Value
The value appearing on the face of the bond, unless the value is otherwise specified by the issuing company. Face value is ordinarily the amount the issuing company promises to pay at maturity. Face value, sometimes called "par value," is not an indication of market value.

401K
A tax-qualified employee benefit plan where employee contributions are made with pre-tax dollars. Also called a cash or deferred arrangement (CODA).

403b
A tax-qualified employee benefit plan where employee contributions are with pre-tax dollars. Also called a tax sheltered annuity (TSA).

IRA
Individual Retirement Account. A pension plan with major tax advantages. Effective in 1982, any worker can begin an IRA and obtain a tax deduction for his cash contributions presently up to $2,000 annually and $250 for a non-working spouse. IRAs permit investment through intermediaries like mutual funds, insurance companies, and banks or directly in stocks and bonds through registered reps.

Illiquid Asset
An asset not readily convertible to cash.

Itemized Assets
All assets listed individually.

Joint Tenancy
Form of property registration. In a joint tenancy arrangement, all parties listed on the deed own equal parts of that property and their parts are not divided. For example, one joint tenant cannot sell his or her part without the other. Joint tenancy registration normally bypasses probate.

Keogh Plan
Keogh Plan, now known as an "unincorporated pension plan," is a tax-advantaged personal retirement program that can be established by a self-employed individual. Currently, annual contributions to a plan can be up to $15,000. Such contributions and reinvestments are not taxed as they accumulate but will be when withdrawn, presumably at retirement when taxable income may be less. At the time of publication of this book, legislation was making huge changes in Keogh plans, so check current literature before quoting figures to clients.

Leverage
The effect on the per-share earnings of the common stock of a company when large sums must be paid for bond interest or preferred stock dividends, or both, before the common stock is entitled to share in earnings. Leverage may be advantageous for the common stock when earnings are good, but may work against the common stock when earnings decline. Leverage also refers to mortgage funds used in financing of real estate and other types of limited partnerships. Also the use of borrowed money with invested funds to increase returns.

Market Price
In the case of a security, market price is usually considered the last reported price at which the stock or bond sold.

Money Market Funds
A mutual fund whose investments are in high-yield money market instruments such at Treasury securities, CDs, bankers acceptances, and commercial paper. Its intent is to make such instruments, normally purchased in large denominations by institutions, available indirectly to individuals.

Municipal Bond
See "Bond"

Mutual Fund
An investment company that offers shares to the public in addition to redeeming shares on demand as required by law. While in common use, the term "mutual fund" has no meaning in law.

National Association of Securities Dealers (NASD)
An association of brokers and dealers in the over-the-counter securities business. The NASD has the power to expel members who have been declared guilty of unethical practices. The NASD wants, amoung other objectives, to "adopt, administer, and enforce rules of fair practice and rules to prevent fraudulent and manipulative acts and practices, and in general to promote just and equitable principles of trade for the protection of investors."

Notes
Usually, a term used interchangeably with bonds. It can also include paper evidencing indebtedness on real estate, as well as unsecured debts of all kinds.

Oil and Gas Partnerships
A limited partnership in which the investor, along with other investors, buys a portion of a program that will either search for, drill for, pump, or buy and sell oil and gas.

Present Working Assets
Those assets in a client's estate that the financial planner has to work with. These are assets in the investor's control that will benefit the investor durings his or her lifetime but excludes assets that would normally be released because of death or retirement.

Qualified Retirement Plan
A retirement plan that meets the rules and regulations of the IRS in that contributions are made on a tax-deferred basis.

Real Estate Syndicators
A group of investment bankers who together underwrite and distribute real estate. The term "syndicator" is applied to people who perform similar services with other types of investments as well.

Registered Representative
A full-time, licensed employee of a broker/dealer, who has met the requirements of an exchange as to background and knowledge of the securities business. Also known as an "account executive" or "customer's broker." Licensed to discuss and sell securities.

Research and Development or Venture Capital Programs
Limited partnerships whose purpose is to finance the study of some product or process that will eventually be brought to market.

Reserve Assets
Those assets that will be released at the time of death or retirement, such as net insurance protection of life insurance or a residence the investor lives in, or pension.

Single-Premium Whole Life Insurance

A type of whole life insurance in which the premium is paid single payment, rather than monthly or annually, as is common with "regular" whole life. Such policies are often purchased for their tax advantages more than their death benefits.

Speculative Stocks

In a sense, all common stocks are speculations because they are not guaranteed or insured. More commonly, the term denotes stocks in companies that are starting up or in financial difficulty. In reference to investments in general speculative implies a higher degree of risk.

Treasury Bill

Short-term U.S. government paper with no stated interest rate. T-bills are sold at a discount in competitive bidding and reach maturity in 13 weeks, in 26 weeks, or in one year.

Trust Deed

Generally, a trust deed is paper indicating that a piece of real property is security for a debt, evidenced by a note. In some states, it is called a "land contract." In California, the term also refers to mortgages.

Yields

The dividends or interest paid by a stock or bond, expressed as a percentage of the current price. Also known as return. A stock with a current market value of $20 a share that has paid $1 in dividends in the preceding 12 months is said to yield 5 percent ($1.00/$20.00). The current return on a bond is figured in the same way.

Zero-Coupon Bond

Bonds sold at deep discounts and on which interest is paid at maturity, rather than over the life of the bond.

INDEX

After-tax yields
  how to estimate, 78, 80-81
  need to estimate, 68, 69
Age and planning
  to age 35, 9-12, 117-119
  age 35 to age 50, 12-13, 119-120
  age 51 to 65, 13-14, 120
  age 65 and over, 14-15
Annuities
  life insurance, 167
  place in portfolio, 85, 86, 95
  as tax-advantaged investments, 78, 85
Automobile insurance
  actual cash value (ACV), 108
  amount of coverage, 108-110
  and liability, 101, 108-110
  in no-fault states, 108
Automobile ownership, 22, 101

Balance, in portfolio, 83, 84
Bank savings
  place in portfolio, 67, 70, 86, 95
  risks associated with, 63-64, 66
Bonds
  and age, 86-87
  place in portfolio, 67, 68, 70, 83, 85-86, 95
  risks compared with stocks, 65, 66, 67
Business ownership, gathering data on, 60, 61

Cable TV, place in portfolio, 93

Capital accumulation, 4, 147, 153-155
Cash and equivalents
  gathering data on, 46, 48
  need for emergency reserve, 84, 85
  place in portfolio, 70, 83, 84, 93, 94, 95
Cash flow
  and credit card debt, 150-151
  from growth investments, 86
  management of, 146, 147-151
  and taxes, 76, 77
  three-bin system and, 147-150
  using negative income for, 39
Clifford Trust, 165
Collectibles, 70, 93
Collision insurance, 108
Commodities, place in portfolio, 93
Common stock
  gathering data on, 51, 52
  management of, 87
  place in portfolio, 67, 68, 70, 75, 83, 88-89
  risks compared with bonds, 65, 66, 67
  in small companies, 67
Community property, 118-119, 135-136
Comprehensive auto insurance, 108
Credit card debt, 150-151
Credit union accounts, 70, 86

Deflation hedges
  examples of, 12, 13, 70
  need for, 66, 83
  place in portfolio, 83, 86-87, 95
  table of, 87

Dental insurance, 46
Diamonds, 92
Disability
  definitions in insurance policies, 44, 84, 111, 112-113
  income needed for, 46, 47, 84, 110-111
  risk of (table), 111
  Social Security coverage for, 111
Disability insurance
  cancellation and renewal, 113
  disability definition, 44, 84, 111, 112-113
  employee-sponsored insurance for, 111-112
  monthly benefit, 112
  period of coverage, 112
  private insurance for, 111-112
Diversification
  achieving balance, 75, 94, 95
  need for, 11, 66, 67, 70-71, 75, 83
  within stock or capital pools, 67, 68
Durable power of attorney, 136-137

Earthquake insurance, 107
Education
  cost of, 35, 161
  financing of, 12, 162-168
  investments for, 166-167
  setting goals for, 22, 34, 35, 161-162
Employment of children, 165, 167
Energy investments
  estimating value, 57, 58
  and OPEC, 90
  place in portfolio, 70, 71, 90-91
Entertainment, 22
Equipment leasing, 77, 93
Equity kicker, 87
Estate planning
  to age 35, 12, 117-119
  age 35 to 50, 13, 119-120
  age 51 to 65, 14, 120
  and attorney, 117, 136-137
  and children, 119, 133
  and community property, 118-119, 121, 135-136
  and estate size, 121, 122
  examples of, 117-121
  gifting and, 15, 29, 120-121, 133-134
  goal of, 4
  and life insurance, 137-144
  and method of ownership, 135-136
  probate process and, 124-126
  setting goals for, 29, 32-33, 35
  and Social Security, 140, 145
  and taxes, 120-121, (table) 123, 134-135
  unified credit trust, 121, 126
  for unmarried young person, 117-118
  use of trusts in, 29, 119, 126, 128
  See also Probate; Will
Exotics
  description of, 70, 91-92, 93
  investment in, 57, 59
  place in portfolio, 70, 91-93

Financial goals, and success, 2-3, 147
Financial independence, 4, 14, 23-24, 151
Financial planner, duties of, 3
Financial planning
  affect of age on, 9-15
  components of, 4, 23-25
  documents used in, 27-28
  and limitations, 12, 23-25
  need for, 1-2, 146
  need to monitor, 4, 7, 12, 28
  process of, 4-5, 27-60
  and use of worksheets, 28-60
  who should do, 2-3
  See also Capital accumulation; Cash flow; Estate planning; Investment
Fixed-income securities, 49, 52
Flood insurance, 107
Future cost
  factors (table), 152
  and investment, 153

Goals
  assigning priorities to, 18, 24-25, 155-156
  as foundation of plan, 4, 17-18, 24-25, 146
  and future costs, 19 (table), 22, 146, 151-152
  kinds of, 23-24
  in portfolio building, 83
Gold, 90-91, 94, 95
Guest property coverage, 106

Health, impact on financial security, 14, 15
Home furnishings, 22
Home ownership, 22
Homeowner's insurance
  all-risk coverage, 103
  comprehensive personal liability, 106
  condominium, 106-107
  contents coverage, 105
  cost-of-construction adjustment, 44, 104
  dwelling coverage, 103-104
  guaranteed replacement cost endorsement, 104, 105
  personal property coverage, 104-105

Illiquidity, 83, 84, 87, 89
Income categories, 77
Income shifting, 163-164
Individual ownership, 135
Individual Retirement Account (IRA), 93, 156-157
Inflation hedges
  examples of, 13, 15, 70
  need for, 66, 83, 87 (table)
  place in portfolio, 86-87, 95
Insurance
  and age, 12-15, 140, 144
  casualty and liability, 39, 40-41, 42, 44, 101, 102-103
  coverage needed, 101, 109-110
  deductibles, 39, 44, 102, 105, 107, 114
  duration of benefits, 44
  goal of, 4, 70, 102, 103
  policy coverage, 39, 44, 46, 102-103, 106
  and scheduled property, 44, 105
  umbrella, 109, 110
  See also Automobile insurance; Dental insurance; Disability insurance; Homeowner's insurance; Life insurance; Medical insurance.
Interest rates, 65, 66
Investment
  and age, 85, 86-87, 93-95
  analysis of, 71, 72, 75, 83, 96-99
  basic concepts for building portfolio, 68-69, 83-84
  deflation hedges, 12, 13, 66, 70, 83, 86-87, 91
  duration of, 84-85
  education on, 85-86
  expenses of, 68-69
  gathering data on, 46-60, 62, 96
  goals, 4, 83-84
  inflation hedges, 13, 15, 66, 70, 83, 86-87, 91
  and liquidity, 70, 83
  management of, 68, 86, 87-88, 146-147
  monitoring of, 71-75, 96, 98, 147
  restructuring of, 96-99
  sample portfolios, 93-95
  selecting, 70-71, 96-99
  risks, 66, 85, 89, 93, 94, 95
  and Tax Reform Act of 1986, 75-77
  See also individual kinds of investments.

Joint tenancy, 135

Leverage
  affect on gains, 11, 89-90
  place in portfolio, 94, 95
Life insurance
  accidental death and dismemberment, 138
  cash value of, 46, 70, 143-144
  endowment, 138, 144

in estate plan, 24, 101, 137-144
irrevocable trusts, 138, 141
ownership of policy, 46, 141
protection provided by, 45, 46
term, 138, 141, 142-143
when needed, 12, 13, 15, 24, 137-138, 144
whole, 138, 141-144, 167
Limited partnership
loss of tax-shelter status, 90-91
place in portfolio, 68, 87, 89, 94, 95
risks of, 68, 87, 89-90
Liquidity
as factor in investment, 70, 83, 84, 86
need for, 83, 84
Living trust, 119, 126, 128

Marginal tax bracket, 79-80
Medical insurance
Health Maintenance Organization (HMO), 113, 114
mentioned, 42-43, 44, 46, 101
provisions of, 113, 114
Medical payments coverage, 106
Money
attitudes toward, 2-3, 8-9, 18
mastery of, 2-3, 18-19, 24-25, 37-38, 39, 84-85, 146, 147-151
roles of, 8
Money market funds, 86
Mortgages, place in portfolio, 87
Mutual funds
gathering data on, 52, 53, 88
global, 88-89
place in portfolio, 67, 68-69, 84, 85, 88-89, 94, 95

Notes receivable
as deflation hedges, 70, 87
gathering data on, 50, 52
place in portfolio, 68, 70, 87

Options, place in portfolio, 93

Passages, 2
Portfolio. See Investment; *individual kinds of investments*
Precious gems, 92
Pre-paid tuition, 167-168
Probate, 124-125
Proportion
and age, 75, 85
as goal in portfolio building, 75, 83

Real estate
estimating after-tax yield on, 55, 57
gathering data on, 52, 54-57
place in portfolio, 68, 70, 89-90, 94-95
Real estate investment trust (REIT), 89
Research and development, 70
Retirement planning
goals, 4, 29, 31
monitoring of, 13
relation to financial independence, 4, 14
See also Estate planning; Retirement plans
Retirement plans
company savings or thrift, 159
deferred compensation or 401(k), 159
defined benefit, 158
establishing for self or corporation, 158
Individual Retirement Account, 150-151
non-qualified deferred compensation, 159
tax-sheltered annuity or 403(b), 159
Return on investment, 56, 57, 83
Risk
at different ages, 65, 94-95
investment, 63-65, 66, 87
and liquidity, 86
purchasing power, 63, 66
retaining or transferring, 101, 102, 105
spectrum of, 63-65, 67
in tax strategies, 77
tolerance for, 83
See also Insurance; Investment; Risk management
Risk management
methods of, 67, 101

monitoring, 14
principles of, 105-106
and protection of assets, 4, 102

Safe deposit box, 105
Saving
   attitudes toward, 8-9, 146
   establish habit of, 10, 146-147
   setting goals for, 146-147
Savings and loan accounts, 86
Scholarships, 167
Series EE bonds, 166
Silver, 92
Social Security
   benefits provided (table), 140
   unreliability of, 145
Student loans, 167

Tax
   affect on financial planning, 2, 15, 75-77
   estimating, 35, 36, 39, 78-79
   goal of planning for, 4, 146, 147
   management strategies, 77, 128-130, 146
   marginal brackets, 78
   state, 79-80
Tax Reform Act of 1986
   affect on investments, 75-76, 90
   and college funding, 163
   and debt, 151
   goals of, 76
   income categories under, 77
   and IRAs, 93, 156-157
   marginal brackets under, 78-80
Tax shelters, 71, 90-91
Tenancy by entirety, 135
Tenancy in common, 135
Testamentary trust, 119
Three-bin system
   accrual account, 148
   capital account, 147
   investment account, 148

operation of, 11, 22, 148, 150
planning for (table), 149
Treasury bills, 68, 70, 86
Trusts
   charitable remainder trust, 132-133
   irrevocable, 131-132
   marital deduction
      exemption, 128, 129-130
      Q-tip, 128, 130
      survivor's, 128-129
   pour-over arrangement, 128
   probate avoidance, 126, 128
   revocable living (inter vivos), 29, 119, 124
   and taxes, 124
   Totten, 130-131
   2503(c) trust, 165-166
   use in estate plan, 13, 119, 128-131

UGMA account, 165
Utility stocks, 75, 89

Vacations, 22
Venture capital
   place in portfolio, 11, 67-68, 70, 93, 94
   risks of, 11, 67-68

Will
   choosing an executor, 119
   choosing a guardian, 119
   and laws of intestate succession, 115, 116
   need for, 115-116
   special bequests, 133
   structuring of, 117
   understanding of, 126
   See also Estate planning; Probate; Trusts

Zero-coupon bonds, 166

MASTERING MONEY Puts You on the Road to Financial Success

Do you know the answers to these questions?

- Where do you stand financially?
- How do you choose investments to make more money?
- Where do you want to be financially in one year? Five years? Ten years?
- How will you accomplish your financial goals? Have you made the right financial decisions?
- Do you need a professional financial advisor?

If you've ever asked yourself any of these questions, you are not alone. Investment options abound, and with that range of options comes growing confusion about which ones are best for an individual's situation. A great many people wonder at what point they should seek professional guidance.

MASTERING MONEY: How To Create Your Own Financial Plan will help you get organized and focus on the answers to those questions based on your own individual financial picture. By completing the easy-to-follow worksheets and summarizing your own "big picture," you'll be able to create a basic financial plan and then decide for yourself: *Where* you want to go . . . *How* you want to get there . . . and *If* you need help. This book answers your many questions about seeking professional advice. . .

- What information must I provide?
- How much money do I have to make?
- How much does a financial plan cost?
- What do I have to do before seeking advice?
- How and where do I find a good financial planner?

If you want to master your financial picture, you need *MASTERING MONEY: How To Create Your Own Financial Plan!*

Longman Financial Services Publishing
a division of Longman Financial Services Institute, Inc.
520 North Dearborn Street
Chicago, Illinois 60610-4975

Distributed by
Longman Trade
Naperville, IL

Reorder Number: 5606-23
ISBN: 0-88462-589-3
$15.95